P9-ARM-431

Woman,
Thou Art Loosed!

The Book and the Devotional
for Women

Woman, Thou Art Loosed!

The Book and the Devotional for Women

T. D. JAKES

INSPIRATIONAL PRESS

NEW YORK

Unless otherwise indicated, all Scripture quotations are taken from
the *King James Version* of the Bible.

Previously published as two separate volumes:
WOMAN, THOU ART LOOSED!
Copyright © 1996 by T.D. Jakes.

Scripture quotations marjed NIV are taken from the *Holy Bible, New
International Version®*. NIV®. Copyright 19763, 1978, 1984 by
International Bible Society. Used by permission of Zondervan
Publishing House. All rights reserved.

WOMAN, THOU ART LOOSED! DEVOTIONAL
Copyright © 1997 by T.D. Jakes.

All rights reserved. No part of this work may be reproduced or
transmitted in any form or by any means, electronic or mechanical,
including photocopying, recording, or any information storage and
retrieval system, without permission in writing from:
Albury Publishing, 2448 East 81st Street, Suite 5700,
Tulsa, OK 74137

First Inspirational Press edition pubished in 2000.

Inspirational Press
A division of BBS Publishing Corporation
450 Raritan Center Parkway
Edison, New Jersey 08837

Inspirational Press is a registered trademark of
BBS Publishing Corporation
Published by arrangement with Albury Publishing, 2448 East 81st Street,
Suite 5700, Tulsa, OK 74137

Distributed by World Publishing
Nashville, TN 37214
www.worldpublishing.com

Library of Congress Catalog Card number: 98-75433
ISBN: 0-88486-355-7
Printed in the United States of America.

Contents

Woman, Thou Art Loosed!

Healing the Wounds
of the Past

DEDICATION

I want to dedicate this book to the memory of my father, the late Rev. Ernest L. Jakes, Sr. It is also dedicated in tribute to my mother, Mrs. Odith P. Jakes, whose unfailing love has defined motherhood and provided my first encounter with excellence. And to my sister, Jackie, who kissed away my childhood tears. And finally, to my lovely wife, Serita, whose gentle breeze has often kept my sails full of the wind of destiny.

CONTENTS

CHAPTER ONE

Infirm Woman

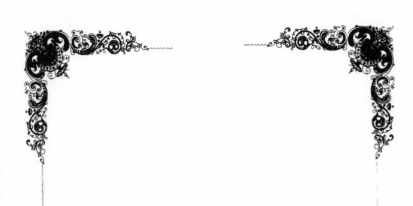

It is important to remember that for every person, there will be a problem. Even more importantly, for every problem, our God has a prescription!

"And, behold, there was a woman which had a spirit of infirmity eighteen years, and was bowed together, and could in no wise lift up herself. And when Jesus saw her, he called her to him, and said unto her, Woman, thou art loosed from thine infirmity."

{Luke 13:11-12}

The Holy Spirit periodically lets us catch a glimpse of the personal testimony of one of the patients of the Divine Physician Himself. This woman's dilemma is her own, but perhaps you will find some point of relativity between her case history and your own. She could be like someone you know or have known; she could even be like you.

There are three major characters in this story. They are the person, the problem, and the prescription. It is important to remember that for every person, there will be a problem. But even more importantly, for every problem, our God has a prescription!

Jesus' opening statement to the problem in this woman's life is not a recommendation for counseling—it is a challenging command! Often much more is involved in maintaining deliverance than just discussing past trauma. Jesus did not counsel what should have been commanded. I am not, however, against seeking the counsel of godly men. On the contrary, the Scriptures say:

"Blessed is the man that walketh not in the counsel of the ungodly, nor standeth in the way of the sinners, nor sitteth in the seat of the scornful." {Psalm 1:1}

"Where no counsel is, the people fall: but in the multitude of counsellors there is safety." {Proverbs 11:14}

What I want to make clear is that after you have analyzed the condition, after you have understood its origin, it will still take the authority of God's Word to put the past under your feet! This woman was suffering as a result of something that attacked her eighteen years earlier. I wonder if you can relate to the long-range aftereffects of past pain? This kind of trauma is as fresh to the victim today as it was the day it occurred. Although the problem may be rooted in the past, the prescription is a present word from God! The Word is the same yesterday, today and forevermore {Hebrews 13:8}. That is to say, the Word you are hearing today is able to heal your yesterday!

A PERSONAL WAR

When Jesus said, "Woman, thou art loosed," He did not call her by name. He wasn't speaking to her just as a person. He spoke to her femininity. He spoke to the song in her. He spoke to the lace in her. Like a crumbling rose, Jesus spoke to what she could, and would have been. I believe the Lord spoke to the twinkle that existed in her eye when she was a child; to the girlish glow that makeup can never seem to recapture. He spoke to her God-given uniqueness. He spoke to her gender.

Her problem didn't begin suddenly. It had existed in her life for eighteen years. We are looking at a woman who had a personal war going on inside her. These struggles must have tainted many other areas of her life. The infirmity that attached to her life was physical.

However, many women also wrestle with infirmities in emotional traumas. These infirmities can be just as challenging as a physical affliction. An emotional handicap can create dependency on many different levels. Relationships can become crutches. The infirm woman can place such weight on people that it strains a healthy relationship. And many times such emotional handicaps will spawn a series of unhealthy relationships.

> *"For thou hast had five husbands; and he whom thou now hast is not thy husband: in that saidst thou truly."* {John 4:18}

Healing cannot come to a desperate person rummaging through other people's lives. One of the first things that a hurting person needs to do is break the habit of using other people as a narcotic to numb the dull aching of an inner void. The more you medicate the symptoms, the less chance you have of allowing God to heal you.

CLINGING OR LOVING?

Another destructive tendency that can exist with any abuse is the continual increasing of dosage. So avoid addictive, obsessive relationships. If you are becoming increasingly dependent upon anything other than God to create a sense of wholeness in your life, you are abusing your relationships. Clinging to people is far different from loving them. It is not so much a statement of your love for them as it is a crying out of your need for them. Like lust, it is intensely selfish. It is taking and not giving.

Love is giving. God is love. God proved His love not by His need of us, but by His giving to us.

> *"For God so loved the world, that he gave his only begotten Son, that whosoever believeth in him should not perish, but have everlasting life."*   *[John 3:16]*

The Scriptures plainly show that this infirm woman had tried to lift herself. People who stood on the outside could easily criticize and assume that the infirm woman lacked effort and fortitude. But that is not always the case. Some situations in which we find ourselves defy willpower. We feel unable to change. The Scriptures say this woman "could in no wise lift up herself." This implies she had employed various means of self-ministry.

SPIRITUAL AILMENTS

Isn't it amazing how the same people who lift up countless others, often cannot lift themselves? This type of person may be a tower of faith and prayer for others, but impotent when it comes to their own limitations. This type of person may be the one others rely upon. Sometimes we esteem others more important than ourselves and we always become the martyr. It is wonderful to be self-sacrificing, but watch out for self-disdain! If we don't apply some of the medicine that we use on others to strengthen ourselves, our patients will be healed and we will be dying.

> *"I shall not die, but live, and declare the works of the Lord."*   *[Psalm 118:17]*

Many things can engender disappointment and depression. In this woman's case, a spirit of infirmity had gripped her life. A spirit can manifest itself in many forms. For some it may be low self-esteem caused by child abuse, rape, wife abuse or divorce. I realize that these are natural problems, but they are rooted in spiritual ailments.

One of the many damaging things that can affect us today is divorce, particularly among women, who often look forward to a happy relationship. Little girls grow up playing with Barbie and Ken dolls, dressing doll babies and playing house. Young girls lie in bed reading romance novels, while little boys play ball and ride bicycles in the park. Whenever a woman is indoctrinated to think success is *romance*, then experiences the trauma of a failed relationship, she comes to a painful awakening.

PUTTING PERSPECTIVE ON THE PAST

Divorce is not merely separating; it is the tearing apart of what was once joined together. Whenever something is torn, it does not heal easily. But Jesus can heal a broken or torn heart!

> *"The Spirit of the Lord is upon me, because he hath anointed me to preach the gospel to the poor; he hath sent me to heal the brokenhearted, to preach deliverance to the captives, and recovering of sight to the blind, to set at liberty them that are bruised."*
>
> *[Luke 4:18]*

Approximately five out of ten marriages end in divorce. Those broken homes in which it occurs leave a trail of broken dreams, people and children. Only the Master can heal these victims in the times in which we live. Only He can treat the long-term effects of this tragedy.

One of the great healing balms of the Holy Spirit is forgiveness. To forgive is to break the link between you and your past. Sadly, though, many times the person hardest to forgive is the one in the mirror. Although many rage loudly about others, they secretly blame themselves for a failed relationship. But regardless of who they may be holding responsible, there is no healing in blame!

When you begin to realize that your past does not necessarily dictate the outcome of your future, you can finally release the hurt. It is impossible to inhale new air until you exhale the old.

I pray that as you continue reading, God will give the grace of releasing where you have been, so you can receive what God has for you now. Exhale, then inhale; there is more for you.

LET THE LITTLE CHILDREN COME TO ME....
{MATTHEW 19:14}

Perhaps one of the more serious indictments against our civilization is our flagrant disregard for the welfare of our children. Child abuse, regardless of whether it is physical, sexual or emotional, is a terrible issue for an innocent mind to wrestle with. It is horrifying to think that little children who survive the peril of the streets, the public schools, and the aggravated society in which we live, come home to be abused in what should be a haven.

Recent statistics suggest that three in five young girls in this country have been or will be sexually assaulted. If that many are reported, I shudder to think of how many are never reported and are covered with a shroud of secrecy.

THE ABUSED ARE IN OUR MIDST

If by chance you are a pastor, please realize that these figures are actually faces in your choir, committees, etc. They reflect a growing amount of our congregational needs. Although this book focuses on women, many men also have been abused as children. And I fear that God will judge us for our blatant disregard of this need in our messages, ministries and prayers. I would even suggest that our silence contributes to the shame and secrecy that Satan attaches to these victimized persons.

So whenever I think on these issues, I am reminded of what my mother used to say. I was forever coming home with a scratch or cut from schoolyard play. When I did, my mother would take the band-aid off, clean the wound and say, "Things that are covered don't heal well." And mother was right. Things that are covered do not heal well.

Perhaps Jesus was thinking on this order when He called the infirm woman to come forward. It takes a lot of courage even in church today to receive ministry in sensitive areas. But the Lord is the kind of physician who can pour on the healing oil. So uncover your wounds in His presence and allow Him to gently heal your injuries. One woman even found healing in the hem of His garment {Mark 5:25-29}. There is a balm in Gilead! {Jeremiah 8:22.}

THE DEATH OF TRUST

However, even when a victim survives, there is still a casualty. It is the death of trust. Surely you realize that little girls tend to be trusting and unsuspicious. But when those who should nurture and protect them violate that trust through illicit behavior, multiple scars result. It is like programming a computer with false information; you can get out of it only what has been programmed into it.

When a man tells a little girl that his perverted acts are normal, she has no reason not to believe that what she is being taught is true. She is devoted to him and allows him to fondle her and further misappropriate his actions toward her. Usually the abuser is someone very close, with access to the child at vulnerable times. But fear is also a factor. Many children lay down with the cold taste of fear in their mouths. They believe the abuser could and would kill them for divulging his liberties against them. And some, as the victims of rape, feel physically powerless to wrestle with the assailant.

What kind of emotions might this kind of conduct bring out in the later life of this person? I am glad you asked. It would be easy for this kind of little girl to grow into a young lady who has difficulty trusting anyone! Maybe she will learn to deal with the pain inside by getting attention in illicit ways. Drug rehabilitation centers and prisons are full of adults who were abused children needing attention.

INTIMIDATED BY INTIMACY

Not every abused child takes such drastic steps. Often their period of behavioral disorder dissipates with time. Still, the abused child struggles with her own self-worth. She reasons, "How can I be valuable if the only way I could please my own father was to have sex with him?" This kind of childhood can affect how later relationships progress. Intimidated by intimacy, she struggles with trusting anyone. Insecurity and jealousy may be constant companions to this lady who can't seem to grasp the idea that someone could love her.

There are a variety of reactions to child abuse. Some avoid people who really care, being attracted to those who do not treat them well. Relating to abuse, they seem to sabotage good relationships and struggle for years in worthless ones. Others have become emotionally incapacitated to the degree that they need endless affirmation and affection just to maintain the courage to face ordinary days.

UNPROGRAMMING LIFE'S POORLY PROGRAMMED EVENTS

The pastor may tell this lady that God is her heavenly Father. But that doesn't help, because the problem is her point of reference. We frame our references around our own experiences. If those experiences are distorted, our ability to comprehend spiritual truths can be off center. I know that may sound very negative for someone who is in that circumstance. But what do you do when you have been poorly programmed by life's events? I've got good news! You can reprogram your mind through the Word of God.

> *"Do not conform any longer to the pattern of this world, but be transformed by the renewing of your mind. Then you will be able to test and approve what God's will is—his good, pleasing and perfect will."*   *[Romans 12:2] [NIV]*

The Greek word *metamorphoo* is translated as "transformed" in this text. Literally, it means to change into another form! You can have a complete metamorphosis through the Word of God.

It has been my experience as a pastor who does extensive counseling in my own ministry and abroad, that many abused people, women in particular, tend to flock to legalistic churches who see God primarily as a disciplinarian. Many times the concept of fatherhood for them is a harsh code of ethics. This type of domineering ministry may appeal to those who are performance-oriented.

MORALITY OR LEGALISM?

I understand that morality is important in Christianity. However, there is a great deal of difference between morality and legalism. It is important that God not be misrepresented. He is a balanced God. He is not an extremist.

> *"The Word became flesh and made his dwelling among us. We have seen his glory, the glory of the One and Only, who came from the Father, full of grace and truth."*   *[John 1:14] [NIV]*

The glory of God is manifested only when there is a balance between grace and truth. Religion doesn't transform. Legalism doesn't transform. For the person who feels dirty, harsh rules may create a sense of self-righteousness. But God doesn't have to punish you to heal you. Jesus has already prayed for you.

"Sanctify them through thy truth: thy word is truth."

[John 17:17]

Jesus simply shared grace and truth with that one hurting woman. He said, "Woman, thou art loosed." Jesus our Lord was a great emancipator of the oppressed. It does not matter whether someone has been oppressed socially, sexually or racially; our Lord is an eliminator of distinctions. Anyone can believe the Word of God and be free.

"There is neither Jew nor Greek [racial], there is neither bond nor free [social], there is neither male nor female [sexual]: for ye are all one in Christ Jesus."　　　*[Galatians 3:28]*

I feel it is important to point out that this verse deals with unity and equality in regard to the covenant of salvation. That is to say, God is no respecter of persons. He tears down barriers that would promote prejudice and separation in the Body of Christ. Yet it is important also to note that while there is no distinction in the manner in which we receive any of those groups, there should be an appreciation for the uniqueness of their individuality.

CULTURAL RAPE

There is a racial, social and sexual uniqueness that we should not only accept, but also appreciate. It is cultural rape to teach other cultures or races that the only way to worship God is the way another race or culture does. Unity should not come at the expense of uniqueness of expression. We should also tolerate variance in social classes. It is wonderful to teach prosperity as long as it is understood that the Church is not an elite organization for spiritual yuppies only, who exclude other social classes.

And if uniqueness is to be appreciated racially and socially, it is certainly to be appreciated sexually. Male and female are one in Christ. Yet they are unique, and that uniqueness is not to be tampered with. Let the male be masculine and the female be feminine!

It is a sin for a man to misrepresent himself by conducting himself as a woman. I am not merely speaking of homosexuality. I am also talking about men who are feminine in their mannerisms. Many of these men may not be homosexual in their behavior, but the Bible says they must be healed of feminine mannerisms, and vice versa. It is equally sad to see a masculine woman. Nevertheless, God wants them healed, not hated!

> *"Know ye not that the unrighteous shall not inherit the kingdom of God? Be not deceived: neither fornicators, nor idolaters, nor adulterers, nor effeminate, nor abusers of themselves with mankind."*　　　　　　　　　　　　*[1 Corinthians 6:9]*

I realize that these behavioral disorders are areas that require healing and prayer. My point is simply that unity does not negate uniqueness. God is saying, "I don't want men to lose their masculine uniqueness." This is true racially, socially and sexually.

God can appreciate our differences and still create unity. It is like a conductor who can orchestrate extremely different instruments into producing a harmonious, unified sound. Together we produce a sound of harmony that expresses the multifaceted character of God.

Having established the uniqueness of unity, let us now discuss some aspects of the uniqueness of the woman. By nature a woman is a receiver. She is not physically designed to be a giver. Her sexual and emotional fulfillment becomes somewhat dependent on the giving of her male counterpart (in regard to intimate relationships).

A CERTAIN VULNERABILITY

There is a certain vulnerability that is a part to being a receiver. In regard to reproduction (sexual relationships), the man is the contributing factor while the woman is the receiver. And what is true of the natural is true of the spiritual. Men tend to act out of what they perceive to be facts, while women tend to react out of their emotions.

If your actions and moods are not a reaction to the probing of the Holy Spirit, then you are reacting to the subtle taunting of the enemy. He is trying

---

Effeminate: Strong's #3120 "*malakos* (mal-ak-os'); of uncertain affinity; soft, i.e. fine (clothing); figuratively a catamite: effeminate, soft" (*Strong's Exhaustive Concordance of the Bible*, Hendrickson Publishers, n.d.)

to produce his destructive fruit in your home, heart, and even in your relationships. So *receiver*, be careful what you *receive!* Moods and attitudes that Satan would offer, you need to resist. Tell the enemy, "This is not me, and I don't receive it." It is his job to offer it...and your job to resist it. If you do your job, all will go well.

> *"Submit yourselves, then, to God. Resist the devil, and he will flee from you."*   *[James 4:7] [NIV]*

Don't allow the enemy to plug into you and violate you through his subtle seductions. He is a giver, and he is looking for a receiver. You must discern his influence if you are going to rebuke him. Anything that comes and any mood that is not in agreement with God's Word, is Satan trying to plug into the earthly realm through your life. He wants you to believe you cannot change. He loves prisons and chains!

ACCEPTING LIPS

Statements like, "This is just the way I am," or "I am in a terrible mood today," come from lips that accept what they ought to reject. So never allow yourself to settle for anything less than the attitude God wants you to have in your heart. Don't let Satan have your day, your husband, or your home. Eve could have thrown the devil out of Eden!

> *"Neither give place to the devil."*   *[Ephesians 4:27]*

It is not enough to reject the enemy's plan. You must nurture the Word of the Lord. You need to draw the promise of God and His vision for the future to your breast. It is a natural law that anything not fed will die. And whatever you have drawn to your breast is what is growing in your life. So, breast-feeding holds several advantages for what you are feeding. First, it hears your heartbeat. Second, it is warmed by your closeness. And third, it draws nourishment from you.

But be cautious. Be sure you are nurturing what you want to grow, and starving what you want to die. As you read this, you may feel that life is passing you by. You may be experiencing success in one area, and gross defeat in others.

You need a burning desire for the future—the kind of desire that overcomes past fear and inhibitions. You will remain chained to your past and all the secrets therein until you decide ENOUGH IS ENOUGH!

THERE IS AN EARTHQUAKE COMING INTO YOUR PRISON!

I am telling you that when your desire for the future peaks, you can break out of prison. I challenge you to sit down and write thirty things you would like to do with your life and scratch them off, one by one, as you accomplish them. There is no way you can plan for the future while dwelling in the past at the same time.

I feel an earthquake coming into your prison! It is midnight—the turning point of days! It is your time for a change. So praise God and escape out of the dungeons of your past!

> *"And at midnight Paul and Silas prayed, and sang praises unto God: and the prisoners heard them. And suddenly there was a great earthquake, so that the foundations of the prison were shaken: and immediately all the doors were opened, and every one's bands were loosed."* [Acts 16:25-26]

Have you ever noticed how hard it is to communicate with distracted people who will not give you their attention? They almost seem weird. They do not respond! There is a principle to learn here. Paul and Silas were completely preoccupied with God in the midst of their pain. Pain will not continue to rehearse itself in the life of a preoccupied, distracted person.

Every woman has something she wishes she could forget. Forgetting isn't a memory lapse; it is a memory release! Like carbon dioxide the body can no longer use, exhale it and let it go out of your spirit. Set your mind on God, and let God set you free.

> *"Brethren, I count not myself to have apprehended: but this one thing I do, forgetting those things which are behind, and reaching forth unto those things which are before, I press toward the mark*

for the prize of the high calling of God in Christ Jesus. Let us there-
fore, as many as be perfect, be thus minded: and if in any thing ye
be otherwise minded, God shall reveal even this unto you."
                                                    [Philippians 3:13-15]

Jesus set the infirm woman free. She was able to stand upright. The crip-pling condition of her infirmity was removed by the God who cares, sees and calls our infirmities to the dispensary of healing and deliverance. You can call upon Him even in the middle of the night. Like a 24-hour medical center, you can reach Him at any time. He is touched by the feeling of your infirmity.

"For we have not an high priest which cannot be touched with
the feeling of our infirmities; but was in all points tempted like as
we are, yet without sin."   *[Hebrews 4:15]*

In the name of our High Priest, Jesus Christ, I curse the infirmity that has
bowed the backs of God's women. I pray that as we share together out of the Word of God, the Holy Spirit will roll you into God's recovery room where you can fully realize that your trauma is over.

And I am excited to say that God never loosed anybody that He wasn't going to use mightily. May God reveal His healing and purpose as we con-tinue to seek Him.

CHAPTER TWO

Broken Arrows

*Children are living epistles
that should stand as evidence
to the future that the past
made some level of
contribution.*

"Lo, children are an heritage of the Lord: and the fruit of the womb is his reward. As arrows are in the hand of a mighty man; so are children of the youth. Happy is the man that hath his quiver full of them: they shall not be ashamed, but they shall speak with the enemies in the gate."   *[Psalm 127:3-5]*

*T*he birth of a child is still the greatest miracle I have ever seen. Standing in the sterile white environment of that hospital maternity ward with the smell of disinfectant strong on my hands like some strange new cologne, they handed me my link into the future. They handed me my ambassador to the next generation. Blinking, winking, squirming little slice of love, wrapped in a blanket and forever fastened to my heart...we had just had a baby! To me a piece of heaven had been pushed through the womb of our consummated love.

LIVING EPISTLES

Children are living epistles that should stand as evidence to the future that the past made some level of contribution. The psalmist David wrote a brief note that is as loud as an atomic bomb which speaks to the heart of men concerning their attitude toward their offspring. Remember, this was David, the man whose indiscretion with Bathsheba had produced a love child.

Though inappropriately conceived, David's baby was loved nonetheless. David loved it so much that he laid upon the ground in sackcloth and ashes, praying feverishly for mercy, as his child squirmed in the icy hands of death. Then, suddenly, a cold silence slowly grew in his tent. The squirming stopped. The crying stilled. David's baby had gone into eternal rest.

ARROWS IN OUR HANDS

If anybody knows the value of children, it is those who just left theirs in the ground. *"As arrows are in the hand of a mighty man; so are children of the youth,"* says King David, whose arrow they lowered into the ground.

So why did David compare children to arrows? Maybe it was because of their potential to be propelled into the future. Perhaps it was for the intrinsic gold mine that lies in the heart of every child who is "shot" through the womb. Or maybe he was trying to tell us that children go where we, their parents, aim them. Could it be that we, as parents, must be responsible enough to place them in the kind of bow that will accelerate their success and emotional well-being? I think so. How happy I am to have my quiver full of arrows!

AN ARROW SHOT

If someone must be hurt, if it ever becomes necessary to bear pains, weather strong winds, or withstand trials and opposition, let it be adults...not their children. I was my father's arrow and my mother's heart. My father is dead, but his arrows are yet soaring in the wind. You will never know him; he is gone. However, my brother, my sister and I are flying, soaring, scientific proof that he was, and through us, continues to be.

So don't worry about me; I am an arrow shot. If I don't succeed, I have had the greatest riches known to man. I have had an opportunity to test the limits of my destiny. Whatever happens will happen. I can accept the fate before me. But whether preferred or rejected, let the record show: I am here. My father aimed me, and now I pray, "Oh, God, let me hit my target!" If I miss and plummet to the ground, then at least I can say, "I have been shot!"

BROKEN ARROWS

It is for the arrows of this generation that we must pray. We must pray for those who are being aimed at the streets and drugs and perversion. Not all of them, but some of them, have been broken in the quiver!

I write to every empty-eyed child I have ever seen sit at my desk with tears and trembling lips struggling to tell their unmentionable secret.

I write to the trembling voice of every caller who spoke into a telephone the secret they could not keep and could not tell.

I write to every husband who holds a woman every night who was a child lost in space, a rosebud crushed before you met her, a broken arrow shaking in the quiver.

And I write to every lady who hides behind her silk dresses and leather purses a terrible secret that makeup can't seem to cover, and long showers will not wash.

Some people call them abused children. Some call them victimized. Some call them statistics. But I call them broken arrows.

Whose hand is this that fondles the bare, flat chest of a little girl? Whose fingers linger upon the flesh he helped to create? Why has the love that should be mama's come to snuggle under daughter?

"Can someone tell me how to rinse the feeling of fingers off my mind?" This is the cry of little children all over this country. This is the cry of worried minds clutching dolls and riding bicycles. Of little girls and even little boys sitting on school buses who got more for Christmas than they could ever show and tell.

MENDING ARROWS

Today the Church must realize that the adult problems we are fighting to correct, are often rooted in the ashes of such childhood experiences. How delicate is the touch of a surgeon's hand. Who needs surgery under a butchering hacksaw? So it is in the ministry. There is a different prerequisite for effectiveness than what the textbooks alone can provide. Ours is not a medicine that can be mixed by a pharmacist. Our patients' wounds are in the heart. We don't need medicine; we need miracles.

I always laugh at the carnal mind that picks up books like this to critique the approach of the prophet. They weigh the words of divine wisdom against the data they have studied. Many have more faith in a textbook written by a person whose eyes may be clouded by their own secrets, than to rely upon the word of a God who knows the end from the beginning.

Whatever a psychologist learned, he either read in a book, heard in a lecture, or discovered in an experiment. I do appreciate the many who have been helped through these precious hearts. Yet I know that, at best, they are practicing an uncertain method on people as they ramble through the closets of a troubled person's mind. What they need is divine intervention!

If there is something minor wrong with my car, like a radiator hose needing replacement or a tire that needs to be changed, I can take it almost anywhere. But if I suspect there is serious trouble with it, I always take it to the dealer. The manufacturer knows his product better than the average mechanic. So like the dealership, ministers may work with, but need not be intimidated by, the sciences of the mind! Child abuse is no radiator hose.

God is not practicing. He is the manufacturer. He is accomplished. We need to share God-given, biblical answers to troubling questions as we deal with the highly sensitive areas of sexually abused children.

COMPASSION AND CHANGE

I earnestly believe that where there is no compassion, there can be no lasting change. As long as Christian leadership secretly jeers and sneers at the perversion that comes into the Church, there will be no healing. Perversion is the offspring of abuse! As long as we crush what is already broken by our own prejudices and phobias, there will be no healing. The enemy robs us of our healing power by robbing us of our concern.

Compassion is the mother of miracles! When the storm had troubled the waters and the disciples thought they would die, they didn't challenge Christ's power; they challenged His compassion. They went to the back of the ship and said, "...Carest thou not that we perish?" {Mark 4:38}. They understood that if there is no real compassion, then there can be no miracle.

Until we, as priests, are touched with the feelings of our parishioners' illnesses rather than just being turned off by their symptoms, they will not be healed. Also, to every husband who wants to see his wife healed and to every mother who has a little girl with a woman's problem: The power to heal is in the power to care.

ARE YOU A BROKEN ARROW?

If you are a broken arrow, please allow someone into your storm. I know you usually do not allow anyone to come to your aid. And I realize a breach of trust may have left you leery of everyone. But the walls you have built to protect yourself have also imprisoned you.

BE LOOSED!

The Lord wants to *loose* you out of your dungeon of fear! He does care. No one would take hours away from themselves and from their family praying for you, preaching to you, or even writing this to you if they didn't care. *Rise and be healed in the name of Jesus!*

What happened to the disciples as their ship was tossed and they questioned the Lord's concern? Jesus rebuked the storm! How could they have thought that the God who was sailing with them didn't care about the storm? When Jesus said, "...Peace, be still...!" {Mark 4:39} there was a great calm.

Jesus does care. He is full of compassion. And to you today, He is still saying, "Peace, be still!"

> *"But when he saw the multitudes, he was moved with compassion on them, because they fainted, and were scattered abroad, as sheep having no shepherd."*　　　　　*[Matthew 9:36]*

> *"And Jesus went forth, and saw a great multitude, and was moved with compassion toward them, and he healed their sick."*　　　　　*[Matthew 14:14]*

> *"And Jesus, moved with compassion, put forth his hand, and touched him, and saith unto him, I will; be thou clean."*　　　　　*[Mark 1:41]*

> *"And Jesus, when he came out, saw much people, and was moved with compassion toward them, because they were as sheep not having a shepherd: and he began to teach them many things."*　　　　　*[Mark 6:34]*

> *"Then the lord of that servant was moved with compassion, and loosed him, and forgave him the debt."*　　　　　*[Matthew 18:27]*

Preceding miracle after miracle, compassion provoked Christ's power. We can build all the churches we want. We can decorate them with fine tapestry and ornate artifacts. But if people cannot find a loving voice within our hallowed walls, they will pass through unaltered by our clichés and religious rhetoric.

LOOKING CHILD ABUSE IN THE FACE

We can no longer ostracize the victim and let the assailant escape! Every time you see some insecure, vulnerable, intimidated adult who has unnatural fear in her eyes, low self-esteem or an apologetic posture, she is saying, "Carest thou not that I perish?"

Every time you see a bra-less woman in men's jeans, choosing to act like a man rather than to sleep with one, and every time you see a handsome young man who could have been someone's father walking like someone's mother—you may be looking child abuse in the face. If you think it's ugly, you're right. And if you think it's wrong, you're right again. But if you think it can't be healed, you're dead wrong! If you look closely into these eyes I've so feebly tried to describe, you will sense that something in this person is weak, hurt, maimed or disturbed, but fixable.

PAIN ISN'T PREJUDICED

These splintered, broken arrows come in all colors and forms. Some are black, some are white. Some are rich, some are poor. One thing about pain, though...it isn't prejudiced. Camouflaged, behind the walls of otherwise successful lives, successful people often wrestle with secret pain. So we must not narrow the scope of our ministries. Many people bear no outward signs of trauma as dramatic as I have described. Yet there are tragedies in their lives severe enough to have destroyed them, had God not held them together.

To God be the glory. He is a magnificent Healer!

Each person who has been through these adversities has their own story. Some have been blessed by not having to experience any such circumstance. Let the strong bear the infirmities of the weak! God can greatly use you to restore wholeness to others who walk in varying degrees of brokenness. After all, every car accident doesn't have the same assessment of damage. Many people have sustained injury without while still loving the unrighteous. Most of us have had some degree of cracking, submitting to the ineffective narcotics of a sinful and often perverted lifestyle.

But to those who have fallen prey to Satan's snares, we must teach righteousness. The fact that we have persevered is a testimony to all who understand themselves to be broken arrows.

> *"And they brought young children to him, that he should touch them: and his disciples rebuked those that brought them. But when Jesus saw it, he was much displeased, and said unto them, Suffer the little children to come unto me, and forbid them not: for of such is the kingdom of God. Verily I say unto you, Whosoever shall not*

> *receive the kingdom of God as a little child, he shall not enter therein. And he took them up in his arms, put his hands upon them, and blessed them."*
>
> *[Mark 10:13-16]*

It is interesting to me that just before this account took place in Scripture, the Lord was ministering on the subject of adultery and divorce. When He brought the subject up, someone brought the children to Him so He could touch them.

BROKEN HOMES PRODUCE BROKEN CHILDREN

Broken homes often produce broken children. It is the little ones who are often caught in the crossfire of angry parents. It reminds me of a newscast report I heard on the Gulf War. It was a listing of the many young men who were accidentally killed by their own military. They were killed innocently in the confusion of the battle. The newscaster used a term I had not heard before. He called it "friendly fire." I thought, *What is friendly about bleeding to death with your face buried in the hot sand of a strange country? I mean, it doesn't help much when I am dead!* Many children are wounded by the friendly fire of angry parents.

I wonder who these nameless persons were who had the insight and wisdom to bring the children to the Master? They brought the children to Him that He might touch them. What a strange interruption to a discourse on adultery and divorce. Here came these little children dragging dirty blankets and blank gazes into the presence of God while He was dealing with grown-up problems. When He saw them, He took time from His busy schedule, not so much to counsel them, but to touch them. That's all it takes.

A HIGH CALLING

I salute all the wonderful people who work with children. Whether through children's church or public school, you have a very high calling. Don't forget to touch their lives with a word of hope and a smile of encouragement. It may be the only one some of them will receive. You are the builders of our future. So be careful, you may be building a house that we will have to live in!

What was wrong with these disciples that made them angry at some nameless person who aimed these little arrows at the only answer they might ever have gotten to see? Jesus stopped teaching on the cause of divorce and marital abuse to touch the victim. He stopped to minister to the effect of the abuse and told them to suffer the little children to come. Suffer the suffering to come!

It is hard to work with hurting people, but the time has come for us to suffer the suffering to come. Anything, whether an injured animal or a hospital patient, if it is hurt, is unhappy. We cannot get a wounded lion to jump through hoops! Hurting children as well as hurting adults can carry the unpleasant aroma of bitterness. But in spite of the challenge, it is foolish to give up. So they brought the "ouch" to the band-aid, and He stopped the message of His mission.

Imagine tiny hands outstretched, little faces upturned, perching like sparrows on His knee. They came to get a touch, but Jesus always gives us more than we expect. He held them with His loving arms. He touched them with His sensitive hands. But most of all, He blessed them with His compassionate heart!

I am concerned that we maintain our compassion. How can we be in the presence of a loving God and not love these little ones? When Jesus blessed the children, He challenged the adults to become as children. Oh, to be a child again! To allow ourselves the kind of relationship with God that we may have missed as a child!

Sometimes we need to allow the Lord to adjust the damaged places of our past. I am glad to say that God provides arms which allow grown children to climb up like little children to be nurtured through the tragedies of early days. Isn't it nice to toddle into the presence of God and let Him hold you in His arms? In God, we can become children again. Salvation is God giving us a chance to start over again. He will not abuse the children that come to Him.

CLIMB INTO YOUR FATHER'S ARMS

It is so important that we learn how to worship and adore our God. There is no better way to climb into His arms. Even if you were exposed to grownup situations when you were a child, God can reverse what you have been through. He will let the grown-up person experience the joy of being a child in His presence!

Through praise, I approach Him like a toddler on unskillful legs. In worship, I kiss His face and am held by the caress of His anointing. He has no ulterior motive. His caress is safe and wholesome.

> *"Because thou shalt forget thy misery, and remember it as waters that pass away: and thine age shall be clearer than the noonday; thou shalt shine forth, thou shalt be as the morning. And thou shalt be secure, because there is hope; yea, thou shalt dig about thee, and thou shalt take thy rest in safety. Also thou shalt lie down, and none shall make thee afraid; yea, many shall make suit unto thee."*   *{Job 11:16-19}*

It is inconceivable to the injured that the injury can be forgotten. However, as I mentioned in chapter one, to forget isn't to develop amnesia. It is to reach a place where the misery is pulled from the wounded one's memory, as a stinger is pulled out of an insect bite. Once the stinger is gone, healing is inevitable.

The above passage in Job points out so eloquently that the memory is as "waters that pass away." Stand in a stream with waters around your ankles, and the waters passing by at that moment, you will never see again. So it is with the misery that has challenged your life: Let it go, let it pass away. And he says, the brilliance of morning is in sharp contrast to the darkness of night. Simply stated, it was night, but now it is day.

Perhaps David understood the aftereffects of traumatic deliverance when he said, "...Weeping may endure for a night, but joy cometh in the morning" {Psalm 30:5b}. There is such a security that comes when we are safe in the arms of God. It is when we become secure in our relationship with God that we begin to allow the past to fall from us as a garment. We may remember it, but we choose not to wear it!

RESTING IN HIS PRESENCE

I am convinced that resting in the relationship we have with God heals us from the feelings of vulnerability. It is a shame that many Christians have not yet rested in the promise of God. Everyone needs reassurance. Little girls as well as grown women need that sense of security. In the process of creating Eve, the mother of all living, His timing was crucial. In fact, God did not unveil her until everything she needed was provided. From establishment to relationship, all things were in order. He knew the woman would tend to need stability. It is innate. He knew she would want no sudden changes that would disrupt or compromise her security.

MEANT TO BE COVERED

Woman was meant to be covered. Originally Adam was her covering. He was to nurture and protect her. My sister, you were made to be covered even as a child. If someone "uncovered" you, there is a feeling of being violated. Even when these feelings are suppressed, and they often are, they are still powerful.

I think it is interesting that when the Bible talks about incest, it uses the word *uncover*. Sexual abuse violates the covering of a family and the responsible persons whom we looked to for guidance. This stripping away of right relationship leaves us exposed to the infinite reality of corrupt, lustful imaginations. Like fruit peeled too soon, it is damaging to uncover what God had wanted to remain protected!

Who among us can re-peel a banana once it has been peeled? The Bible says, "...With men it is impossible, but not with God: for with God all things are possible" {Mark 10:27}.

> *"None of you shall approach to any that is near of kin to him, to uncover their nakedness: I am the Lord."*   {Leviticus 18:6}

To molest a child is to uncover them. It leaves them feeling unprotected. Do you realize that one of the things the blood of Jesus Christ does is cover us? Like Noah's sons who covered their father's nakedness, the blood of Jesus will cover the uncovered. He will not allow you to spend the rest of your life exposed and violated.

God spoke a message through Ezekiel to the nation of Israel with an illustration of an abused woman. He spoke about how, as a child, this little girl was not cared for properly. But that He passed by and swaddled and cared for her as a baby. He also said the baby would have bled to death if He hadn't stopped the bleeding.

> *"Then I passed by and saw you kicking about in your blood, and as you lay there in your blood I said to you, 'Live!' I made you grow like a plant of the field. You grew up and developed and became the most beautiful of jewels. Your breasts were formed and your hair grew, you who were naked and bare. Later I passed by, and when I looked at you and saw that you were old enough for love, I spread the corner of my garment over you and covered your*

> *nakedness. I gave you my solemn oath and entered into a covenant*
> *with you, declares the Sovereign Lord, and you became mine. I*
> *bathed you with water and washed the blood from you and put*
> *ointments on you. I clothed you with an embroidered dress and put*
> *leather sandals on you. I dressed you in fine linen and covered you*
> *with costly garments."*   *[Ezekiel 16:6-10] [NIV]*

Did you know that God can stop the bleeding of an abused child? Even as you grow older, He still watches out for you! He will cover your nakedness. Reach out and embrace the fact that God has been watching over you all of your life. My sister, He covers you, He clothes you, and He blesses you! Rejoice in Him in spite of the broken places. God's grace is sufficient for your needs and your scars. He will anoint you with oil.

GOD'S INTENSIVE CARE

The anointing of the Lord be upon you now! May it bathe, heal and strengthen you as never before. For the hurting, God has intensive care. There will be times in your life when God nurtures you through crisis situations. You may not even realize how many times God has already intervened to relieve the tensions and stresses of day-to-day living. Because every now and then, He does us a favor. Yes, a favor—something we didn't earn or can't even explain except as the loving hand of God. He knows when the load is overwhelming. And many times He moves (it seems to us) just in the nick of time.

The Bible instructs men to dwell with women according to knowledge {1 Peter 3:7}. It will pay every husband to understand that many, many women do not deal easily with such stress as unpaid bills and financial disorder. Because of the way God created women, a feeling of security is a plus, especially in reference to the home. That same principle is important in our relationship with God. He is constantly reassuring us that we might have a consolation and a hope for the soul, the mind and emotions, steadfast and unmovable. He gives us security and assurance.

> *"Because God wanted to make the unchanging nature of his*
> *purpose very clear to the heirs of what was promised, he confirmed*
> *it with an oath. God did this so that, by two unchangeable things*
> *in which it is impossible for God to lie, we who have fled to take*
> *hold of the hope offered to us may be greatly encouraged."*
>   *[Hebrews 6:17-18] [NIV]*

BROKEN ARROW FEAR

"Also thou shalt lie down, and none shall make thee afraid..." is the Word of God to you {Job 11:19}. God wants to bring you to a place of rest, where there is no pacing the floor and no glaring through frightened eyes at those with whom you are involved. Like a frightened animal backed into a corner, we can become fearful and angry because we don't feel safe. So Christ says, "Woman, thou art loosed!"

There is no torment like inner-torment. How can you run from yourself? No matter what you achieve in life, if the clanging, rattling chains of old ghosts are not laid to rest, you will not have any real sense of peace and inner joy. God says, "None shall make thee afraid." And "...perfect love casteth out fear..." {1 John 4:18}.

It is a miserable feeling to spend your life in fear. Many grown women live in a fear that resulted from broken arrow experiences. This kind of fear can manifest itself in jealousy, depression and many other distresses. As you allow the past to pass over you as waters moving in the sea, you will begin to live and rest in a new assurance. God loves you so much that He is even concerned about your rest. So take authority over every flashback and every dream that keeps you linked to the past. Even as we share together here, the peace of God will do a new thing in your life. I encourage you to claim Job 11:16-19 as yours.

SIMPLER DAYS

I was raised in the rich, robust Appalachian mountains of West Virginia where the plush greenery accentuates the majestic peaks of the rugged, mountainous terrain. The hills sit around the river's edge like court stenographers, recording the events of the ages without expression or interference. I learned as a child how to entertain myself by running up and down the trails and scenic paths of our community, splashing in the creek beds and singing songs to the wind. This kind of simplistic joy is, to me, characteristic of that time when children were not as complex as they are now.

If you know much about the Appalachian mountains, you know they were the backyard for many, many Indians in days gone by. During my childhood, occasionally my classmates or I would find old Indian memorabilia in the rocks and creek beds in the hills. There are many large, man-made hills that the Indians called mounds, which served as cemeteries for the more affluent members of the tribes.

The most common things we found were discarded arrowheads that were carved to a point and beaten flat. Perhaps an Indian brave from the pages of history had thrown away an arrow, assuming he had gotten out of it all the use that he possibly could. Though worthless to him, it was priceless to us as we retrieved it from its hiding place and saved it in a safe and sacred place.

GOD GATHERS BROKEN ARROWS

In the same way, I believe God gathers discarded children who, like arrows, have been thrown away from the quiver of vain and ruthless people. If children are like arrows in the quiver of a mighty man, then broken arrows thrown away by that same man belong to our God. He is forever finding treasure in the discarded refuse of our confused society.

> *"And they shall be mine, saith the Lord of hosts, in that day when I make up my jewels; and I will spare them, as a man spareth his own son that serveth him."*   *(Malachi 3:17)*

Please, Holy Spirit, translate these meager words into a deluge of cleansing and renewal. I pray that you who have been marred, would allow the reconstructive hand of the Potter to mend the broken places in your lives. Amidst affairs and struggles, needs and incidents, may the peace and calmness of knowing God cause the birth of fresh dreams. But most of all, may it lay to rest old fears.

CHAPTER THREE

That Was Then

Many have more faith in a textbook written by a person whose eyes may be clouded by their own secrets, than to rely on the Word of God who knows the end from the beginning.

Many Christians experienced the new birth early in their childhood. It is beneficial to have the advantage of Christian ethics. I'm not sure what it would have been like to have been raised in the Church insulated from worldliness and sin. Sometimes I envy those who have been able to live victoriously all of their lives. But most of us have not had that kind of life. My concern is the many persons who have lost their sensitivity for others and who suffer from spiritual arrogance. Jesus condemned the Pharisees for their spiritual arrogance, yet many times that same self-righteous spirit creeps into the Church.

UNHOLY HOLINESS

There are those who define holiness as what one wears or what a person eats. For years churches displayed the name "holiness" because they monitored a person's outward appearance. But they weren't truly looking at character. Often, they were carried away with whether someone should wear makeup or jewelry when thousands of people were destroying themselves on drugs and prostitution. Priorities were confused. Unchurched people who came to church had no idea why the minister would emphasize outward apparel when people were bleeding inside.

The fact is, we were all born in sin and shaped in iniquity. We have no true badge of righteousness that we can wear on the outside. God concluded all are in sin so He might save us from ourselves {Galatians 3:22}. It wasn't the act of sin, but the state of sin, that brought us into condemnation. We were all born in sin. Equally and individually we were shaped in iniquity without one race or sociological group escaping the fact of Adam's sinful heritage.

MAJORING ON THE MINORS

No one person needs any more of the blood of Jesus than the other. Jesus died once and for all. Humanity must come to God on equal terms. Each individual is totally helpless to earn his or her way to Him. When we come to Him with this attitude, He raises us up by the blood of Christ. He doesn't raise us up because we do good things. He raises us up because we have faith in the finished work on the cross.

Many in the Church were striving for holiness. What we were striving to perfect had already fallen and will only be restored at the second coming of the Lord. We were trying to perfect flesh. But flesh is in enmity against God, whether we paint it or not.

The Church frequently has, and still does, major on the minors. When that begins to happen, it is a sign that the Church has lost touch with the world and with the inspiration of the Lord. It is no longer reaching out to the lost. A church that focuses on the external has lost its passion for souls. When we come into that position, we have attained a pseudo-holiness. It's a false sanctity.

WHAT IS HOLINESS?

To understand holiness, we must first separate the pseudo from the genuine, because when you come into a church, it is possible to walk away feeling like a second-class citizen. Many start going overboard trying to be a super spiritual person in order to compensate for an embarrassing past. You can't earn deliverance. You have to just receive it by faith. Christ is the only righteousness that God will accept. If outward sanctity had impressed God, Christ would have endorsed the Pharisees.

However, there is a sanctity of your spirit that comes through the blood of the Lord Jesus Christ which sanctifies the innermost part of your being. Certainly, once you get cleaned up in your spirit, it will be reflected in your character and conduct. You won't dress like Mary Magdalene did before she met the Master. The Spirit of the Lord will give you boundaries. On the other hand, people must be loosed from the chains of guilt and condemnation. Many women in particular have been bound by manipulative messages that specialize in control and dominance.

THE ONLY HOSPITAL FOR WOUNDED SOULS

The Church must open its doors and allow people who have a past to enter in. What often happens is they're spending years in the back pew trying to pay through obeisance for something in the past. Congregations are often unwilling to release reformed women. Remember, the same blood that cleanses the man can restore the woman also.

The Bible never camouflaged the weaknesses of the people God used. God used David and God used Abraham. We must divorce our embarrassment about wounded people. Yes, we've got wounded people. Yes, we've got hurting people. And sometimes they break the boundaries becoming lascivious and out of control. When they do, we have to readmit them into the hospital and allow them to be treated again. But that's what the Church is designed to do. The Church is the only hospital for wounded souls.

The staff in a hospital understands that periodically people get sick and they need a place to recover. Now, I'm not condoning the sin. I'm just explaining that it's a reality. Many of those in Scripture were unholy. The only holy man out of all the characters in the Bible is Jesus Christ, the righteousness of God.

FOCUSING ON HURTING PEOPLE

We have all wrestled with something, though it may not always be the same challenge. My struggle may not be yours. If I'm wrestling with something that's not a problem for you, you do not have the responsibility of judging me when all the while you are wrestling with something equally as incriminating.

Jesus' actions were massively different from ours. He focused on hurting people. Every time He saw a hurting person, He reached out and ministered to their need.

Once when He was preaching, He looked through the crowd and saw a man with a withered hand. He immediately healed him {Mark 3:1-5}. He sat with the prostitutes and the winebibbers, not the upper echelon of His community. In fact, Jesus surrounded Himself with broken, bleeding, dirty people. He called a woman who was crippled and bent over {Luke 13:11-13}. She had come to church and sat in the synagogue for years and years. Noboby had helped that woman until Jesus saw her. When He did, He called her to the forefront.

At first when I thought about His calling her, I thought, *How rude to call her.* Why didn't He speak the word and heal her in her seat? Perhaps God wants to see us moving toward Him. We need to invest in our own deliverance. We will bring a testimony out of a test. I also believe that someone else there who saw Jesus ministering had problems. When we can see someone else overcoming a handicap, it helps us to overcome.

HEALING THE WOUNDS OF THE PAST

We can't know how long it took the woman to get up to the front. Handicapped people don't move as fast as others do. As believers, we often don't grow as fast as other people grow because we've been suffering for a long time. We are incapacitated. Often what is simple for one person is extremely difficult for another. But Jesus challenged this woman's limitations. He called her anyway.

Thank God He calls women with a past. He reaches out and says, "Get up! You can come to Me." Regardless of what a person has done, or what kind of abuse one has suffered, He still calls. We may think our secret is worse than anyone else's. But rest assured that He knows all about it, and still draws us with an immutable call.

Jesus said, "Come unto me, all ye that labour and are heavy laden, and I will give you rest" {Matthew 11:28}.

So no matter how difficult life seems, people with a past need to make their way to Jesus. Regardless of the obstacles within and without, they must reach out to Him. You may have a baby out of wedlock cradled in your arms, but keep pressing on. You may have been abused and molested and never able to talk to anyone about it, but don't cease reaching out for Him. You don't have to tell everyone your entire history. Just know that He calls, on purpose, women with a past. He knows your history and He called you anyway.

God will give you a miracle. He will do it powerfully in public. And many will say, "Is this the same woman who was bent over and wounded in the church?" Perhaps others will think, "Is this the same woman who had one foot in the church and the other in an affair?"

JESUS WAS INTIMATE WITH "COLORFUL" PEOPLE

Many of the people who were a part of the ministry of Jesus' earthly life were people with colorful pasts. Some had indeed always looked for the Messiah to come. Others were involved in things that were immoral and inappropriate.

A good example is Matthew. He was a man who worked in an extremely distasteful profession. He was a tax collector. Few people today like tax collectors. Their reputation was even worse at that time in history. Matthew collected taxes for the Roman empire. He had to have been considered a traitor by those who were faithful Jews. The Romans were their oppressors. How could he have forsaken his heritage and joined the Romans?

And tax collectors did more than simply receive taxes for the benefit of the government. They were frequently little better than common extortioners. They had to collect a certain amount for Rome, but anything they could collect above that set figure was considered the collector's commission. Therefore, they frequently claimed excessive taxes. They often acted like common thieves.

But regardless of his past, Jesus called Matthew to be a disciple. He later served as a great apostle and wrote one of the books of the New Testament. Much of the history and greatness of Jesus would be lost to us were it not for Jesus calling Matthew, a man with a past. We must maintain a strong line of demarcation between a person's past and present.

PEOPLE WITH A PAST

These were the people Jesus wanted to reach. And He was criticized for being around such questionable characters. Everywhere He went the oppressed and the rejected followed Him because they knew that He offered mercy and forgiveness.

> *"And it came to pass, as Jesus sat at meat in the house, behold, many publicans and sinners came and sat down with him and his disciples. And when the Pharisees saw it, they said unto his disciples, Why eateth your Master with publicans and sinners? But when Jesus heard that, he said unto them, They that be whole need not a physician, but they that are sick."* [Matthew 9:10-12]

People with a past have always been able to come to Jesus. He makes them into something wonderful and marvelous. It is said that Mary Magdalene was a prostitute. Christ was moved with compassion for even this base kind of human existence. He never used a prostitute for sex, but He certainly loved them into God's kingdom.

When Christ was teaching in the temple courts, there were those who tried to trap Him in His words. They knew that His ministry appealed to the masses of lowly people. They thought that if they could get Him to say some condemning things, the people wouldn't follow Him anymore.

> *"And the scribes and Pharisees brought unto him a woman taken in adultery; and when they had set her in the midst, they say unto him, Master, this woman was taken in adultery, in the very act. Now Moses in the law commanded us, that such should be stoned: but what sayest thou? This they said, tempting him, that they might have to accuse him. But Jesus stooped down, and with his finger wrote on the ground, as though he heard them not. So when they continued asking him, he lifted up himself, and said unto them, he that is without sin among you, let him first cast a stone at her."*　　　　　　　　　　　　　　*(John 8:3-7)*

Clearly Jesus saw the foolish religious pride in their hearts. He was not condoning the sin of adultery. He simply understood the need to meet people where they were and minister to their need. He also saw the pride in the Pharisees and ministered correction to that pride. He saw the wounded woman and ministered forgiveness. Justice demanded that she be stoned to death. But God's mercy threw the case out of court.

Have you ever wondered where the man was who had been committing adultery with this woman? She was caught in the very act. So surely they knew who the man was. There still seems to be a double standard today when it comes to sexual sin. Often we look down on a woman because of her past, but overlook who she is now. Jesus, however, knew the power of a second chance.

> *"When Jesus had lifted up himself, and saw none but the woman, he said unto her, Woman, where are those thine accusers? hath no man condemned thee? She said, No man, Lord. And Jesus said unto her, Neither do I condemn thee: go, and sin no more."*　　　　　　　　　　　　　　　　　*(John 8:10-11)*

There are those today who are very much like this woman. They have come into the Church. Perhaps they have made strong commitments to Christ and have the very Spirit of God living within them. Yet they walk as cripples. They have been stoned and ridiculed. They may not be physically broken and bowed over, but they are wounded within. Somehow the Church must find room to throw off condemnation and give them life and healing.

The blood of Jesus is efficacious, cleansing the woman who feels unclean. So how can we reject what He has cleansed and made whole? Just as He said to the woman then, He proclaims today: "Neither do I condemn thee: go, and sin no more." How can the Church do any less?

THE CHAINS THAT BIND

The chains that bind are often from events that we have no control over. The woman who is abused is not responsible for the horrible events that happened in her past. Other times the chains are there because we have willfully lived lives that bring bondage and pain. But regardless of the source, Jesus comes to set us free. He is unleashing the women of His Church. He forgives, heals and restores. Women can find the potential of their future because of His wonderful power operating in their lives.

CHAPTER FOUR

The Victim Survives

Stand in a stream with waters around your ankles. The waters that pass by you at that moment, you will never see again. So it is with the misery that has challenged your life: Let it go, let it pass away.

ow I would like to share what is perhaps one of the most powerful stories in the Bible. It takes place in ancient Israel. The chosen people had become a great empire. Israel was at its zenith under the leadership of a godly king named David. There can be no argument that David frequently allowed his passions to lead him into moral failure. However, he was a man who recognized his failures and repented. He was a man who sought God's heart.

Although David longed to follow God, some of his passions and lusts were inherited by his children. Maybe they learned negative things from their father's failures. That is a tendency we must resist. We ought not repeat the failure of our fathers. We are most vulnerable, however, to our father's weaknesses.

"And it came to pass after this, that Absalom the son of David had a fair sister, whose name was Tamar; and Amnon the son of David loved her. And Amnon was so vexed, that he fell sick for his sister Tamar; for she was a virgin; and Amnon thought it hard for him to do any thing to her. But Amnon had a friend, whose name was Jonadab, the son of Shimeah David's brother: and Jonadab was a very subtil man. And he said unto him, Why art thou, being the king's son, lean from day to day? wilt thou not tell me? And Amnon said unto him, I love Tamar, my brother Absalom's sister. And Jonadab said unto him, Lay thee down on thy bed, and make thyself sick: and when thy father cometh to see thee, say unto him, I pray thee, let my sister Tamar come, and give me meat, and dress the meat in my sight, that I may see it, and eat it at her hand. So Amnon lay down, and made himself sick: and when the king was come to see him, Amnon said unto the king, I pray thee, let Tamar my sister come, and make me a couple of cakes in my sight, that I may eat at her hand. Then David sent home to Tamar saying, Go now to thy brother Amnon's house, and dress him meat. So Tamar went to her brother Amnon's house; and he was laid down. And she took flour, and kneaded it, and made cakes in his sight, and did bake the cakes. And she took a pan, and poured them out

*before him; but he refused to eat. And Amnon said, Have out all
men from me. And they went out every man from him. And Amnon
said unto Tamar, Bring the meat into the chamber, that I may eat
of thine hand. And Tamar took the cakes which she had made, and
brought them into the chamber to Amnon her brother. And when
she had brought them unto him to eat, he took hold of her, and
said unto her, Come lie with me, my sister. And she answered him,
Nay, my brother, do not force me; for no such thing ought to be
done in Israel: do not thou this folly. And I, whither shall I cause
my shame to go? and as for thee, thou shalt be as one of the fools
in Israel. Now therefore, I pray thee, speak unto the king; for he
will not withhold me from thee. Howbeit he would not hearken
unto her voice: but, being stronger than she, forced her, and lay
with her. Then Amnon hated her exceedingly; so that the hatred
wherewith he hated her was greater than the love wherewith he
had loved her. And Amnon said unto her, Arise, be gone. And she
said unto him, There is no cause: this evil in sending me away is
greater than the other that thou didst unto me. But he would not
hearken unto her. Then he called his servant that ministered unto
him, and said, Put now this woman out from me, and bolt the door
after her. And she had a garment of divers colours upon her: for
with such robes were the king's daughters that were virgins appar-
elled. Then his servant brought her out, and bolted the door after
her. And Tamar put ashes on her head, and rent her garment of
divers colours that was on her, and laid her hand on her head, and
went on crying. And Absalom her brother said unto her, Hath
Amnon by brother been with thee? but hold now thy peace, my sister: he is thy brother; regard not this thing. So Tamar remained
desolate in her brother Absalom's house. But when king David
heard of all these things, he was very wroth."*

{2 Samuel 13:1-21}

The name *Tamar* means "palm tree." Tamar is a survivor. She stands in
summer and spring. She even faces fall with leaves when other trees lose
theirs. She still stands. When the cold blight of winter stands up in her face,
she withstands the chilly winds and remains green throughout the winter.
Tamar is a survivor. And like her, you are a survivor. Through hard times God
has granted you the tenacity to endure stresses and strains.

ABUSE IS ABNORMAL USE

It's hard for me as a man to fully understand how horrible rape is for women. I can sympathize, but the violation is incomprehensible. I don't feel as vulnerable to being raped as a woman would. However, I have come to realize that rape is another creature inflicting his will on someone without her permission. It is more than just the act of sex. It is someone victimizing you. There are all kinds of rape: emotional, spiritual and physical. And there are many ways to be victimized. Abuse is abnormal use. It is terrible to misuse or abuse anyone.

GUILTY BY VICTIMIZATION

Many women feel guilty about things they had no control over. They feel guilty about being victimized. Often their original intention was to help another, but in the process they were damaged. Tamar must have been one of them.

Tamar was the king's daughter, and she was a virgin. She was a "good girl." She didn't do anything immoral. It is amazing that her own brother would be so filled with desire that he would go to such lengths to destroy his sister. He thought he was in love. But it wasn't love, it was lust. He craved her so intensely that he lost his appetite for food. He was visibly distorted with passion. Love is a giving force, while lust is a selfish compulsion centralized on gratification.

TWISTED AMNON

It is frightening to think about the nights that Amnon plotted and conjured Tamar's destruction. The intensity of his passion for her was awesome. So much so, that even his father and cousin recognized something had altered his behavior. He was filled with lustful passion for her.

Amnon draws a picture for us of how badly the enemy wants to violate God's children. He is planning and plotting your destruction. He has watched you with wanton eyes. He has great passion and perseverance. That is why Jesus told Peter, "...Satan hath *desired* to have you, that he may sift you as wheat: but I have prayed for thee..." {Luke 22:31-32}. Satan lusts after God's children. He wants you. He craves you with an animalistic passion. He awaits an opportunity for attack. In addition, he loves to use people to fulfill the same kinds of lust upon one another.

Desire is a motivating force. It can make you do things you never thought yourself capable of doing. Lust can make a man break his commitment to himself. It will cause people to reach after things they never thought they would reach for.

Like Peter, you may have gone through some horrible times, but Jesus intercedes on your behalf. No matter what struggles women have faced, confidence is found in the ministry of our High Priest. He prays for you. Faith comes when you recognize that you can't help yourself. Only trust in Christ can bring you through. Many have suffered mightily, but Christ gives the strength to overcome the attacks of Satan, and of human, selfish lust.

ALLOW CHRIST TO COME INTO THE
DARK PLACES OF YOUR LIFE

Often, the residual effects of being abused linger for many years. Some never find deliverance because they never allow Christ to come into the dark places of their life. Jesus has promised to set you free from every curse of the past. If you have suffered abuse, please know that He will bring you complete healing. He wants the whole person well in body, emotions and spirit. He will deliver you from all the residue of your past. Perhaps your incident is over, but the crippling damage remains. Let Him deal with the crippling that's left in your life.

MANIPULATING THE MATERNAL

One of the things that makes many women particularly vulnerable to different types of abuse and manipulation is their maternal instinct. Wicked men frequently capitalize on this tendency in order to have their way with women. Mothers like to take care of little helpless babies. It seems that the more helpless a man acts, the more maternal a woman can become. Women instinctively are nurturers, reaching out to needy people in order to nurture, love and provide inner strength. But all too often, these healthy desires are taken advantage of by those who would fulfill their own lusts. The gift of discernment must operate in your life. There are many wonderful men. But I must warn you about Amnon. He is out there, and he is dangerous.

TWO KINDS OF RAPE

The number of cases of violence within relationships and marriages is growing at an alarming rate. The incidence of date rape is reaching epidemic proportions. And the fastest growing number of murders today is happening within relationships. Husbands and wives, and girlfriends and boyfriends are killing one another. Some women have taken to murder in order to escape the constant violence of an abusive husband. It is important that you do not allow loneliness to coerce you into Amnon's bed.

Another form of abuse is more subtle. There are those men who often coerce women into a sexual relationship by claiming that they love them. Deception is emotional rape! It is a terrible feeling to be used by someone. Looking for love in all the wrong places leads to a feeling of abuse.

A deceiver may continually promise that he will leave his wife for his lover. His lover holds on to that hope, but it never seems to come true. So he makes every kind of excuse possible for taking advantage of her. And she, because of her vulnerability, follows blindly along until the relationship has gone so far that she is trapped.

Men who have sex with women without being committed to them are just as guilty of abuse as a rapist. A woman may have given her body to such a man, but she did so because of certain expectations. When someone uses another person for sex by misleading them, it is the same as physical rape. The abuse is more subtle, but it amounts to the same thing. Both the abuser and the victim are riding into a blazing inferno. Anything can happen when the victim has had enough.

SUFFERING THE EXTREMES OF LOW SELF-ESTEEM

Some women suffer from low self-esteem. They are victims and they don't even know it. Perhaps that's you. Do you think it's your fault every time something goes wrong? It's not your fault if you are being abused in this way. However, it is your fault if you don't allow God's Word to arrest sin and weakness in your life. It is time to let go of every ungodly relationship. Do it now!

When Tamar came into that ancient Israeli bedroom, her brother took advantage of her maternal instincts. He told her that he needed help. He sought her sympathy. Then once she gave in to his requests for help, he violently raped her. Although the circumstances may be different, the same thing is happening today.

AMNON IS AMONG US

The kind of violent act that Amnon performed that night was more than an offense against a young lady. He offended God and society by committing incest. There are those who attend church who are incestuous. It sill happens today, but God is saying ENOUGH IS ENOUGH!

Some have been abused, misused and victimized. Some even played a part in their own demise. Then there are those who live in fear and pain because of the immoral relationships that took place in the home.

If you know this kind of pain, the Lord wants to heal you. Those who have a desperate need for male attention, usually come from a situation where there has been an absence of positive male role models in the home. Perhaps you didn't get enough nurturing as a girl. Therefore, it becomes easy to compromise and do anything to find male acceptance and love.

THE LORD IS CALLING!

The Lord is calling the hurting to Him. He will fill that void in your life. He wants to be the father you never had who will mend your heart with a positive role model. Through His Spirit, He wants to hold and nurture you. Millions have longed for a positive hug and nurturing embrace from fathers without ever receiving what they longed for. There is a way to fill that emptiness inside. It is through relationship with God.

Men, God is healing us so we can recognize that a woman who is not our wife is to be treated as our sister. Women must learn that they can have a platonic relationship with men. A brotherly and sisterly love does not include sexual intimacy. It does not include self-gratification.

There is a place in the heart of most women for an intimate, yet platonic relationship. Big brothers tend to protect their little sisters. They tend to watch for traps that may be placed in the sister's way. But abused women have confused ideas about relationships and may not understand a healthy platonic relationship with the opposite sex. This confusion comes from the past. One lady said she could never trust a man who didn't sleep with her. Actually, she had a long history of victimization that led to her poor view of relationships.

"MEN" ARE NOT THE ENEMY

Society often places a woman's worth on her sexual appeal. But nothing is further from the truth. Self-esteem cannot be earned by performance in bed. Society suggests that the only thing men want is sex. Although the male sex drive is very strong, all men are not like Amnon.

Men, in general, are not the enemy. We cannot use Amnon as a basis to evaluate all men. So don't allow an Amnon experience to taint your future. Draw a line of demarcation and say to yourself, "That was then—and this is now!"

THE CHURCH IS GOD'S CEDAR CHEST!

The Song of Solomon shows a progression of the relationship between the author and his wife. First she was his sister. Then she became his bride. He also wrote of protecting a little sister. There are many new converts in the Church who should be treated as little sisters. Solomon says, "...inclose her with boards of cedar" {Song of Solomon 8:9}. The Church is God's cedar chest!

God's people are to nurture and protect one another. It makes no difference how tempestuous our past life has been. Even in the face of abuse, God still cares. Allow Him the privilege of doing what Absalom did for Tamar. He took her in. He gave her a place of comfort, a place to abide.

> *"He that dwelleth in the secret place of the most High shall abide under the shadow of the Almighty."* {Psalm 91:1}

Tamar laid outside Amnon's door a fragmented, bruised rose petal. Her dreams were shattered. Her confidence was violated. Her virginity was desecrated. But Absalom took her into his domain. Did you know that God has intensive care? He will take you in His arms. His love is flowing into broken lives all over the country. So don't believe for one moment that no one cares. God cares, and the Church is learning to become a conduit of His concern. At last, we are in His school of love. Jesus said, "By this shall all men know that ye are my disciples, if ye have love one to another" {John 13:35}. Love embraces the totality of the other person.

SCARS FROM THE PAST

It is impossible to completely and effectively love someone without being included in that other person's history. Our history has made us who we are. The images, scars and victories that we live with have shaped us into the people we have become. We will never know who a person is until we understand where they have been.

The secret of being transformed from a vulnerable victim to a victorious, loving person is found in the ability to open your past to someone responsible enough to share your weaknesses and pains with. "Bear ye one another's burdens, and so fulfil the law of Christ," writes Paul in Galatians 6:2. You don't have to keep reliving it. You can release it.

TAKE THE FIRST STEP

There can be no better first step toward deliverance than to find a Christian counselor to share your past with. Then, come out of hiding. Of course, some care should be taken. No one is expected to air their personal life to everyone or everywhere. However, if you seek God's guidance and the help of confident leadership, you will find someone who can help you work through the pain and suffering of your victimized past.

The Church is a body. No one operates independent of another. We are all in this walk together and therefore can build one another up. Let's carry some of the load with which our sisters are burdened.

Tamar was victimized brutally, yet she survived. There is hope for the victim. If you are a victim, there is no need to feel weak if you have Jesus Christ. His power is enough to bring about the kinds of changes that will set you free. He is calling, through the work of the Holy Spirit, for you to be set free.

CHAPTER FIVE

Walk Into the Newness

If you are a woman living today, and you're not learning spiritual warfare, you're in trouble. The enemy may be taking advantage of you.

mnon was wicked. He brutally raped his sister Tamar. He destroyed her destiny and her future. He slashed her self-esteem. He spoiled her integrity. He broke her femininity like a twig under his feet. He assassinated her character. She went into his room a virgin with a future, but when it was over, she was a bleeding, trembling, crying mass of pain.

This is one of the saddest stories in the Bible. It reveals what people can do to one another if left alone without God. When Amnon and Tamar were left alone, he assassinated her. Tamar's body may have survived, but her femininity was destroyed. She felt she would never be the woman she should have been because it happened.

Have you ever had anything happen to you that changed you forever? Something you went through that somehow, like a palm tree, you survived? Something you knew would never let things be the same again?

Perhaps you have spent every day since then "bowed over," and you can in "no wise lift up yourself." You shout. You sing. You skip. But when no one is looking, when the crowd is gone and the lights are out, you are still that trembling, crying, bleeding mass of pain that is abused, bowed, bent backward, and crippled.

Maybe you are in the Church, but you are in trouble. People move all around you, and you laugh, even entertain them. You are fun to be around. But they don't know. You can't seem to talk about what happened in your life.

The Bible says Tamar was in trouble. The worst part about it was, after Amnon had abused her, he didn't even want her. He had messed up her life and spoiled what she was proud of. He assassinated her future and damaged her prospects. He destroyed her integrity and self-esteem. He had changed her countenance forever. And afterward, he didn't even want her. All Tamar could say was, "What you're doing to me now is worse than what you did to me at first." Or, "Raping me was horrible, but not wanting me is worse!" {2 Samuel 13:16.}

When women feel unwanted, it destroys their sense of esteem and value. Some of you have gone through divorces, tragedies and adulterous relationships, and you've been left feeling unwanted. You just can't shout over that sort of thing. You can't leap over that kind of wall. It injures something about you that changes how you relate to everyone else for the rest of your life.

When Amnon rejected Tamar after he raped her, she also pleaded with him, "Don't throw me away." She was fighting for the last strands of her femininity. But Amnon called a servant and told him to, "Throw her out." The Bible even says he hated her with a greater intensity than the love he felt for her before his violation {2 Samuel 13:15}.

AMNON DOESN'T LOVE YOU

God knows that the Amnon in your life really does not love you. He's out to abuse you. His servant picked Tamar up, opened the door and threw the victimized woman out. Then as she laid on the ground outside the door—with nowhere to go—he told his servant to, "Lock the door."

What do you do when you are trapped in a transitory state, neither in nor out? When you're left lying at the door, torn up and disturbed, trembling and intimidated? The Bible says Tamar cried.

What do you do when you don't know what to do? When you're filled with regrets, pains, nightmare experiences, and are seemingly unable to find relief? Tamar stayed on the ground. And she cried.

Tamar had a coat, a cape of many colors. It was a sign of her virginity and of her future. She was going to give it to her husband one day. But she sat there and ripped it up. When she did, she was saying, "I have no future. It wasn't just that he took my body. He took my future. He took my esteem and value away."

Many of you have been physically or emotionally raped and robbed. And you have survived. But you left a substantial degree of self-esteem on Amnon's bed. Have you lost the road map that directs you back to where you were before?

A CALL OUT IN THE SPIRIT

There is a call out in the Spirit for hurting women. The Lord says, "I want you." No matter how many men like Amnon have told you, "I don't want you," God is saying, "I want you. I've seen you bent over. I've seen the aftereffects of what happened to you. I've seen you at your worst moment. And still, I want you." God hasn't changed His mind. He loves you with an everlasting love.

When Jesus encountered the infirm woman of Luke 13, He called out to her. There may have been many fine women present that day, but the Lord didn't call them forward. He reached around all of them and found that crippled woman in the back. And when He called forth that wounded, hurting woman with a past, He issued the Spirit's call to every other like her who has had their self-esteem destroyed by the intrusion of vicious circumstances.

The infirm woman must have thought, "He wants me. He wants me. I'm frayed and torn, but He wants me. I have been through trouble. I have been through this trauma, but still, He wants me." Perhaps she thought no one would ever want her again. But Jesus wanted her. He had a plan.

She may have known that it would take a while for her life to be put completely back together. She had many things to overcome. She was handicapped. She was probably filled with insecurities. Yet Jesus called her forth to give her His touch.

TURN YOURSELF TOWARD HOME

If you can identify with the feelings of this infirm woman, then know that Jesus is waiting on you and that He wants you. He sees your struggling and He knows all about your pain. He knows what happened to you eighteen years ago, ten years ago, or even last week. With patience He waits for you, as the father waited for the prodigal son. Jesus says to the hurting and crippled, "I want you enough to wait for you to hobble your way back home."

Now God says, "I'm going to deliver you and heal you. Now I'm going to renew you and release you. I'm going to tell you who you really are. Now I'm ready to reveal to you why you had to go through what you did to become what you shall become."

And God is saying, "Now I'm going to tell you a secret, something between you and Me that no one else knows. Something that Amnon didn't know, your boyfriend didn't know, and your first husband didn't know. Something that your father, uncle, brother or whoever abused you had no knowledge of. Come closer and let Me tell you. You are the daughter of a King. Your Father is the King."

YOU ARE A PRINCESS!

When the infirm woman came to Jesus, He proclaimed her freedom as she stood erect for the first time in eighteen years. When you come to Jesus, He will cause you to stand in His strength. You will know how important you are to Him. Part of your recovery will be to learn how to stand up and live in the "now" of His life, instead of the "then" of yours. That was then—but this is now.

I proclaim to the abused: There is healing going into your spirit right now. I speak life to you. I speak deliverance to you. I speak restoration to you. All in the mighty name of Jesus, in the invincible, all-powerful, everlasting name of Jesus. I proclaim victory to you. You will recover the loss you suffered at the hands of your abuser. You will get back every stolen item. Jesus will heal that broken twig. He will rebuild your self-esteem, your self-respect, and your integrity.

GIVE HIM ALL YOUR SECRETS

All you need do is to allow His power and anointing to touch your hurting places. He will take care of the secrets. He touches the places where you've been assassinated. He knows the woman you would have been, the woman you should have been, the woman you could have been. God is healing and restoring her in you as you call out to Him.

The enemy wanted to change your destiny through a series of events, but God will restore you to wholeness as if the events had never happened. The triumphant woman locked inside shall come forth to where she belongs. He's delivering her. He's releasing her. He's restoring her. He's building her back. He's bringing her out. He's delivering by the power of His Spirit. "...Not by might, nor by power, but by my spirit, saith the Lord of hosts" {Zechariah 4:6}.

GOD'S ANOINTING IS REACHING OUT TO YOU

The anointing of the living God is reaching out to you. He calls you forth to set you free. When you reach out to Him and allow the Holy Spirit to have His way, His anointing is present to deliver you. Demons will tremble. Satan wants to keep you at the door, but never let you enter. He wants to keep you down. Now his power is broken in your life.

Tamar knew the feeling of desertion. She understood that she was cast out. However, the Bible explains that Absalom came and said, "I'm going to take you in."

You too have been lying at the door. Perhaps you didn't have anywhere to go. You may have been half in and half out. You were broken and demented and disturbed. But God sent Absalom to restore his sister.

In this instance, Absalom depicts the purpose of real ministry. Thank God for the Church. It is the place where you can come broken and disgusted, and be healed, delivered and set free in the name of Jesus.

Jesus said, "The Spirit of the Lord is upon me, because he hath anointed me to preach the gospel to the poor; he hath sent me to heal the broken-hearted, to preach deliverance to the captives, and recovering of sight to the blind, to set at liberty them that are bruised" {Luke 4:18}.

You may have thought that you would never rejoice again. But God declares that you can have freedom in Him now! The joy that He brings can be restored to your soul. He identifies with your pain and suffering. He knows what it is like to suffer abuse at the hands of others. Yet He proclaims joy and strength. He will give you the garment of praise instead of the spirit of heaviness {Isaiah 61:3}.

HOLD UP YOUR HANDS AND HEAD

Once you have called out to Him, you can lift up your hands in praise. No matter what you have suffered, you can hold up your head. Regardless of who has hurt you, hold up your head! Forget how many times you've been married. Put aside those who mistreated you. You may have been a lesbian. You may have been a crack addict. It doesn't matter who you were. You may have even been molested. You can't change where you have been, but you can change where you are going.

> *"Lift up your heads, O ye gates; even lift them up, ye everlasting doors; and the King of glory shall come in. Who is this King of glory? The Lord of hosts, he is the King of glory. Selah."*
> *{Psalm 24:9-10}*

He will restore to you that which the cankerworm and the locust ate up {Joel 2:25}. He says, "I'm going to give it back to you." Maybe you wrestle with guilt. You've been hearing babies crying in your spirit. You feel so dirty. You've had abortions. You've been misused and abused. The devil keeps bringing up to you your failures of the past. But God is saying:

> *"Come now, and let us reason together, saith the Lord: though your sins be as scarlet, they shall be as white as snow; though they be red like crimson, they shall be as wool."*   *{Isaiah 1:18}*

All my life I have had a tremendous compassion for hurting people. When other people would put their foot on them, I always tended to have a ministry of mercy. Perhaps it is because I've had my own pain. When you have suffered, it makes you able to relate to other people's pain. So the Lord settled me in a ministry that just tends to cater to hurting people. Sometimes when I minister, I find myself fighting back tears. And sometimes I can hear the cries of anguished people in the crowd.

WALK INTO THE NEWNESS!

Like Tamar, you are a survivor. So you should celebrate it! Instead of agonizing over your tragedies, you should celebrate your victory and thank God you made it. I charge you to step over your adversity and walk into the newness. It is like stepping from a storm into the sunshine. Just step into it now.

God has blessed me with two little boys and two little daughters. As a father, I have found that I have a ministry of hugs. When something happens, and I really can't fix it, I just hug them. I can't change how other people treated them. I can't change what happened at school. I can't make the teacher like them. And I can't take away the insults. But I can hug them!

The Church needs to develop a ministry of hugs. I believe the best nurses are the ones who have been patients. They have compassion on the victim. If anyone understands the plight of women, it ought to be women. And if anyone understands the needs of the infirm, it ought to be the Church. The touch of the Master sets us free. The touch of a fellow pilgrim lets us know we are not alone in our plight.

RECEIVE YOUR FREEDOM NOW

The Holy Spirit is calling for the broken, infirm women to come to Jesus. He will restore and deliver. How do we come to Jesus? We come to His Body, the Church. It is in the Church that we can hear the Word of God. The Church gives us strength and nourishment. The Church is to be the place where we share our burdens and allow others to help us with them. The Spirit calls; the burdened need only heed the call.

There are three tenses of faith! When Lazarus died, Martha, his sister, said, "Lord, if You would have been here, my brother would not have died."

This is historical faith. Its view is digressive. Then when Jesus responded, "Lazarus will live again," Martha replied, "I know he will live in the resurrection." This is futuristic faith. It is progressive. But Martha also acknowledged God's working in the present when she said, "But *even now* You have the power to raise him up again." {See John 11:21-27.}

I feel like Martha. Even now, after all you've been through, I know that God has the power to raise you up again! This is the present tense of faith. Walk into the newness, even now.

CHAPTER SIX

Origins of Femininity

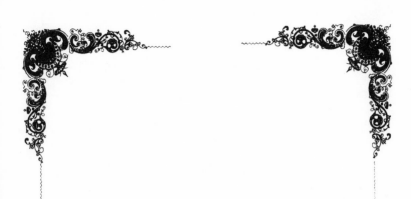

God will reward those who
persevere in seeking Him.
He may not come when you
want Him to, but He will be
right on time.

early every home in America is wired for electricity. Walls are covered with receptacles that deliver the electric current. But in order to take advantage of the power, something must be plugged into the receptacle. The receptacle is the female, and the plug is the male.

Women were made like receptacles because they were made to be receivers in every area of life. Men were made to be givers. They were made to give physically, sexually and emotionally, and to provide for others in life.

The woman was made, or fashioned, out of the man, to be his help meet. She was made to help him meet and accomplish his task. Through their union, men and women find wholeness in each other. In other words, a power saw has great potential for cutting, but it is ineffective until it is plugged in. The receptacle helps the power saw meet its purpose. Without that receptacle, the power saw, although mighty, remains limited.

A CERTAIN VULNERABILITY

However, there is a certain vulnerability built into the receptacle because of the different kinds of plugs it may be connected with. Receptacles, like women, are open. They are open by nature and design. Men are closed. Therefore, women must be careful what they allow to plug into them that will draw their strength. The wrong plugs may seek your help and drain your power.

Because God recognizes your vulnerability, He determined that those who would plug into the woman sexually would have to have a covenant. It was never God's intention for humanity to have casual sex. His design has always included the commitment of a covenant. So He purposed that a man who has sexual relations with a woman would be committed to her for life. And that nothing short of this commitment would meet His standards.

GOD WANTS YOU COVERED

God wants you covered like the electrical outlet is covered, so no one can tamper with your intended purpose. The married woman is covered by her husband. The single woman is covered by her chastity and morality. It is dangerous to be uncovered.

Originally, God created humanity perfect and good.

> *"And God said, Let us make man in our image, after our likeness: and let them have dominion over the fish of the sea, and over the fowl of the air, and over the cattle, and over all the earth, and over every creeping thing that creepeth upon the earth."*
>
> *(Genesis 1:26)*

God placed Adam in the garden He prepared for him with one simple rule: Man was not allowed to eat of the tree of the knowledge of good and evil. God wanted mankind to rely on Him for moral decisions. History records the consequences of man's attempts at making his own moral decisions after the fall. The history is bleak.

Although God had made a wonderful place for Adam to live, the man remained less than complete. He needed a woman. Keep in mind, though, that she was needed to complete his *purpose*, not his *person*. Therefore, if you are not complete as a person, marriage will not help you.

> *"And the Lord God caused a deep sleep to fall upon Adam, and he slept: and he took one of his ribs, and closed up the flesh instead thereof; and the rib, which the Lord God had taken from man, made he a woman, and brought her unto the man."*
>
> *(Genesis 2:21-22)*

In Genesis 3 we see that Eve allowed herself to be taken advantage of by Satan, who plugged into her the desire to see, taste, and be wise. The enemy took advantage of her weakness.

> *"And the man said, The woman whom thou gavest to be with me, she gave me of the tree, and I did eat."*   *(Genesis 3:12)*

Eve had given her attention over to someone else.

> *"And the Lord God said unto the woman, What is this that thou hast done? And the woman said, The serpent beguiled me, and I did eat."*
>
> *(Genesis 3:13)*

Adam's anger is shown in his statement in Genesis 3:12, "You gave her to be with me!" to which the woman answered, "Well, I couldn't help it. He plugged into and beguiled me."

BE CAREFUL ABOUT WHO UNCOVERS YOU

You've got to be careful who you let uncover you, because, as with Eve, they can lead you to complete destruction. Notice what God did next:

> *"And the Lord God said unto the serpent, Because thou hast done this, thou art cursed above all cattle, and above every beast of the field; upon they belly shalt thou go, and dust shalt thou eat all the days of thy life: and I will put enmity between thee and the woman, and between thy seed and her seed; it shall bruise thy head, and thou shalt bruise his heel."* *{Genesis 3:14-15}*

A SPECIAL ENMITY

There is a special enmity that has been established between femininity and the enemy. There is a special conflict the enemy seeks with you. That's why you must do spiritual warfare. You must do so because of your vulnerability in certain areas, and the enmity that rages between Satan and you. So, be on your guard.

THIS IS WAR

Women do tend to be more prayerful than men once they get committed. But if you are a woman living today, and you are not learning spiritual warfare, you are in trouble. The enemy may be taking advantage of you. He is attracted to you because he knows you were designed as a receptacle to help meet someone's vision.

If the enemy can get you to help meet his vision, you will have great problems. Why? Because God said, "And I will put enmity between thee and the woman, and between thy seed and her seed..." {Genesis 3:15}.

Now, God didn't say only "her seed and your seed." He said, "Between you and the woman." Stop and think about it. There is a special fight waged between you and the devil. Who are the victims of the most rapes in this country? Who are the victims of the most child abuse? Who are the victims of much of the sexual discrimination in the job market? And who has the most trouble getting together, unifying with each other, and collaborating? Satan has a special war with you.

Satan is continually attacking femininity. Mass populations of women have increased throughout the country. Isaiah 4:1 says the time will come when there will be seven women to every one man. According to recent statistics, we are living in those times right now. Where you have more need than supply, there is growing enmity between the woman and the enemy.

GET TRAINED FOR WAR!

If godly women do not learn how to start praying and doing effective spiritual warfare, they will not discern what is plugging into them. Perhaps you become completely vulnerable to moods and attitudes and dispositions. Perhaps you are doing things, and you don't know why. Look out, something's plugging into you. If you are tempted to rationalize, "I'm just in a bad mood. I don't know just what it is. I'm just evil. I'm tough," don't believe it, because something's plugging into you.

> *"Unto the woman he said, I will greatly multiply thy sorrow and thy conception; in sorrow thou shalt bring forth children; and thy desire shall be to thy husband, and he shall rule over thee."*
>
> *[Genesis 3:16]*

God explained that birthing would come through sorrow. Everything you bring forth comes through pain. If it didn't come through pain, it probably wasn't worth much.

If you are going to *bring forth*, and I'm not merely talking about babies, I'm talking about birthing vision and purpose—you will do so with sorrow and pain. If you are going to bring forth anything in your career, in your marriage or your life, or if you are going to develop anything in your character through becoming a fruitful woman—it is going to come through sorrow. It will come through the things you suffer. And, you will enter into strength through sorrow.

SORROW IS NOT THE OBJECT: IT IS ONLY THE CANAL

Sorrow is not the object; it is simply the canal the object comes through. Many of you are mistaking sorrow for the baby, instead of the canal. In that case, all you have is pain. You ought to have a child for every sorrow. By that I mean, for every sorrow, for every intense groaning in your spirit, you ought to have something to show for it.

So don't let the devil give you sorrow without any seed. Be aware that any time you have sorrow, it is a sign that God is trying to get something through you and to you.

WOMEN GIVE LIFE LEGAL ENTRY

Women are the producers. You are the ones through whom life passes. Every child who enters into this world must come through you. Even Jesus Christ had to come through you to obtain legal entry into the world. It was required that He come through you. So you are a channel and an expression of God's blessings. If there is to be any virtue, any praise, any victory, any deliverance, it's got to come through you.

But Satan also wants to use you for legal entry into this world. He wants to use you to get into your family. That's how he destroyed the human race with the first family. He knows that you are the entrance of all things. And that you are the doors of life. So be careful what you let plug into and come through you. Close the doors to the enemy's planting. Then know that when travail comes into your spirit, it is because you are going to give birth.

And you will give birth! That is why you suffer pain. Your spirit is signaling you that something is trying to get through. So don't become so preoccupied with the pain that you forget to push the baby. Sometimes you are pushing the pain and not the baby, and you are so engrossed with what is hurting you that you are not doing what it takes to produce fruit in your life.

So when you see sorrow multiply, let it be a sign to you that God is getting ready to send something to you. Don't settle for the pain and not get the benefit. Hold out. Disregard the pain and get the promise. Understand that God has promised some things to you that He wants you to have. And know that you have got to stay there on the table until you get to the place where you ought to be in the Lord. After all, the pain is forgotten when the baby is born.

What is the pain when compared to the baby? Some may have dropped the baby. That happens when you become so engrossed with the pain that you leave the reward behind. Your attention gets focused on the wrong thing. You can be so preoccupied with how bad it hurts that you miss the joy of a vision giving birth.

A PAINFUL EXAMPLE

Wouldn't it be foolish for a woman to go into labor, go through all of its pain, stay on the delivery table for hours and hours, then to simply get up and walk out of the hospital without her baby? Certainly it would. But this is exactly what happens when you become preoccupied with how bad the past hurts you. Maybe you have walked away and left your baby lying on the floor.

For every struggle in your life, God accomplished something in your character and in your spirit. So why hold the pain and drop the baby when you can hold the baby and drop the pain? Again, you are holding on to the wrong thing in life if all you do is concentrate on past pain. Release the pain. Pain doesn't release itself. It's got to be released. So *release* your pain. Allow God to loose you from the pain. He wants to separate you from what has afflicted you to be left with the baby, not the problem.

BRING FORTH

When God said, "...In sorrow thou shalt bring forth children..." {Genesis 3:16} it included every area of your life. It is in your character. It is true in your personality. And it is true in your spirit as well as in your finances. So bring forth, ladies! If it comes into this world, it has to come through you. If you are in a financial rut, bring forth! If you are in need of healing for your body, bring forth! Understand that it must be brought forth. It doesn't just happen by accident.

CRY IF YOU MUST, BUT PUSH

When the midwife tells a woman, "Push," the baby will not come forth if the woman doesn't push him. God will not allow you to become trapped in a situation without escape. But you have got to push while you are in pain if you intend to produce. I am told that when the pain is at its height, that is when they instruct you to push—not when the pain recedes. So when the pain is at its ultimate expression, that is the time you need to push.

As you begin to push in spite of the pain, the pain recedes into the background because you become preoccupied with the change rather than the problem. So push! You don't have time to cry. Push! You don't have time to be suicidal. Push! This is not the time to give up. Push! because God is about to birth a promise through you.

Cry if you must, and groan if you have to, but keep on pushing because God has promised that if it is to come into the world, it has got to pass through you.

Now let's talk about the conflict between past pain and future desire that remains. Here is the conflict. God said,

> "...in sorrow thou shalt bring forth children; and thy desire
> shall be to thy husband, and he shall rule over thee."
>
> *{Genesis 3:16}*

In other words, woman, you will have so much pain in producing the child that if you don't have a balance between past pain and future desire, you will quit producing. So God says, "After the pain, your desire shall be to your husband." Pain is swallowed by desire.

IMPREGNATED WITH DESTINY

Impregnated with destiny, women of promise must bear down in the Spirit. The past may hurt and the pain may be genuine. But you must learn to get in touch with something other than your pain. If you do not have desire, you won't have the tenacity to resurrect. Desire will come back. After the pain is over, desire follows, because it takes desire to be productive again.

CHAPTER SEVEN

A Womb-Man

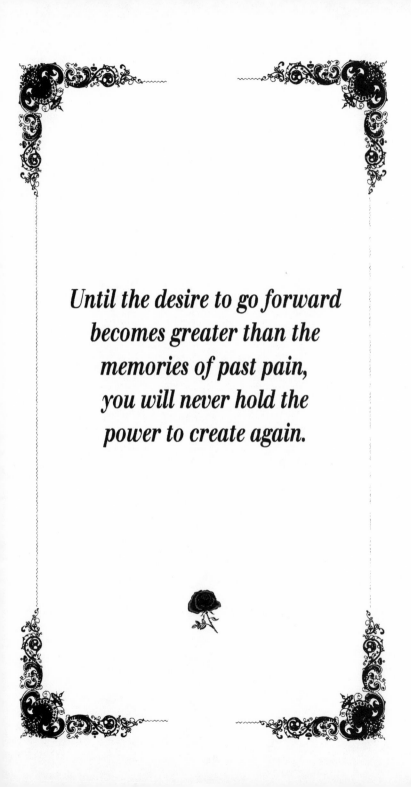

*Until the desire to go forward
becomes greater than the
memories of past pain,
you will never hold the
power to create again.*

I have been in the delivery room with my wife as she was giving birth. I have witnessed the pain and suffering that she has endured. I believe that there were times of such intense pain that she would have shot me if she only had the chance. But her desire made her continue. She didn't simply give up. She endured the pain so new life could be born. Then once the child was born, the pain was soon forgotten.

Until your desire to go forward becomes greater than the memories of past pain, you will never hold the power to create again. However, when desire comes back into your spirit and begins to live in you again, it will release you from the pain.

GO FORTH WITH GOD'S VISION

God wants to give us the strength to overcome past pain to move forward into new life. Solomon wrote, "Where there is no vision, the people perish..." {Proverbs 29:18}. So vision is the desire to go ahead. Until you have a vision to go ahead, you will always live in yesterday's struggles.

God is calling you to *today*, but the devil wants you to live in *yesterday*. The devil is always telling you about what you cannot do. His method is to bring up your past. He wants to draw your attention backward.

God wants to put desire in the spirit of broken women. There wouldn't be any desire if there wasn't any relationship. You can't desire something that's not there. The very fact that you have a desire is in itself an indication that better days are coming. David said, "I had fainted, unless I had believed to see the goodness of the Lord in the land of the living" {Psalm 27:13}. So expect something wonderful to happen.

When I was a boy, we had a dog named Pup. Don't let the name fool you, though. He was a mean and ferocious animal. He would eat anyone who came near him. We had him chained in the back of the house to a four-by-four post. The chain was huge. And we never imagined that he could possibly tear himself loose from that post. When he would chase something, the chain would snap him back. We often laughed at him, as we stood outside his reach.

One day, Pup saw something that he really wanted. It was out of his reach. However, the motivation before him became more important than what was behind him. So he pulled that chain to the limit. Then all at once, instead of drawing him back, the chain snapped and Pup was loose to chase his prey.

That's what God will do for you. The thing that used to pull you back, you will snap, and you will be liberated by a goal because God has put greatness before you. You can't receive what God wants for your life by looking back. He is mighty. He is powerful enough to destroy the yoke of the enemy in your life. And He is strong enough to bring you out and loose you, deliver you, and set you free.

PLANT GOD'S SEED OF TRUTH

What you need is a seed in the womb that you believe is enough to produce an embryo. And you must be willing to feed that embryo for it to grow and become visible. When it will not be hidden anymore, it will break forth in life as answered prayer. It will break forth. No matter how hard others try to hold it back, it will break forth.

So put the truth in your spirit and feed, nurture and allow it to grow. Quit telling yourself, "You're too fat, too old, too late, or too ignorant." Quit feeding yourself that garbage. That will not nourish the baby. Too often we starve the embryo of faith that is growing within us. It is unwise to speak against your own body. Women tend to speak against their bodies, opening the door for sickness and disease. Speak life to your own body and celebrate who you are. You are the image of God.

READ THE SCRIPTURES

Scriptures remind us of who we are.

> *"I will praise thee; for I am fearfully and wonderfully made:*
> *marvellous are thy works; and that my soul knoweth right well."*
> *(Psalm 139:14)*

These are the words that will feed our souls. The truth will allow new life to swell up within us. Feed the embryo within with such words as these.

> *"When I consider thy heavens, the work of thy fingers, the moon and the stars, which thou hast ordained; what is man, that thou art mindful of him? and the son of man, that thou visitest him?"*
> *{Psalm 8:3-4}*

> *"And the Lord shall make thee the head, and not the tail; and thou shalt be above only, and thou shalt not be beneath...."*
> *{Deuteronomy 28:13}*

> *"I can do all things through Christ which strengtheneth me."*
> *{Philippians 4:13}*

The Word of God will provide the nourishment that will feed the baby inside.

BECAUSE WE CAN'T SEE IT DOESN'T MEAN GOD WON'T DO IT

The book of Hebrews provides us with a tremendous lesson on faith. When we believe God, we are counted as righteous. Righteousness cannot be earned or merited. It comes only through faith. We can have a good report simply on the basis of our faith. Faith becomes the tender, like money is the legal tender in this world that we use for exchange of goods and services. Faith becomes the tender, or the substance, of things hoped for, and the evidence of things not seen. By it the elders obtained a good report {Hebrews 11:1-2}.

> *"Through faith we understand that the worlds were framed by the word of God, so that things which are seen were not made of things which do appear."*   *{Hebrews 11:3}*

The invisible became visible and was manifested. God wants us to understand that just because we can't see it doesn't mean that He won't do it.

FAITH BEGINS WITH A WORD

What God wants to do in us begins as a word that gets into our spirit. Everything that is tangible started as an intangible. It was a dream, a thought, a word of God. In the same way, what man has invented began as a concept in someone's mind. So just because we don't see it doesn't mean we won't get it.

There is a progression in the characters mentioned in this chapter of Hebrews. Abel worshiped God by faith. Enoch walked with God by faith. You can't walk with God until you worship God. The first calling is to learn how to worship God. When you learn how to worship God, then you can develop a walk with God. So stop trying to get people to walk with God who won't worship. If you don't love God enough to worship Him, you will never be able to walk with Him. If you can worship like Abel, then you can walk like Enoch.

ENOCH AND NOAH

Enoch walked, and by faith, Noah worked with God. You can't work with God until you walk with God. And you can't walk with God until you worship God. So if you can worship like Abel, you can walk like Enoch. And if you walk like Enoch, you can work like Noah.

> *"But without faith it is impossible to please him: for he that cometh to God must believe that he is, and that he is a rewarder of them that diligently seek him."*　　　*{Hebrews 11:6}*

God will reward those who persevere in seeking Him. He may not come when you want Him to, but He will always be right on time. If you will wait on the Lord, He will strengthen your heart. He will heal you and deliver you. He will lift you up and break those chains. God's power will loose the bands from around your neck. He will give you the garment of praise for the spirit of heaviness {Isaiah 61:3}.

ABRAHAM

Abraham was a great man of faith. The writer of Hebrews mentions many areas of his faith. Abraham looked for a city whose builder and maker was

God {Hebrews 11:10}. However, he is not listed in the faith "hall of fame" as the one who produced Isaac. You would think if Abraham was famous for anything, it should have been for producing Isaac. However, he is not applauded for that.

SARAH

> "Through faith also Sara herself received strength to conceive
> seed, and was delivered of a child when she was past age, because
> she judged him faithful who had promised." {Hebrews 11:11}

When it comes to bringing forth the baby, the Scriptures do not refer to a man; they refer to a womb-man.

Sarah needed strength to conceive seed when she was past childbearing age. So God met her need. She believed that He was capable of giving her a child regardless of what the circumstances looked like. From a natural perspective, it was impossible. The enemy certainly didn't want it to happen. God, however, performed His promise.

GO FORTH WITH A SARAH VISION

Why would you allow your vision to be incapacitated for the lack of a man? Many women have unbelieving husbands at home. Have faith for yourself. Be a womb-man. It doesn't matter whether someone else believes or not. Cling to the truth that He is doing a good work in you. Each of us needs our own walk with God. So stand back and thank God. Believe God and know that He is able to do it.

Sarah didn't stand on her husband's faith; she stood on her own.

YOU ARE GOD'S WOMAN

You are God's woman. You are not called to sit by the window waiting on God to send you a husband. So you had better have some faith yourself and believe God down in your own spirit. If you would believe God, He would perform His Word in your life. No matter the desire or the blessing that you seek, God has promised to give you the desires of your heart {Psalm 37:4}.

GOD WILL TURN IT AROUND

Recognize that where life has seemed irrational and out of control, God will turn it around. When trouble was breaking loose in my life, and I thought I couldn't take it anymore, God intervened and broke every chain that held me back. He will do no less for you.

Abraham had many promises from God regarding his descendants. God told Abraham that his seed would be as the "sands of the sea and the stars of heaven" {Genesis 22:17}. So there were two promises of seed given to Abraham.

First of all, God said his seed would be as the sands of the earth. That promise represents the natural, physical nation of Israel. These were the people of the Old Covenant. However, God didn't stop there. He also promised that Abraham's seed would be as the stars of heaven. These are the people of the New Covenant, the exalted people. The Church. We are exalted in Christ Jesus. So we too are seed of Abraham. We are the stars of heaven.

But God had more plans for Abraham's descendants than to simply start a new nation on earth. He planned a new spiritual kingdom that will last forever. The plan started as a seed, but it ended up as stars.

MULTIPLIED BLESSING

Now can you see why Sarah herself had to receive strength to conceive a seed when she was past childbearing age? The only thing that stood between the seed and the stars was her—the woman. The old man gave her a seed and she gave him the stars of heaven. In the same way, God wants whatever He gives you to be multiplied in the womb of your spirit. Then when you bring it forth, it shall be greater than the former.

The enemy wants to multiply fear in your life. In fact, he wants you to become so afraid that you won't be able to figure out what you fear. You may be afraid of living in your own home. Some are afraid to correct their children. Others fear standing up in front of others. Intimidated and afraid, many do not deliver a prophecy. So God wants to set you free from fear by filling you with faith.

SAY GOODBYE TO YESTERDAY

But in order to move forward, we must be willing to give up yesterday and go on toward tomorrow. We have to trust God enough to allow Him to come in and plow up our lives. Perhaps He needs to root out closet skeletons and replace them with new attitudes.

Sometimes women are so accustomed to being hurt that if anyone comes near them, they become defensive. Some may look tough and angry toward men, but God knows that behind that tough act, they are simply afraid. God deals directly with the issues of the heart. He lets you know you don't have to be afraid. And the plans of God are good. He is not like the people who have hurt and abused you. He wants only to help you be completely restored.

BREAK THE CHAINS OF THE PAST

However, the enemy tries to chain us to the circumstances of the past to keep us from reaching our potential. Satan has assigned fear to block up your womb. It blocks up your womb and causes you to be less productive than you like. He wants to destroy the spirit of creativity within you. But God wants you to know that you have nothing to fear. You can be creative. He will make you into the womb-man that He wants you to be.

Maybe you have been tormented and in pain. You have been upset. You have been frustrated and it is hindering your walk. But God is releasing you from fear.

> *"For God hath not given us the spirit of fear; but of power, and of love, and of a sound mind."*   *[2 Timothy 1:7]*

You need to allow God an opportunity in your life. Then you will start seeing beauty at all different stages of your life. Maybe you have been afraid of aging. If you have, God will give you the strength to thank Him for every year.

Although we must be careful not to become trapped by the past, we should look back and thank God for how He has kept us through the struggles. If you're like me, you will want to say, "I would never have made it if You had not brought me through." So celebrate who you have become through His assistance. In every circumstance, rejoice that He was with you in it.

HEALTH INTO DRY BONES

I believe God is bringing health into dry bones. Bones that were bowed over, bones that were bent out of shape, bones that made you upset with yourself. All are giving way to the life of the Spirit. Perhaps you respond to your history with low self-esteem. God will heal the inner wound and teach you how important you are to Him. You do make a difference. The world would be a different place if it were not for you. You are a part of His divine plan.

When the angel came to Mary and told her what God was going to do in her life, Mary questioned how it could be possible {Luke 1:34}. Perhaps God has been telling you things He wants to do in your life, but you have questioned Him. Perhaps your circumstances do not seem to allow you to accomplish much. And maybe you lack the strength to accomplish the task alone. Or perhaps, like Mary, you are thinking only in the natural and that you must have a man to do God's will.

> *"And the angel answered and said unto her, The Holy Ghost shall come upon thee, and the power of the Highest shall overshadow thee: therefore also that holy thing which shall be born of thee shall be called the Son of God."*   {Luke 1:35}

If you have been wondering how God will make things come to pass in your life, remember that He will accomplish the task. No man will get the credit for your deliverance. Just as He told Mary, "The Holy Ghost shall come upon thee," the same is true of godly women today. The Holy Spirit will fill you. He will impregnate you. He will give life to your spirit. He will put purpose back into you. He will renew you. And He will restore you.

God had a special plan for Mary. She brought forth Jesus. And He has a special plan for us. Unlike Mary, however, we aren't privileged to see the future. We don't know what kind of good things He has in store for us. But, He does have a plan. God's women are to be womb-men. They are to be creative and bring forth new life. That is exactly what God wants to do with those who are broken and discouraged.

SIMPLY BELIEVE

If great things came from those who never suffered, we might think that they accomplished those things of their own accord. When a broken person submits to God, God gets the glory for the wonderful things He accomplishes—

no matter how far that person has fallen. The anointing of God will restore you and make you accomplish great and noble things. Believe it!

The hidden Christ that's been locked up behind your fears, your problems and your ministry, will come forth in your life. You will see the power of the Lord Jesus do a mighty thing.

After the angel told Mary those words, do you know what she said? "And Mary said, Behold the handmaid of the Lord; be it unto me according to thy word. And the angel departed from her" {Luke 1:38}. Mary said, "Be it unto me according to thy word." Not according to my marital status. Not according to my job. Not according to what I deserve. But, "Be it unto me according to thy word."

Mary knew enough to believe God and to submit to Him. She was taking an extreme risk. To be pregnant and unmarried brought dire consequences in those days. Yet she willingly gave herself over to the Lord.

Mary had a cousin named Elizabeth who was already expecting a child. The child in Elizabeth's womb was to be the forerunner of the Messiah. When the two women came together to share their stories, the Bible says that the baby leaped in Elizabeth's womb and that she was filled with the Holy Ghost {Luke 1:41}.

You need to know that the things you had stopped believing God for will start leaping in your spirit again. God will renew you! Often, women have been working against each other, but God will bring you together. You will come together like Mary and Elizabeth and cause your babies to leap in your womb. The power of the Lord Jesus will do a new thing in your life. Just let Him. The Holy Ghost will come upon you and restore you.

FOLLOW YOUR DREAM

If you are a woman who has had a dream and sensed a promise, reach out to Him. Every woman who knows they have another woman inside of them who is yet to come forth can reach their hearts toward God. When they do, He will meet those inner needs and cause them to live at their potential. He will restore what was stolen by your suffering and abuse. He will take back from the enemy what was swallowed up in your history.

He wants to bring you together, sisters. Every Mary needs an Elizabeth. He needs to bring you together. So stop your wars and fighting. Drop your guns. Throw down your swords. Put away your shields. God put something in your sister that you need. When you come together, powerful things will happen.

Satan attempts to keep us from our potential. He allows and causes horrible things to happen in lives so those lives will take on a different outlook. The fear of abuse can only be removed by the power of the Holy Spirit. There is great potential in women who believe. But that potential may be locked up at times because of ruined histories. Let God wipe the slate clean. He will likely use others to help in the process, but it is His anointing that will bring forth new life from deep within.

CHAPTER EIGHT

Anoint Me... I'm Single!

The Scripture calls unmarried women virgins because God is of the opinion that if you do not belong to a man, you belong strictly to Him.

*S*ome of you do not understand the benefits of being single. In reality, while you are not married, you really ought to be involved with God. Because when you get married, you direct all of the training that you had while you were unmarried toward your spouse. The apostle Paul addressed this issue in his first letter to the church at Corinth.

> *"But I would have you without carefulness. He that is unmarried careth for the things that belong to the Lord, how he may please the Lord: But he that is married careth for the things that are of the world, how he may please his wife. There is difference also between a wife and a virgin. The unmarried woman careth for the things of the Lord, that she may be holy both in body and in spirit: but she that is married careth for the things of the world, how she may please her husband."*
>
> *(1 Corinthians 7:32-34)*

Single women often forget some very important advantages they have. At five o'clock in the morning you can lie in bed and pray in the Spirit until half-past seven, and not have to answer to anyone. You can worship the Lord whenever and however you please. You can lie prostate on the floor in your house and worship, and no one will become annoyed about it. "...The unmarried woman careth for the things of the Lord...."

Often, those who minister in churches hear unmarried women complain about their need for a husband. And rarely does a single woman boast about the kind of relationship she is free to build with the Lord. Are you complaining about how you need someone? If you are, quit complaining and start taking advantage of the time you don't have to worry about cooking meals and caring for a family. While a woman is single, she needs to recognize that she has the unique opportunity to build herself up in the Lord without the drains that can occur later.

BECOME FAITHFUL IN YOUR SINGLENESS

This time is in your life for you to charge up the battery cells. It's time to pamper; a time to take luxurious baths in milk and honey. You can lie there in the bath and worship the Lord. It's a ministry you have. So before you ask God for another man, take care of Him. If you are not ministering to His needs, and are always before Him asking Him to give you one of His princes to minister to, your prayers are not being heard because you are not being faithful to Him. When you become faithful in your singleness, then you will be better prepared to be faithful with a husband.

If you disregard the perfect husband, Jesus, you will certainly disregard the rest of us. If you ignore the one who provides oxygen, breath, bone tissue, strength, blood corpuscles, and life itself, you will certainly not be able to have regard for any earthly husband. The Lord wants to make sweet love to you. I'm not being carnal, I'm being real. He wants to hold you. He wants you to come in at the end of the day and say, "Oh, Lord, I could hardly make it today. Whew, I went through so much, I'm so glad I have You in my life. They tried to devour me, but I thank You for this we have together. I just couldn't wait to get alone to worship and praise and magnify You. You're the One who keeps me going. You're the lover of my soul, my mind, my emotions, my attitude, and my disposition. Hold me. Touch me. Strengthen me. Let me hold You. Let me bless You. I've set the night aside for us. Tonight is our night. I'm not so busy that I don't have time for You. For if I have no time for You, surely I will have no time for a husband. My body is Yours. Nobody touches me but You. I am holy in body and in spirit. I am not committing adultery in our relationship. My body is Yours."

DON'T ASK FOR SAUL

The Scripture calls unmarried women virgins because God is of the opinion that if you do not belong to a man, you belong strictly to Him. God thinks you are His. God's heart was broken with the ancient nation of Israel. It was broken because Israel came to Him and said, "...Make us a king to judge us like all the nations" {1 Samuel 8:5}. God had thought He was their King. But when they preferred a man over Him, He gave them Saul, and Israel went to the dogs.

TAKE THE TIME TO WORSHIP HIM

There is nothing wrong with wanting to be married. I am simply saying that you need to take care of the Lord while you are waiting. Minister to Him. Let Him heal and loose you while you worship Him. Single women ought to be the most consecrated women in the Church.

Instead of singles being envious of married women, the married ought to be jealous of singles. You are the ones whose shadows ought to fall on people and they be healed. Why? Because you are in a position and posture of prayer. The Lord has become your necessary food. While some married women are dependent on their husbands, single women can learn to be dependent on the Lord. God has no limitations. A married woman may have a husband who can do some things, but God can do everything. What a privilege to be married to Him. As He told Joel, "...and upon the handmaids...will I pour out my spirit," {Joel 2:29}, God has a special anointing for the woman who is free to seek Him. Her prayer life should explode in miracles!

GOD IS YOUR EDGE

That does not mean it is wrong for you to want physical companionship. God ordained that need. While you are waiting, though, understand that God thinks He is your husband. So be careful how you treat Him. He thinks He is your man. That's why He does those special favors for you. It is God who made you into a beautiful woman. He has been taking care of you, even when you didn't notice His provision. He is the source of every good thing. He keeps things running, and provides for your daily care. It is He who opened those doors for you. He has been your edge, your friend, and your companion.

Those who are married seek to please their spouse, while unmarried people are much freer to seek and please the Lord. There is a special relationship of power between God and the single believer. Paul wrote, "Let every man abide in the same calling wherein he was called" {1 Corinthians 7:20}. In other words, the person who is single should be abiding, not wrestling, in singleness. Rather than spending all of our effort trying to change our position, we need to learn to develop the position in which He has placed us. Isn't that what this means: "...I have learned, in whatsoever state I am, therewith to be content" {Philippians 4:11}. I speak peace to you today.

SANCTIFY YOURSELF

Maybe you haven't been living like you really should. Maybe your house hasn't been the house of prayer that it really could have been. I want you to take this opportunity to begin sanctifying your house and body. Maybe your body has been mauled and pawed by all sorts of people. That doesn't matter. I want you to sanctify your body unto the Lord, and give your body as a living sacrifice to God {Romans 12:1}. If you can't keep your vow to God, you would never be able to keep your vow to a man. So give your body to God and sanctify yourself.

When God picks a wife for one of His royal sons, He will pick her from those who are faithful and holy unto Him. He may pass over those who didn't keep a vow to Him. If you are to marry a king, he will have claimed you to be a queen. So begin to sanctify yourself! Bring your body before God. Bring your nature before God. Bring your passion to Him and allow God to plug into your need.

Allow God to strengthen you until you can tell the devil, "My body belongs to God; my whole body belongs to God. I am God's. From the crown of my head to the soles of my feet, all that I am belongs to God. Early in the morning will I seek His face. I lie upon my bed at night and call on His name. I will touch Him and embrace Him. He is the God of my salvation."

THE MINISTRY OF MARRIAGE

Marriage is ministry. If you are single, your ministry is directly unto the Lord. But if you are married, your ministry is through your spouse. Those who are married are instructed in Scripture to learn godly devotion through relationship with their spouse.

> *"Husbands, love your wives, even as Christ also loved the church, and gave himself for it; that he might sanctify and cleanse it with the washing of water by the word."*
>
> *{Ephesians 5:25-26}*

Marriage is the one place in human society where true love can be expressed in a great way. Marriage partners are to give self-sacrificially to one another. Just as Jesus gave Himself for the Church, husbands and wives are to give one another as selfless gifts of love. Marriage is not a place for seeking self-gratification. It is the place where we seek to gratify another.

The sacredness of marriage is found in the relationship between Christ and the Church. Jesus continues to intercede on behalf of the Church, even after He gave His all for us. He is the greatest advocate of believers. He stands before God to defend and proclaim our value.

YOU ARE YOUR HUSBAND'S GREATEST ADVOCATE

Similarly, husbands and wives are to be bonded together to the extent that they become the greatest advocate of the other. Not demanding one's own way, but always seeking to please the other.

There can be no doubt that God has special plans for each one of us. The woman who is single needs to recognize her position and seek to please God in every way. Single means to be "whole." So enjoy being a whole, single person. The greatest visitation of the Holy Ghost in history happened to an unmarried woman named Mary. Before Joseph could have relations, the Holy Ghost came upon her. And that same life-giving anointing wants to come upon you. So stop murmuring and complaining. His presence is in the room! Worship Him! He is waiting on you.

CHAPTER NINE

A Table for Two

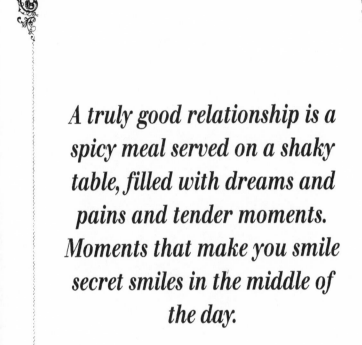

A truly good relationship is a spicy meal served on a shaky table, filled with dreams and pains and tender moments. Moments that make you smile secret smiles in the middle of the day.

"So the Lord God caused the man to fall into a deep sleep; and while he was sleeping, he took one of the man's ribs and closed up the place with flesh. Then the Lord God made a woman from the rib he had taken out of the man, and he brought her to the man."
{Genesis 2:21-22} [NIV]

*T*he first female mentioned in the Bible was created mature, without a childhood or an example to define her role and relationship to her husband. She was created a woman while Adam was asleep. When the Lord "brought her to the man" is the first hint of marriage. I believe life would be better if we still allowed God to bring to us what He has for us.

The only evolution I can find in the Bible is the woman, who evolved out of man. She is God's gift to man. When God wanted to be praised, He created man in His own likeness and in His image. Then when God saw that it was not good for man to be alone, He gave man someone like himself. Adam said the woman was "...bone of my bones, and flesh of my flesh..." {Genesis 2:23}. His attraction to her was her likeness of him. He called her "womb man" or woman. Like the Church of Christ, Eve was his body and his bride.

"For no man ever yet hated his own flesh; but nourisheth and cherisheth it, even as the Lord the church: for we are members of his body, of his flesh, and of his bones. For this cause shall a man leave his father and mother, and shall be joined unto his wife, and they two shall be one flesh. This is a great mystery: but I speak concerning Christ and the church."   *{Ephesians 5:29-32}*

SUPERFICIAL COMPONENTS

Man and woman were both made of the same material. Adam said, "She is bone of my bone." He said nothing of her size, body build, or hair color. These superficial components are like placing a product in an attractive container. The container may get the consumer to try it. But only the product will keep the consumer coming back. His attraction goes much deeper than externals.

These outward attractions are certainly an advantage, but be assured that when it comes to marriage, no one ever stayed together simply because they were attractive.

FLESH IS JUST FLESH

I don't know whether I agree with those who say there is only one person in the world for you. I personally would be afraid that out of the billions of people on this planet, I wouldn't be able to find them. However, I do know that when you find a person with whom you are compatible, there is a bonding that consummates marriage that has nothing to do with sex. I also understand how you could feel this person to be the only choice in the world. Let's face it, everyone you meet isn't bone of your bone! It is so important that you do not allow anyone to manipulate you into choosing someone with whom you have no bond. When Ezekiel speaks about those dry bones in the valley, he says, "...the bones came together, bone to his bone" {Ezekiel 37:7}. So every person must pray and discern if the other is someone they could cleave to the rest of their life.

The term *cleave* (joined) used in Genesis 2:24 from which Paul quoted in Ephesians 5:29-32 is translated from the Hebrew word, *debaq*. It means "to impinge, cling or adhere to; figuratively, to catch by pursuit or follow close after." [See Strong's Exhaustive Concordance of the Bible, #1692.] There is a great need in most of our lives to cleave, to feel that this is where we belong. But it is sad to realize our society has become so promiscuous that many have mistaken the thrill of a weekend fling for the cleaving of two thirsty souls in loving commitment.

BEFORE AND AFTER

If you are reading this book and are not married, I encourage you to con-sider these issues carefully as you pray and seek God for companionship. Find ten couples who have been married twelve years or longer. Then look at their wedding album to see how many of them have drastically changed. When you do you will realize that if those initial impressions were all that held a marriage together, they would probably have already come to an end.

Certainly, you owe it to your spouse and yourself to be all that you can. Still, there is much more involved in marriage than the superficial.

A HOLY BOND

Marriage is so personal that no one is able to stand outside of another relationship to see why they bond. If you are married, understand that your spouse isn't running for office. He shouldn't have to meet the approval of all your family and friends. And don't expect everyone to see what you see in each other that cleaves and sticks you together.

Have you made the commitment to stay together? The secret to cleaving is leaving. "For this cause shall a man *leave* his father and mother..." {Mark 10:7}. If you enter into marriage and keep your former options open, whether mental, emotional or physical, your marriage will never work. When the tugging of adversity tries the bonds of your matrimony, you will fall apart. So you must leave and cleave to your spouse. It is very unhealthy to cleave to someone other than your spouse for support.

LEAVE AND CLEAVE

Now we all need wholesome friendships. However, none should have more influence over you than your spouse (that is, after God). Some of you could save your marriages right now if you would leave some of your extra-martial ties and cleave to your spouse!

It is not always a matter of feelings. The just shall live by faith. We use this verse for so many other things, so why not about marriage? Romans 1:17 says, "For therein is the righteousness of God revealed from faith to faith: as it is written, The just shall live by faith." Believe God for your marriage! It will not be your feelings that heal your relationship; it will be your faith. Did you know that you cannot trust your own feelings?

CLEAVE IN FAITH

I counsel people all the time who sit with tears streaming down their weary faces and say, "I just can't trust him." I've got news for you. You can't trust yourself either! Your feelings will swing in and out. But your faith will not move. Cleaving implies that you don't want to get away. A marriage erodes like the banks of a river do—a little each day.

BE YOURSELF

There is a certain way a woman treats a man when she is fulfilled. It takes faith to treat a frustrated marriage with the same kind of respect that you would treat a prosperous relationship with. Many times you may feel yourself holding back from who you would like to be so you can maintain a strong exterior. All I am simply saying is don't allow another person to cause you to play a role that isn't really who you are.

I realize that many of you may be in the middle of an awful relationship, but I can't counsel what I can't see. For specific needs, I recommend pastoral care and counseling. Nevertheless, I do want to warn you that suppressing the gentle side of you as a defense will not stop you from being hurt! If you suppress who you are, you will fall into depression! It is terrible to arrest who you are in an attempt to "fight fire with fire." The best way to fight fire is with water! The winning way of a woman is not in her words, it is in her character.

> *"Wives, in the same way be submissive to your husbands so that, if any of them do not believe the word, they may be won over without words by the behavior of their wives, when they see the purity and reverence of your lives."*   *{1 Peter 3:1-2} [NIV]*

> *"For this is the way the holy women of the past who put their hope in God used to make themselves beautiful. They were submissive to their own husbands, like Sarah, who obeyed Abraham and called him her master. You are her daughters if you do what is right and do not give way to fear."*   *{1 Peter 3:5-6} [NIV]*

A LESSON FROM PETER

Recently, while teaching a seminar, a lady raised her hand and said, "I am a widow. I lost my husband and he died unsaved." She continued, "I claimed 1 Peter 3:1, and at the end of his life he still was not saved."

She was obviously wrestling with grief, so I responded, "That scripture doesn't mean the responsibility of getting the husband saved rests on the wife. It just says that a submissive, quiet woman creates an atmosphere so he may be won." Then I rebuked the condemning spirit of guilt and she worshiped God under the anointing of the Holy Spirit.

This passage in Peter was not given to abuse women; it was given to instruct them about what works well in the home. Faith is not loud and fleshly. It is quiet and spiritual. Believe me when I say I know this to be effective. No one can do anything to make another person get saved. You can't make them come home. You can't make someone love you. But you can create an atmosphere where your conduct is not undermining your prayers! This is what Peter means.

LEARNING TO ACT AND TALK

Women tend to be vocal while men tend to be physical. Women feel that everything needs to be discussed. And communication is crucial to a healthy relationship, it is just that men don't always talk with words.

Men communicate through touch even in male to male relationships. A pat on the back, or a two-handed handshake, means "I like you." Some think that men always communicate through sex. But that isn't always the case. When a coach playfully slaps a basketball player on the rump, he is not being sexual. He is saying, "Good job!" We must learn each other's method of communication.

So instead of always feeling like you are neglected, ask your husband to share with you why he does what he does. Or better still, observe his method of communication and teach him yours.

TEACH YOUR LANGUAGE

Then in all your getting, get understanding! It is terrible to be misunderstood! I am a giver. So whenever I feel affection, the first thing I want to do is to buy a gift for my wife. I was shocked to find that although my wife will acknowledge the gifts, she will also go into orbit over cards! To me this is insane! She keeps cards that are so old they've turned yellow. I read cards and enjoy them, but I seldom keep them. So we spent the first few years of our marriage teaching each other our language.

BABBLING IN BABEL

Your husband may really think he's telling you something that you keep complaining about not getting. And he may feel like, "What more does she want? I told her that I loved her. I did this and that and the other." You may be living in the Tower of Babel. That was the place where families divided because they could not understand each other's language. So sit down and learn each other's language before frustration turns your house into the Tower of Babel. At Babel all work ceased and arguing began. If you are arguing, it is because frustration exists between you. People who don't care don't argue. No one argues over what they would rather leave!

But when you approach your husband, do not corner him. Catch him at a time when he won't feel interrogated. You would be surprised at how men tend to avoid open confrontation. I have seen big, burly, macho men intimidated about telling their 100-pound wives about how they were going to do something they feared she wouldn't like. Even men who are physically abusive still have moments when they feel anxiety about facing their wives. Solomon wrote, "It is better to dwell in the corner of the housetop, than with a brawling woman and in a wide house" {Proverbs 25:24}. So unless you are trying to drive him away, remember you could win the argument and still lose the man.

LIVING IN PENTECOST

A man's communication is different. I am not suggesting that men can't learn the communication method of their wives. I am merely saying that spouses must learn to appreciate each other's language. Remember, I briefly discussed faith for your marriage. And faith calls those things that are not as though they were {Romans 4:17}. So everything you plan to do for him *when* he changes, do it now. Do it by faith. Then God will turn your Tower of Babel into a Pentecost! At Pentecost each person heard the message in their own language {Acts 2:6}. I pray that God would interpret the language of your spouse and that your love be fruitful and productive.

NAKED AND NOT ASHAMED

> *"And the Lord God called unto Adam, and said unto him, Where art thou? And he said, I heard thy voice in the garden, and I was afraid, because I was naked; and I hid myself."*
>
> *{Genesis 3:9-10}*

Take it off—take it all off! No, not your clothes! It's the fig leaves that must go. Marriage is at its best when both parties can be naked and not be ashamed. It is important that your husband be able to take it off, to take it all off. There is no resting place for the man who hides in his own house. That's why the Lord asked Adam, "Where art thou?" When men are restored to their rightful place in the home, the family will come out of chaos. Listen as Adam exposes the tendency of most men to avoid open confrontation in these, the four points of his confession: (a) I heard thy voice. (b) I was afraid. (c) I was naked. (d) I hid myself. When women become confrontational, it's not that men don't hear you. But when men become afraid or exposed (naked), they have a tendency to hide.

BE TRANSPARENT

Marriage needs to be transparent. Fear will not heal, it will only hide. So both you and your spouse need to be able to expose your vulnerabilities without fear or condemnation. Woe to the man who has no place to lay his head.

> *"And they were both naked, the man and his wife, and were not ashamed."*
> *[Genesis 2:25]*

Now I want to share something with you that may sound unorthodox. But I pray it will bless someone. I want to stop by Delilah's house {Judges 16:4-20}. Most women would not want to stop at her house; most men would! Most are not afraid of Delilah; most women would not like her. Her morals are inexcusable, but her methods are worth discussing. There are some very important things that every wife must learn from immoral Delilah.

All the colorful exegesis of our preachers have described her as some voluptuous love goddess. They say she walked like a swinging pendulum, smelled like the richest incense, and smiled like the glow of an exquisite candelabra. But, in actuality, the Bible says nothing about Delilah's appearance. Her clothing, makeup or hairdo are not even mentioned.

So what was it about this woman that was so powerful? What was it that attracted and captivated the attention of this mighty man, Samson?

What was it about this woman that kept drawing him back into her arms?

What was it about this woman that, when none of the warriors could get to Samson, the Philistine government put her on the payroll because of what she knew about men?

And what was it that made Samson keep going back to her bed even when he knew she was trying to kill him?

Samson could not leave her alone—he desperately needed her. What was it about this "fatal attraction" of the Old Testament?

WHERE CAN THE MIGHTY LAY HIS HEAD?

This discussion is for women married to men working in high-stress positions—men who are powerful and full of purpose—men who are the envy of everyone around them. Samson was one of them. Jesus described well the problem of such highly motivated men when He said, "...Foxes have holes, and birds of the air have nests; but the Son of man hath not where to lay his head" {Luke 9:58}.

Where can the mighty man lay his head? Where can he become vulnerable? Where can he take off his armor and rest for a few hours? He doesn't want to quit; he merely needs to rest.

IS YOUR HOME A PLACE WHERE THE MIGHTY CAN LAY HIS HEAD?

Is your home a restful place to be? Is it clean and neat? Is it warm and inviting? If it's not, Delilah's place is ready. And I am sure that she has problems, but he doesn't have to solve them as soon as he comes home from fighting the enemy. She knows he is tried, so she says, "Come, lay your head in my lap."

I know we have pictured Delilah as being as lust-ridden as a porno star. But remember, the Bible doesn't even mention Samson and Delilah's sex life. I am sure it was a factor. But Samson had had sex before. He had gotten up from the bed of the prostitute in Gaza and drove back the Philistines. He was not some high school boy whose mind was blown away by new sexual ideas. No, he was a mighty man.

HOW ARE THE MIGHTY FALLEN?

Wasn't it David who questioned at the demise of Saul, "How are the mighty fallen"? Well, tell David to ask Delilah, or if she is not at home, to ask his own Bathsheba!

Delilah knew that all men are little boys somewhere deep inside. They are little boys who started their lives being touched by women. You sang their first song. You gave their first bath. And when they were tired, they laid their weary heads against your warm breast and lapsed into sleep. They listened at your silky voice calling them, "Momma's little man." You talked to them. You touched them and they felt safe in your arms—not criticized, not ostracized, just safe. Delilah stroked Samson. She talked to him. She gave him a place to lay his head. Even God inhabits the room of a praiser and allows the murmurer to wander. Men, created in the likeness of God, respond to praise. Praise will make a weary man perform.

A woman who knows what to say to a man is difficult to withstand. This was the secret of Delilah. She knew all men had a little boy inside. And that for all men's tears and all their fears, they need a woman's arms. They need your words, and your song.

GIVE YOUR ARMS AND YOUR SONG

Again, marriage is a ministry. And there is much more involved in it than selfish fulfillment. So for the wearied husband, let him come home and relax. Give him your arms and your song. Let your love be centered around giving, not taking. When you marry someone, you marry everything he is, and everything he has been. You inherit his strengths, fears and weaknesses. It is impossible to pick the parts you want and to leave the parts you don't. It's a package deal. But God grants the grace to minister to him. So don't be discouraged if you don't see immediate change. Minister to that little child in him. And remember, it takes time even for a small cut to heal. Healing is a process and it takes time! God will give you the oil of compassion and the sweet wind of a sincere love to pour into your husband's workday wounds. Be there for him. Give him a place to rest his head.

> *"But he that is married careth for the things that are of the world, how he may please his wife. There is difference also between a wife and a virgin. The unmarried woman careth for the things of the Lord, that she may be holy both in body and in spirit: but she that is married careth for the things of the world, how she may please her husband."*   *{1 Corinthians 7:33-34}*

Marriage is so much of a ministry that the apostle Paul teaches the married woman she cannot afford to become so "spiritual" that she is unavailable for the ministry of marriage. The Greek word used for "careth" in this passage (*merimano*) means, "to be anxious about, or to have intense concern" [See Strong's Exhaustive Concordance of the Bible, #3309]. So God is saying through Paul, "I want the married woman to be concerned about pleasing her husband and vice versa."

HONOR GOD'S PRIORITIES

Many married women who spend a great deal of time fellowshipping with single women do not realize that their perspective and availability should be different. Your ministry, as a wife, begins not in the mall, not in the nursing home, but in your own home and to your own spouse. Now, I am certainly not implying that a woman should be locked in the kitchen and chained to the bed! I am simply sharing that priorities need to start in the home before spreading to careers, vocations and ministerial pursuits. For the woman who "careth for," God will anoint you to be successful in the ministry of marriage.

There will be no marriages in Heaven. {See Matthew 22:30.} Marriage is for this world. And inasmuch as it is a worldly institution, married people cannot divorce themselves from the "things of the world." Returning to Paul's words in 1 Corinthians 7:34, notice this definition of the Greek word *kosmos* translated as "world" in our text:

> "...but she that is married careth for the things of the world, how she may please her husband...." [v. 34]

Paul's use of the word *kosmos* implies that there should be a concern for harmonious order in a married couple's house. God gives the gift of marriage, but you must do your own decorating. Decorate your relationship or it will become bland for you and for your spouse. Decoration does not come where there is no concern. So God says, in effect, "I release the married woman from the level of consecration I expect from the single woman so she will be able to spend some time decorating her relationship."

Adorn, Adorning kosmos #2889 in Strong's, "a harmonious arrangement or order, then, adornment, decoration, hence came to denote the world, or the universe, as that which is Divinely arranged. The meaning 'adorning' is found in 1 Peter 3:3. Elsewhere it signifies the world. Cp. kosmos, decent, modest, 1 Timothy 2:9; 3:2. See "World" (*Vine's Expository Dictionary of Biblical Words*, Thomas Nelson Publishers, 1985).

You have an important ministry to your companion. I can hear someone saying, "That is good, but I need to spend time with the Lord." I agree that this is true. The Scripture doesn't say married women are to be carnal. It just sets some priorities. Where there are no priorities, there is a sense of being overwhelmed by responsibility. You can still consecrate yourself as long as you understand you are called to be a companion to your spouse. However you choose to decorate your relationship is holy. So do not neglect each other in the name of being spiritual. God wants you to be together!

> *"The husband should fulfill his marital duty to his wife, and likewise the wife to her husband. The wife's body does not belong to her alone but also to her husband. In the same way, the husband's body does not belong to him alone but also to his wife. Do not deprive each other except by mutual consent and for a time, so that you may devote yourselves to prayer. Then come together again so that Satan will not tempt you because of your lack of self-control."*   *[1 Corinthians 7:3-5] [NIV]*

If you are looking for someone to be your everything, don't look around, look up! God is the only One who can be everything. By expecting perfection from the flesh, you ask more out of someone else than you can provide yourself.

TO BE MARRIED

To be married is to have a partner: someone who is not always there, or always on target, or always anything! On the other hand, should you ever get in trouble and you don't know who to look to for help, you can count on your partner! Marriage is having someone to curl up with when the world seems cold, and life uncertain. It is having someone who is as concerned as you are when your children are ill. It is having a hand that keeps checking your forehead when you aren't well. To be married is to have someone's shoulder to cry on as they lower your parent's body into the ground. It is wrapping wrinkled knees in warm blankets and giggling without teeth! To the person you marry you are saying, "When my time comes to leave this world and the chill of eternity blows away my birthdays and my future stands still in the night, it's your face that I want to kiss good-bye. It's your hand that I want to squeeze as I slip into eternity. And as the curtain closes on all I have attempted to do and be, I want to look into your eyes and see that I mattered. Not what I looked like. Not what I did or how much money I made. Not even how talented I was. I want to look into the teary eyes of someone who loved me and see that I mattered!

A SPICY MEAL SERVED ON A SHAKY TABLE

As I close this chapter, I hope you can relate to what a blessing it is to be alive and what it means to be able to feel and taste life. Lift the glass to your mouth and drink deeply of life. It is a privilege to experience every drop of your marriage relationship. It is not perfect, like a suede jacket, the imperfection just adds to its uniqueness. I am sure that yours, like mine, is a mixing of good days, sad days, and all the challenges of life. But I hope you have learned with me how a truly good relationship is a spicy meal served on a shaky table, filled with dreams and pains and tender moments. Moments that, in those split-second flashbacks, made you smile secret smiles in the middle of the day. Moments so strong that they never die, yet are so fragile they disappear like bubbles in a glass.

It does not matter whether you have something to be envied or something to be developed. If you can look back and catch a few moments, or trace a smile back to a memory, you are blessed! You could have been anywhere doing anything, but instead the maitre d' has seated you at a TABLE FOR TWO!

CHAPTER TEN

Daughter of Abraham

Whatever God gives you, He wants it to be multiplied in the womb of your spirit. When you bring it forth, it shall be greater than the former.

believe it is important that women get healed and released in their spirits. I'm excited about what God is doing. And I believe that God will move freshly in the lives of women in an even greater way.

God knows how to take a mess and turn it into a miracle. If you're in a mess, don't be too upset about it because God specializes in fixing messes. God is saying some definite things about women being set free and delivered to fulfill their purpose in His kingdom.

Let's look once again at the infirm woman in the gospel of Luke, chapter 13:

> "And he was teaching in one of the synagogues on the sabbath. And, behold, there was a woman which had a spirit of infirmity eighteen years, and was bowed together, and could in no wise lift up herself. And when Jesus saw her, he called her to him, and said unto her, Woman, thou art loosed from thine infirmity. And he laid his hands on her: and immediately she was made straight, and glorified God. And the ruler of the synagogue answered with indignation, because that Jesus had healed on the sabbath day, and said unto the people, There are six days in which men ought to work: in them therefore come and be healed, and not on the sabbath day. The Lord then answered him, and said, Thou hypocrite, doth not each one of you on the sabbath loose his ox or his ass from the stall, and lead him away to watering? And ought not this woman, being a daughter of Abraham, whom Satan hath bound, lo, these eighteen years, be loosed from this bond on the sabbath day? And when he had said these things, all his adversaries were ashamed: and all people rejoiced for all the glorious things that were done by him."   [Luke 13:10-17]

When the Lord gets through working on you, all your adversaries will be ashamed. All your accusers will be ashamed of themselves. All the people who contributed to your sense of low self-esteem will be ashamed when God gets through unleashing you. You won't have to prove anything. God will prove it. He will do it in your life. When He gets through showing that you've done the right thing and come to the right place, they will drop their heads and be ashamed.

We have already shown how this woman was so bound by Satan for eighteen years that she could not even straighten herself up. She had a past that tormented her, but Jesus set her free. He unleashed her potential that Satan had bound up.

YOUR DILEMMA

Many women in the Church have not really seen Christ as the answer to their dilemma. They go to church, they love the Lord, they want to go to Heaven when they die, but they still do not see Christ as the solution to their problem. Often, we try to separate our personal life from our spiritual life. Many see Jesus as a way to Heaven and the solution to spiritual problems, but they fail to see that He is the solution to all of life's problems.

Can you imagine how hard life was for that woman who was bowed over? She had to struggle, because of her problem, to come to Jesus. Few of us are crippled in the same way. However, we all face crippling limitations. We can be bowed over financially. We can be bowed over emotionally. We can be bowed over where we have no self-esteem. Jesus wants to see us struggling toward Him. He could have walked to this woman, but He chose not to. He wants to see us struggle toward Him.

He wants you to want Him enough to overcome obstacles and to push in His direction. He doesn't want to just throw things at you that you don't have a real conviction to receive. When you see a humped-over person crawling through the crowd, know that that person really wants help. That kind of desire is what it takes to change your life. And Jesus is your answer.

JESUS IS THE ANSWER

I may seek help by going from one person to another, but only He is the answer. I may be sick in my body, but He is the answer. If my son is dead, or insane on drugs, and I need Him to resurrect my child, He is the answer. If I am having family problems with my brother who is in trouble, He's the answer. It doesn't matter what the problem is, Jesus is the answer.

Jesus touched this woman. There is a place in God where the Lord will touch you and provide intimacy in your life when you are not getting it from other places. But you must be open to His touch. If you can't receive from Him, you may find yourself like the woman at the well, who sought physical gratification {John 4:18}. And if you seek only the physical when you really need intimacy, what you end up getting is simply sex. Sex is a poor substitute for intimacy. It's nice with intimacy, but when it's substituted for intimacy, it's frustrating.

Jesus knew this woman. He was the only one who truly knew her. He touched her and healed her. He unleashed her potential that had been bound for eighteen years. You can accomplish anything once you have been called to Jesus. From that moment on you become invincible.

HINDERING WORDS

However, most likely your words have hindered you. Often, we are snared by the words of our very own mouth. The enemy would love to destroy you with your own words. Satan wants to use *you* to fight against you. He will use your strength to fight against you. Many of you have beat yourself down with the power of your own words and have twisted your own back. The enemy worked you against yourself until you saw yourself as crippled. But now is the time to reverse his plan. If you had enough force to bend yourself, you've got enough force to straighten yourself back up.

TODAY IS YOUR DAY TO STRAIGHTEN UP

The Lord told this woman the truth about herself. He told her she was loosed and set her free. He saw the truth despite what everyone else saw. He saw that she was important.

The religious critics didn't like what Jesus had done. His power showed how powerless their religion was. So they accused Him of breaking the law by performing a miracle on the Sabbath day. But Christ acknowledged their hypocrisy by addressing a common occurrence in their day. They all valued their livestock, He said. Then He reminded them that they would loose their donkey on the Sabbath so that it could get a drink. Then He said surely this woman was more valuable than any animal. And that she could be loosed from her pain and sickness regardless of the day.

GOD IS YOUR LIBERATOR

Sometimes pain can become too familiar. Ungodly relationships often become familiar. Change doesn't come easily. Habits and patterns are hard to break. And sometimes we maintain these relationships because we fear change. However, when we see our value the way Jesus sees us, we muster the courage to break away.

He is your defense. He will defend you before your critics. Now is the time for you to focus on receiving the miraculous and getting the water you could not get before. He is loosing you to water. You haven't been drinking for eighteen years, but now you can get a drink. With Jesus, you can do it.

Have you been a beast of burden? Some of you have been a pack horse for many years. People have dumped on you and you have had to grit your teeth. You have never been allowed to develop without stress and weights, not just because of the circumstances, but because of how deeply things truly affect you. Our God, however, is a liberator.

> *"The Lord is my light and my salvation; whom shall I fear? the Lord is the strength of my life; of whom shall I be afraid? When the wicked, even mine enemies and my foes, came upon me to eat up my flesh, they stumbled and fell. Though an host should encamp against me, my heart shall not fear: though war should rise against me, in this will I be confident. One thing have I desired of the Lord, that will I seek after; that I may dwell in the house of the Lord all the days of my life, to behold the beauty of the Lord, and to inquire in his temple."* (Psalm 27:1-4)

You must reach the point where it is the Lord whom you desire. Singleness of heart will bring about deliverance. Perhaps you have spent all your time and effort trying to prove yourself to someone who is gone. Maybe an old lover left you with scars. The person may be dead and buried, but you are still trying to win his approval.

If this is the case, you may be dedicated to worthless tasks. You may be committed to things and unattainable goals that will not satisfy. Christ must be your ambition.

Luke 13:13b reads, *"...and immediately she was made straight, and glorified God."* Christ dealt with eighteen years of this woman's torment in an instant. One moment with Jesus, and immediately she was well. For some things you don't have time to recover gradually. The moment you get the truth, you are loosed. When this woman got hold of the truth, immediately she was well.

Once you realize that you have been unleashed, you will feel a sudden change. When you come to Jesus, He will motivate you and get you to see that other woman in you. You need to blossom and bring her forth.

Notice the sixteenth verse of Luke 13:

> *"And ought not this woman, being a daughter of Abraham, whom Satan hath bound, lo, these eighteen years, be loosed from this bond on the sabbath day?"*

Jesus called her "a daughter of Abraham." She may have been bent over, but she was still Abraham's daughter. So don't let your condition negate your position.

The woman was unleashed because of who her father was. It had little to do with who she was. The Bible doesn't even mention her name. We will never know who she was until we reach Heaven. But we do know *whose* she was. She was a daughter of Abraham.

FAITH IS AN EQUAL OPPORTUNITY EMPLOYER

Faith is an equal opportunity employer. There is no discrimination in it. Faith will work for you. When you approach God, never worry about the fact that you are a woman. Never become discouraged on that basis when it comes to seeking Him. You will only get as much from God as you can believe Him for.

You won't be able to convince Him, seduce Him, break Him down, or trick Him. God will not move because you cry and act melancholy. Now, you may move me like that. Certainly that works with men, but it doesn't work with God. God only accepts faith.

He wants you to believe Him. He wants you to personalize the truth that you can do all things through Him {Philippians 4:13}. He is trying to teach you right now so when the time for a real miracle does come, you will have some faith to draw from. God wants you to understand that if you can believe Him, you can go from defeat to victory and from poverty to prosperity!

START BELIEVING AND BE SET FREE

Faith is more than a fact—faith is an action. So don't tell me you believe when your actions don't correspond with your conviction. If your actions don't change, you might still think you are bound. But when you finally understand that you are loose, you will start behaving as if you were free.

When you are loose, you can go anywhere. If I had one end of a rope around my neck, I would only be able to walk the length of the rope. But once I am unleashed from that rope, I can walk as far as I want. You are whole; you are loose. You can go anywhere.

Hebrews 11 is a faith "hall of fame." It lists great people of God who believed Him and accomplished great exploits. Abraham is given tremendous attention in this chapter. He is revered by millions as the father of faith. He is the first man in history to believe God to the point where it was counted as righteousness. He was saved by faith. Jesus said that the infirm woman was a daughter of Abraham. Because she was, she was worthy. She had merit because she was Abraham's descendant, the father of faith.

TWO HEROES OF FAITH

There are two contrasting women mentioned in the Hebrews 11 faith "hall of fame." Sarah, Abraham's wife, and Rahab, the Jericho prostitute. Isn't it interesting that a married woman and a prostitute both made it to God's hall of fame. A good, clean, godly woman and a prostitute made it into the book! I can understand how Sarah was included, but how in the world did this prostitute get honored? The answer is, faith. She was listed because God honors faith. That was the one thing Sarah and Rahab had in common; nothing else.

The Bible doesn't talk about Rahab having a husband. She had the whole city. Sarah stayed in the tent and knit socks. She moved wherever her husband went and took care of him. There was no similarity in their lifestyles, just in their faith. God saw the same thing in Sarah that He saw in Rahab. So don't accept the excuse that because you have lived like a Rahab you can't have the faith experience.

RAHAB AND SARAH

God wants you to believe Him. So make a decision and stand on it. Rahab decided to take a stand on the side of God's people. She hid the spies. And she made the decision based on her faith. She took action. Faith is a fact and faith is an action. Rahab took action because she believed God would deliver her when Jericho fell to the Israelites.

Sarah received strength to carry and deliver a child when she was well past childbearing age. She took action because she judged Him faithful who had promised {Hebrews 11:11}. She went through the birth process and delivered a child, not because of her circumstances, but because of her faith. Sarah believed God.

God wants your faith to be developed. Regardless of your position and your past, God raises people up equally. Faith is an equal opportunity business. No matter how many mistakes you have made, it is still faith that God will honor. You see, you may have blown it, but God is in the business of restoring broken lives. You may have been like Rahab, but if you can believe God, He will save your house. You know, He didn't save only Rahab. He saved her entire household. All the other homes in Jericho were destroyed. The only house God saved in the city was the house where this prostitute lived.

ONLY FAITH

You would have thought He would have saved some nice little lady's house. Perhaps He would have saved some cottage housing an old woman, or a little widow's house, with petunias growing next to the sidewalk. But God saved the prostitute's house. Was it because He wanted it? No, He wanted the faith. That is what moves God.

If you believe that your background will keep you from moving forward with God, then you don't understand the value of faith. The thing God is asking from you is faith. Some may live good, clean, separated lives. Maybe you are proud of how holy you are. But He still honors only faith.

If you want to grasp the things of God, you will not be able to because of your lifestyle. It will be because of your conviction. God gave healing to some folks who weren't even saved. They were sinners. Perhaps some of them never did get saved, but they got healed because they believed Him. The thing that moves God is faith. If you believe Him, He will move in your life according to your faith, not according to your experience. There was something in Rahab's house that God called valuable. Faith was there. So God protected her from the fire.

He also saved her things. When the fire was over, Rahab was the richest woman in the city. She was the only woman left in town who owned property. So God will also save your finances. Simply believe Him.

FIVE SISTERS

There was also a group of sisters in the Old Testament who proved that God is interested in what happens to women. Their names were, Mahlah, Noah, Hoglah, Milcah and Tirza.

> *"Then came the daughters of Zelophehad, the son of Hepher, the son of Gilead, the son of Machir, the son of Manasseh, of the families of Manasseh, the son of Joseph; and these are the names of his daughters; Mahlah, Noah, and Hoglah, and Milcah, and Tirzah. And they stood before Moses, and before Eleazar the priest, and before the princes and all the congregation, by the door of the tabernacle of the congregation, saying, Our father died in the wilderness, and he was not in the company of them that gathered themselves together against the Lord in the company of Korah; but died in his own sin, and had no sons."* [Numbers 27:1-3]

Mahlah, Noah, Hoglah, Milcah and Tizrah were five women who were left alone. There were no men left in their family. Their father had wealth and he had no sons. But prior to this time, women were not allowed to own property or to have an inheritance except through their husbands. Only men could own property.

But they appealed their situation to God through Moses.

> *"Why should the name of our father be done away from among his family, because he hath no son? Give unto us therefore a possession among the brethren of our father."*   [Numbers 27:4]

They appealed to Moses for help on the basis of who their father was. They stated their case and looked to him as God's authority. These women couldn't understand why they should not have some of their father's wealth simply because they were born female. If not for their boldness, their uncles would have received all their father's wealth while they would have been poor and homeless, receiving only leftovers from others.

DAUGHTERS OF ABRAHAM

But these women were daughters of Abraham. If you want the enemy to release you, remind him of whose daughter you are. No one would have listened to them if they had not initiated a meeting to plead their case. Perhaps you who have struggled need to call a meeting. Get in touch with people in power and demand what you want, or you will not get it. Speak for yourself. They could not understand why they were being discriminated against because of their gender.

DO YOU NEED TO CALL A MEETING?

One of the reasons Zelophehad's daughters could make a proper case for themselves was they were right. It was time to teach God's people that women have value. Abraham's daughters have worth. They didn't wait for a man to defend them; they took action in faith. And God saw it. He saw faith in those women.

> *"And Moses brought their cause before the Lord. And the Lord spake unto Moses, saying, The daughters of Zelophehad speak right: thou shalt surely give them a possession of an inheritance among their father's brethren; and thou shalt cause the inheritance of their father to pass unto them."*   [Numbers 27:5-7]

When Moses heard the sisters' case, he didn't know what to do, so he asked God. And the women were vindicated. If they had failed, surely they would have been scorned by all the good people of Israel who would have never challenged Moses in such a way. But they succeeded instead and received the wealth of their father. God is no respecter of persons. Faith is based on equal opportunity.

YOU ARE A DAUGHTER OF ABRAHAM

Like the infirm woman, you are a daughter of Abraham if you have faith. You want the inheritance of your father to pass on to you. Why should you sit there and be in need when your heavenly Father has left you everything? Your Father is rich, and He left everything to you. However, you will not get your inheritance until you ask for it. Demand what your Father left you! That degree has your name on it. That promotion has your name on it. That financial breakthrough has your name on it.

There is no need to sit around waiting on someone else to get you what is yours. Nobody else is coming. The One who needed to come has already come. Jesus said, "...I am come that they might have life, and that they might have it more abundantly" {John 10:10}. That is all you need.

LET YOUR FAITH SPEAK

The power to get wealth is in your tongue. You shall have whatever you say. So if you keep sitting around murmuring, groaning and complaining, you use your tongue against yourself. Your speech can keep you bent over and crippled. You may be destroying yourself with your words.

So open your mouth and speak something good about yourself and stand up on your feet. You used your mouth against yourself. Then you spoke against all the other women around you because you treated them just like you treated yourself. So open your mouth now and begin to speak deliverance and power. You are not defeated. You are Abraham's daughter.

ASK FOR YOUR INHERITANCE

When you start speaking correctly, God will give you what you say. But you must say you want it. Jesus said, "And all things, whatsoever ye shall ask in prayer, believing, ye shall receive" {Matthew 21:22}. God willed you something. Your Father left you an inheritance. And if God would bless the sons of Abraham, surely He would bless the daughters of Abraham.

God will give you whatever you ask for {John 14:13}. He will give you a business. He will give you a dream. He will make you the head and not the tail {Deuteronomy 28:13}. God's power will bring all things up under your feet. So believe Him for your household. God will deliver. You don't need a sugar daddy. You have the Jehovah-jireh, the best provider this world has ever known.

> *"For ye are all the children of God by faith in Christ Jesus."*
> *{Galatians 3:26}*

Women are just as much children of God as men are. Everything that God will do for a man, He will do for a woman. So you are not disadvantaged. You can get an inheritance like any man. Generally men don't cry about being single—they simply get on with life and stay busy. The same should be true for you. There is no reason a woman can't be complete in God without a husband.

But if you choose to get married, you should get married for the right reasons. Don't give in to a desperate spirit that forces you to put up with someone less than who you would really want. You could become stuck with someone immature and bear three little boys. Then you would have four boys. That is no way to live. You need someone who has some shoulders and backbone.

You need to marry someone who will hold you, help you, strengthen you, build you up, and be with you when the storms of life are raging. If you want a cute man, buy a photograph. But if you want some help, marry a godly man.

> *"For as many of you as have been baptized into Christ have put on Christ. There is neither Jew nor Greek, there is neither bond nor free, there is neither male nor female: for ye are all one in Christ Jesus."*
> *{Galatians 3:27-28}*

Those ancient Israelite women, the daughters of Zelophehad, thought it was a disgrace for them to be starving when they considered who their father was. Rahab was a harlot until she found faith. But once she had faith, she no longer turned to her old profession. The infirm woman was bowed over until Jesus touched her. But once He touched her, she stood up.

WALK WITH RESPECT

You have put on Christ. So there is no reason to be bent over after you have received His touch. You can walk with respect even when you have past failures. It's not what people say about you that makes you different. It is what you say about yourself, and what your God has said about you, that really matters. Just because someone calls you a tramp doesn't mean you have to act like one. Rahab walked with respect. You will find her name mentioned in the lineage of Jesus Christ. She went from being a prostitute to being one of the great-grandmothers of our Lord and Savior Jesus Christ. You can't help where you've been, but you can help where you're going.

QUIT MAKING EXCUSES

God is not concerned about race. He is not concerned about your being black. You may think, "My people came over on a boat and picked cotton on a plantation." But it doesn't make any difference. The answer isn't in being white. Real spiritual advantage does not come from the color of your skin. It's not the color of your skin that will bring deliverance and help from God; it's the contents of your heart.

Some of us have particular problems based on where we came from, and we've got to deal with them. God says there is neither Greek nor Jew. There is no such thing as a black church. There is no such thing as a white church. There is only one Church, purchased by the blood of the Lamb. We are all one in Christ Jesus.

You may have been born with a silver spoon in your mouth too, but that doesn't make any difference. In the kingdom of God, social status doesn't mean anything. Rahab can be mentioned right next to Sarah because if you believe, God will bless. Faith is the only thing in this world where there is true equal opportunity. Everyone can come to Jesus.

"...There is neither male nor female..." {Galatians 3:28}. God doesn't look at your gender. He looks at your heart. He doesn't look at morality and good works. He looks at the faith that lives within. God is looking in your heart. You are spirit, and spirits are sexless. That's why angels don't have sexes; they simply are ministering spirits. Don't think of angels in terms of gender. They can manifest themselves as men, but angels are really ministering spirits. All people are one in Christ Jesus.

Christ saw the worth of the infirm woman because she was a daughter of Abraham. She had faith. He will unleash you also from the pain you have struggled with and the frustrations that have plagued you. Faith is truly equal opportunity. If you will but dare to believe that you are a daughter of Abraham, you will find the power to stand up straight and be unleashed. The potential that has been bound will be truly set free.

CHAPTER ELEVEN

A Woman Without Excuse

Many see Jesus as a way to heaven and the solution to spiritual problems, but they fail to see that He is the solution to all of life's problems.

ttitudes affect the way we live our lives. A good attitude can bring success. But a poor attitude can bring destruction. An attitude results from perspective. I'm sure you understand what perspective is. Everyone seems to have a different perspective. It comes from the way we look at life, and the way we look at life is often determined by our history.

The events of the past can cause us to have an outlook or perspective on life that is less than God's perspective. The little girl who was abused learns to defend herself by not trusting men. This attitude of defensiveness often stretches into adulthood. If we have protected ourselves a certain way in the past with some measure of success, then it is natural to continue that pattern throughout life. So we must learn how to look beyond our perspective to change old ways and attitudes.

The infirm woman whom Jesus healed was made completely well by His touch. She couldn't help herself no matter how hard she tried, but Jesus unleashed her. He lifted a heavy burden from her shoulders and set her free.

Today, many of us have things we need to be separated from, or burdens we need to have lifted. We will not function effectively until those things are lifted off of us. We can function to a certain point under a load, but we can't function as effectively as we would if the thing was lifted off of us. Perhaps some of you right now have things that are burdening you down.

You need to commend yourselves for having the strength to function under pressure. Unfortunately, we often bear the weight of our burdens alone, since we don't feel free to tell anyone about our struggles. So whatever strides you have made, be they large or small, you have made them against the current.

HAVE YOUR PROBLEMS BECOME A SECURITY BLANKET?

It is God's intention that we be set free from the loads we carry. Many people live in co-dependent relationships. Others are anesthetized to their problems because they have had them so long. Perhaps you have become so accustomed to having a problem that even when you get a chance to be delivered, you find it hard to let it go. Problems can become like a security blanket.

But Jesus took away this woman's excuse. He said, "...Woman, thou art loosed from thine infirmity." And the moment He said that, it required something of her that she hadn't had to deal with before. For eighteen years she could excuse herself because she was handicapped. But the moment He told her the problem was gone, the woman had no excuse.

STRAIGHTEN OUT YOUR ATTITUDE

Before you get out of trouble, you need to straighten out your attitude. Until your attitude is corrected, you can't be corrected.

Why should we put up all the ramps and rails for the handicapped if we can heal them? You want everyone to make an allowance for your problem, but your problem needs to make an allowance for God and to humble itself to the point where you don't need special help. I'm not referring to physical handicaps; I'm addressing the emotional baggage that keeps us from total health. You cannot expect the whole human race to move over because you had a bad childhood. They will not do it. So you will end up in depression, frustration, and even confusion. You may even have trouble with relationships because people don't accommodate your hang-up.

One woman I pastored was extremely obnoxious. It troubled me deeply, so I took the matter to God in prayer. The Lord allowed me to meet her husband. And when I saw how nasty he talked to her, I understood why, when she reached down into her reservoir, all she had was hostility. That's all she had taken in. You cannot give out something that you haven't taken in.

A MATTER OF LIFE OR DEATH

Christ wants to separate you from the source of your bitterness until it no longer gives you the kind of attitude that makes you a carrier of pain. Your attitude affects your situation—your attitude, not other people's attitude about you. Your attitude will give you life or death.

One of the greatest deliverances people can ever experience in life is to have their attitude delivered. It doesn't do you any good to be delivered financially if your attitude doesn't change. I can give you $5,000, but if your attitude, your mental perspective, doesn't change, you will be broke in a week because you'll lose it again. The problem is not how much you have, it's what you do with what you have. If you can change your attitude, you might have only $50, but you can take that $50 and learn how to get $5 million.

When God comes to heal, He wants to heal your emotions also. Sometimes all we pray about is our situation. We bring God our shopping list of desires. Fixing circumstances is like applying a band-aid, though. Healing attitudes set people free to receive wholeness.

The woman who was crippled for eighteen years was delivered from her infirmity. The Bible says she was made straight and glorified God. She got a new attitude. However, the enemy still tried to defeat her by using the people around her. Satan doesn't want to let you find health and strength. And he may send another circumstance that will pull you down in the same way, if you don't change your attitude.

When you first read about this woman, you might have thought that the greatest deliverance was her physical deliverance. But I want to point out another deliverance that was even greater. The Bible says that when the Lord laid His hand on her, she was made straight. That's physical deliverance. Then her attitude also changed. How? She entered into praise and thanksgiving and worshiped the Lord. This woman began to leap and rejoice and magnify God and shout the victory like anybody who has been delivered from an eighteen-year infirmity should. But while she was glorifying God over here, the enemy was stirring up strife over there. That's how Satan operates. But she just kept on glorifying God. She didn't stop praising God to answer her accusers.

DEFENSIVE PRAISE

The Lord is your defense. You do not have to defend yourself. When God has delivered you, do not stop what you are doing to answer your accusers. Continue to bless His name, because you do not want your attitude to become defensive. When you have been through difficult times, you cannot afford to play around with moods and attitudes. Depression and defensiveness may make you vulnerable to the devil.

This woman had to protect herself by entering into defensive praise. This was not just praise of thanksgiving, it was defensive praise. Defensive praise is a strategy and a posture of war that says, "We will not allow our attitude to crumble and fall."

When you get to the point that you quit defending yourself or attacking others, you open up a door for the Lord to fight for you.

When this woman began to bless God, she built walls around her own deliverance. She decided to keep the kind of attitude that enabled the deliverance of God to be maintained in her life. When you have been through surgery, you cannot afford to fool around with band-aids.

GOD WILL PULL YOU OUT

When you're in trouble, God will reach into the mess and pull you out. However, you must be strong enough not to let people drag you back into it. Once God unleashes you, don't let anyone trap you into some religious fight. Keep praising Him. For this woman, the more they criticized her, the more she was justified because she just stood there and kept believing God. God is trying to get you to a place of faith. He is trying to deliver you from an attitude of negatives.

When you have had problems for many years, you tend to expect problems. God must have healed this woman's emotions too because she kept praising Him instead of paying attention to the quarrel of the religious folks around her. She could have easily fallen into negative thinking. But instead, she praised God.

Can you imagine what would have happened if she had stopped glorifying God and started arguing? If an argument could have gotten through her doors, this whole scene would have ended in a fight. But she was thankful and determined to express her gratitude.

LET THE WALLS COME DOWN

The Lord wants to speak a word of faith to you. He wants to set you free from every power that has kept you in bondage. But in order for that to be received in your spirit, you must allow Him to come in and instill faith. The emotional walls that surround us have to come down.

Love is eternal. It is not limited by time. When you commit yourself to loving someone, you make that commitment to all the person is. You are who you are because of your history. For me, that means I love my wife and who she has become. But in order for me to love her effectively, she must allow me into her history.

Many couples in a relationship argue over relatively insignificant things. Often, the reason these things are important is because one or the other is reminded of a past event. How can one person love another if he or she doesn't know the other person's history?

TOO NARROW AN APPROACH

The Church has become too narrow in its approach to attitude. We want to keep our attitudes to ourselves and simply take them to God. Although we certainly should take them to Him, we also need to learn to "bear ye one another's burdens..." {Galatians 6:2}.

Thousands walk in fear. The Church could give strength to counter that fear. But thousands have built a wall around them because they do not trust anyone else. The Church can help its members learn to trust one another. Thousands are co-dependent and get their value from a relationship with another person. The Church can point to God's love as the source for self-worth. We must help our members understand that we are not valuable because we love God; we are valuable because He loves us.

Jesus took away the ability of the infirm woman to make excuses for herself and gave her the strength to maintain an attitude of gratitude and praise. The Church today is to be the kind of safe haven that does the same thing. Those who are wounded should be able to come and find strength in our praise.

HAVE AN ATTITUDE OF GRATITUDE

Gratitude and defensive praise are contagious. Although the Bible doesn't specifically say so, I imagine that those who saw what was going on the day Jesus healed the infirm woman were caught up in praise as well. The Church must also find room to join in praise when the broken in our midst are healed. Those who missed the great blessing that day were those who decided to argue about religion.

The Bible describes heaven as a place where the angels rejoice over one sinner who comes into the faith {Luke 15:10}. They rejoice because Jesus heals those who are broken. Likewise, God's people are to rejoice because the brokenhearted and emotionally wounded come to Him.

Christ unleashed power in the infirm woman that day. He healed her body and gave her the strength of character to keep a proper attitude. The woman who is broken and wounded today will find power unleashed within her too when she responds to the call and brings her wounds to the Great Physician.

The True Beauty of a Woman

It's not what people say about you that makes you different. It's what you say about yourself, and what your God has said about you, that really matters.

We are fascinated with beauty. There are contests of all kinds to determine who is the most beautiful of all. Advertisers spend millions of dollars to promote beauty pageants. The beauty industry is one of the largest in America. Women spend huge amounts of money on makeup, fashionable clothing, and jewelry. Plastic surgeons are kept busy cutting and tucking extra flesh and reshaping features to make people more attractive.

But in spite of all this attention, what is the true beauty of a woman? What is it that makes her genuinely attractive? Many feel unattractive because they don't meet a certain image to which they have aspired. Others are constantly frustrated in trying to get someone to notice how attractive they are.

No scientist has ever been able to make a woman. No doctor has been able to create a woman. And no engineer has been able to build a woman. But God has made some fine women. And according to Him, you don't have to look like a TV commercial to be beautiful. No one stays twenty-one forever.

START APPRECIATING YOURSELF

We must learn to thank God for who we are. Don't be a foolish woman watching television and crying because you don't look like the girl who opened up the window in the game show. You are not supposed to look like that. If God had wanted you to look like that, He would have made you like that. So be encouraged, God will send somebody along who will appreciate you the way you are.

And while you are waiting on that person, start appreciating yourself. Remind yourself, "I am valuable to God. I am somebody. And I won't let another use me or abuse me or treat me like I'm nothing. Yes, I've been through some bad times. I've been hurt and I've been bent out of shape. But the Lord touched me and loosed me, and now I am glorifying God and I'm not going back to where I came from."

As I mentioned earlier, there is an important lesson to learn from the account of Samson and Delilah in the Old Testament. {See Judges 16.} The Philistines were his enemies, but they could not kill Samson, until they found a door. The door was named Delilah. The Bible says Samson loved Delilah and that he became so infatuated with her that he made himself vulnerable.

It was not Delilah's beauty that captivated. It was not even her sexuality that destroyed Samson. Samson had known beautiful women before. He had slept with prostitutes. It was not just sexual exercise that caused her to get a grip on this man. What got Samson is what I call, *The Delilah Syndrome.* There is nothing in Scripture to prove that Delilah was beautiful. Maybe she was, but what got Samson was her understanding of the man.

LIFE IS NOT A FAIRY TALE

Beauty and sex appeal are not the areas to concentrate on. Because when you focus on the wrong areas, you don't get the right results. Society teaches you today that if you have the right hair, the right face, the right shape, the right clothes, and the right car, that you will get the right man. Then once you have this, you can expect you will buy the right house, have the right children, live the right life and live happily ever after. But this is simply not true. Life is not a fairy tale.

God put some things into the feminine spirit that a man needs more than anything God put on the feminine body. If a woman knows who she is on the inside, no matter what she looks like, she will have no problem being attractive to a man. If she knows her own self-worth, then when she comes before that man, he will receive her.

INWARDLY ADORNED

The enemy wants you to be so focused on your outer appearance that you won't recognize your inner beauty, your inner strength, your inner glory. Your real value cannot be bought, applied, added on, hung from your ears, or laid on your neck. Your real strength is in more than mere outward apparel and adornment for men. This real thing that causes a man to need you so desperately that he wants to be near you is not what is on the outside of you, but what is in you.

You need to recognize what God has put in you. When God made the woman, He didn't just decorate the outside. He decorated the inside of the woman. He put beauty in her spirit.

The Scriptures talk about not having the outward adornment of gold, silver, and costly array. And the Church took that passage and made a legal doctrine out of it. It was declared that there could be no jewelry, no makeup and no clothing of certain types. We are so negative at times. In fact, we were so busy dealing with the negative that we didn't hear the positive of what God said. God said that He had adorned the woman inwardly.

A WORD TO "BEAUTIFUL" WIVES

> *"Likewise, ye wives, be in subjection to your own husbands...."*
> *{1 Peter 3:1a}*

Notice that this verse in 1 Peter doesn't say women are to be in subjection to all men, just to their own husbands. God did not make you a servant to all men. You have the right to choose who you will be in subjection to—and please choose very carefully.

> *"...that, if any obey not the word, they also may without the word be won by the conversation of the wives."* *{1 Peter 3:1b}*

The word *conversation* here refers to lifestyle. You will not win your husband through lip-service; you will win him through the inward adornment of your beautiful lifestyle. He will see how you are—not what you say. He will watch how you act. He will watch your attitude. He will watch your disposition. A real problem with many women believers today is that with the same mouth they use to witness to their husbands, they are often cursing others. You cannot witness to and win a man while he sits up and listens to you gossip about others.

> *"While they behold your chaste conversation* [lifestyle] *coupled with fear."* *{1 Peter 3:2}*

This next verse of Peter doesn't say anything about your ruby red lips or your long $25 eyelashes. It says your husband should behold your lifestyle, your chaste (beautiful) lifestyle. *Chaste* is a word that means pure. Wives can win a husband by reverencing him.

"Whose adorning let it not be that outward adorning of plaiting the hair, and of wearing of gold, or of putting on of apparel."
{1 Peter 3:3}

Now if this verse means you cannot wear any of these things, then it means you must be naked. Apparel is clothing. The truth that Peter is telling us is that a woman's beauty and strength are not to be found on the outside. There is more to you than clothes. There's more to you than gold. There's more to you than hairdos.

Society promotes the notion that beauty is found in these outer things. However, if you keep working only on these outer things, you will find yourself looking in a mirror to find your value. You could go broke fixing up the outside and still be lonely and alone.

The *Delilah Syndrome* had to do with Delilah's ability to simply provide Samson with a place to rest. Samson felt comfortable around her. The man was tired, so he laid on her and slept. There is nothing in his story to say he loved her for sex. She simply gave him rest. He needed it so desperately that even when he knew she was trying to kill him, he couldn't stay away.

YOU ARE SARAH'S DAUGHTERS

If Satan can work Delilah's strengths against men, then God can use them for men. If you are married, you can enrich your marriage through inner beauty. If you're not married, when you do get married, you will understand that it's not the necklaces you wear that make you attractive. It's not the twists you put in your hair. It's something that God puts in your heart that actually affects the man.

*"But let it be the hidden man of the heart, in that which is not corruptible, even the ornament of a **meek and quiet spirit**, which is in the sight of God of great price."* *{1 Peter 3:4}*

Ladies, God gave you the ornament of a meek and quiet spirit that is more valuable than any other outer form of jewelry. It is worth more than gold. It is more powerful than sexual ability.

When Samson hit Delilah's lap, she calmed him. Can you see what made Adam partake of the forbidden fruit, knowing it was evil? The Bible says Eve was deceived, but that he knew it. Do you see how powerful your influence is? The enemy wants to capitalize on what God put in you. That is why you must watch what goes through your doors.

> *"For after this manner in the old time the holy women also, who trusted in God, adorned themselves...."*   {1 Peter 3:5}

This verse of Peter talks about how women decorated themselves in the times of the patriarchs. Sarah was beautiful because she exhibited inner beauty and lived in obedience to Abraham.

> *"Even as Sara obeyed Abraham, calling him lord: whose daughters ye are, as long as ye do well, and are not afraid with any amazement."*   {1 Peter 3:6}

Here Peter says that you are Sarah's daughters when you are not afraid with any amazement. When you resist the temptation to react to circumstances and maintain a peaceful, meek and quiet spirit in times of frustration, then you are Sarah's daughters.

If you can stay calm in a storm, if you can praise God under pressure, if you can worship in the midst of critics and criticism, God says you are Sarah's daughter.

If you can keep a calm head when the bills are more than the income, and not lose control when Satan says you won't make it, if you can stand in the midst of the storm, you are Sarah's daughter.

If you can rebuke the fear that is knocking at the door of your heart, and tell that low self-esteem it cannot come in, and rebuke all the spirits that are waiting to attack you and take you captive, you are Sarah's daughter.

If you can stand calm in the midst of the storm and say, "I know God will deliver me," you are Sarah's daughter. If you can walk with God in the midst of the storm and trust Him to bring you through dry places, you are Sarah's daughter.

If you can judge God faithful, and know that God cannot lie, understanding that Satan is the father of lies, you are Sarah's daughter.

If you can stand there when fear is trying to get you to overreact and fall apart, you are Sarah's daughter. If you can stand there and push a tear from off the side of your face and smile in the middle of the rain, you are Sarah's daughter.

YOU ARE TRULY BEAUTIFUL

God is adorning you with glory, power and majesty. He will send people into your life to appreciate your real beauty, your real essence. It is the kind of beauty that lasts in a face full of wrinkles, gray hair, falling arches, crow's feet, and all the pitfalls that may come your way. There's a beauty that you can see in a ninety-year-old woman's face that causes an old man to smile. God is decorating you on the inside. He is putting a glory in you that will shine through your eyes. A man will come along and look in your eyes. He will not talk about whether they were blue or whether your eye-shadow was right or not. He will look in your eyes and see trust, peace, love and life.

YOU ARE A WONDERFUL PIECE OF ARTWORK

Appreciate the ornaments of God. Let God give you a new attitude. Let Him wash everything out of your spirit that is against Him. Let go of anger, hate, frustration and bitterness. God wants you unleashed. He repeats today, just as He did 2,000 years ago, "Woman, thou art loosed."

Beauty comes in many ways. However, true beauty is always on the inside. A faithful wife is more precious than words can express. The inner beauty that makes you valuable to God will also make you valuable to others. Some may just take longer to notice it. Regardless of how long it takes, know the attractiveness and beauty that is within.

Perhaps you feel scared by the past. Maybe you think you are unattractive and unworthy. Nothing could be more untrue. God painted a wonderful piece of artwork one day. That painting is you.

CHAPTER THIRTEEN

Every Woman Needs a Sabbath

*You need the calmness of a
Sabbath rest because it is
through the resting of your
spirit that the restoration of
your life begins to occur.*

*W*e have dealt with many aspects of the story of Jesus healing the infirm woman. However, in this chapter I would like to look at an issue underlying the miracle. It does not really concern either the woman or Christ. It concerns the time of her healing: The Sabbath day.

The Sabbath is a day of rest. It is a day of restoration. Following creation, on the seventh day, God rested {Genesis 2:2}. Rest is for the purpose of restoration. It is not just because you're tired. It is during a time of rest that you replenish or receive back those things that were expended or put out. But it is also during the time of restoration that the enemy wants to break off your fellowship with the Lord.

I don't want you to think of rest just in terms of sleep. Please understand that rest and restoration are related concepts. You need the calmness of a Sabbath rest because it is through the resting of your spirit that the restoration of your life begins to occur. The enemy does not want you to have this rest.

It is not a mere coincidence that this woman was healed on the Sabbath day. The Bible goes to great pains to make us aware that it was during the Sabbath that this woman experienced her healing. The Sabbath was meant not only for God to rest, but also for God to enjoy His creation with man. So the issues here are rest and communion.

A SIGN OF THE COVENANT

In the nation of Israel, God used the Sabbath day as a sign of the covenant. It proved that they were His people. They spent time in worship and fellowship with the Lord on the Sabbath. That is what the Sabbath is truly all about. It is real communion between the heart of man and the heart of God.

When Jesus began to minister in a restful situation, needs began to be manifested. The infirm woman's need was revealed in the midst of the Sabbath. You can never get your needs met by losing your head. When you calm down, God speaks.

When you start murmuring and complaining, the only thing God can focus on is your unbelief. But when you start resting in Him, He can focus on your problems and on the areas of your life that need to be touched.

Also, when you begin to enter into real worship with God, that's the best time to have Him minister to your needs. That's the time when God gives restoration in your life. Satan, therefore, wants to break up your Sabbath rest.

THE "RELIGIOUS" AMONG US

Sometimes I would rather deal with rank sinners than with religious people. When Jesus healed this woman on the Sabbath, the religious folks got upset. Why? Because religious people esteem religiosity above God's creation. They are more concerned about keeping doctrine than about helping people. One thing you can't seem to deliver religious people from is their own *religiousness*. But man is God's concern above everything else.

The infirm woman was not sitting around complaining. She was not murmuring. She was not hysterical. She had a problem, but she was calm. She was just sitting there listening to the words of the Master. She had brought her problem with her, but her problem did not dominate her time of worship.

CHRIST IS OUR SABBATH REST

I want to zoom in on the Sabbath day, because what the Sabbath was physically, Christ is spiritually. Christ is our Sabbath rest. He is the end of our labors. We are saved by grace through faith and not by works, lest any man should be able to boast {Ephesians 2:8-9}. Jesus said:

> *"Come unto me, all ye that labour and are heavy laden, and I will give you rest. Take my yoke upon you, and learn of me; for I am meek and lowly in heart: and ye shall find rest unto your souls. For my yoke is easy, and my burden is light."*
>
> *{Matthew 11:28-30}*

The *rest* of the Lord is so complete that when Jesus was dying on the cross, He said, "...It is finished..." {John 19:30}. It was so powerful. For the first time in history, a high priest sat down in the presence of God without having to run in and out bringing blood to atone for the sins of man. When Christ entered in once and for all, He offered up *Himself* for us that we might be delivered from sin.

YOU CAN REST IN HIM

So if you really want to be healed, you've got to be in Him. If you really want to be set free, and experience restoration, you've got to be in Him, because your healing comes in the Sabbath rest. Your healing comes in Christ Jesus. As you rest in Him, every infirmity, every area bent out of place will be restored.

But the devil knows this truth also. So he does not want you to rest in the Lord. Satan wants you to be anxious. He wants you to be upset. He wants you to be hysterical. He wants you to be suicidal, doubtful, fearful and neurotic.

> *"There remaineth therefore a rest to the people of God. For he that is entered into his rest, he also hath ceased from his own works, as God did from his. Let us labour therefore to enter into that rest, lest any man fall after the same example of unbelief."*
> {Hebrews 4:9-11}

Sometimes it takes work to find the place of rest and calm. Our hectic world does not lend itself to quiet and peace. It creates noise and uneasiness. Even though the infirm woman was bowed over and could not lift herself, she rested in the fact that she was in the presence of a mighty God. He is able to do exceedingly and abundantly above all that we may ask or think {Ephesians 3:20}.

Jesus also confronted the woman at the well with some exciting truths.

> *"Jesus answered and said unto her, Whosoever drinketh of this water shall thirst again: but whosoever drinketh of the water that I shall give him shall never thirst; but the water that I shall give him shall be in him a well of water springing up into everlasting life."*
> {John 4:13-14}

In this passage, Jesus was sitting at the well waiting for someone to return. He was relaxed. He was calm and resting. He knew who He was. God doesn't get excited about circumstances.

Another time the disciples and Jesus were on a ship. Then a storm arose that looked like it was about to sink the ship. However, Jesus didn't become concerned about circumstances. In fact, He was sleeping, resting in the middle of the crisis. While everyone else was running all over the boat trying to figure out how they would get into life jackets and into the lifeboats, Jesus was resting. Was Jesus resting because He was lazy? No, He was resting because He knew that He was greater than the storm. When the disciples ran frightened to Him not knowing what to do, Jesus rose up and spoke to the winds and waves and said, "...Peace, be still..." {Mark 4:39}.

YOU DON'T HAVE TO STRUGGLE

When you know who you are, you don't have to struggle. You don't have to work Him up. That was Christ's attitude when the woman at the well met Him. When this woman came down with her waterpot on her shoulder, she was all upset and worried about the water she needed to draw. But when she met Jesus sitting by the well, He began to demonstrate calmness. He told her, "If you drink of the water that you have, you will thirst again, but if you drink of the water that I have, you will never thirst."

> *"The woman saith unto him, Sir, give me this water, that I thirst not, neither come hither to draw. Jesus saith unto her, Go, call thy husband, and come hither."* {John 4:15-16}

Jesus shifted the focus of the conversation to the real need.

> *"The woman answered and said, I have no husband. Jesus said unto her, Thou hast well said, I have no husband: for thou hast had five husbands; and he whom thou now hast is not thy husband: in that saidst thou truly."* {John 4:17-18}

Like this woman, you can get yourself into situations that wound and upset your spirit. These kinds of wounds can't be healed through human effort. You must get in the presence of God and let Him fill those voids in your life. You will not settle it up by going from friend to friend. This woman had already tried that. She had already gone through five men. So the answer is not getting another man. It's getting in touch with *the Man*, Jesus.

Once the woman at the well had been ministered to by Jesus, she threw down her waterpot and ran to tell others about the man she had met at the well. Her mind was no longer focused on her problems. They were focused on Jesus. We too need to get rid of the old, carnal man. Some of those old attachments and old ways of living need to be replaced with the calmness of the Spirit.

This woman could never have rid herself of the old man until she met the new man, Jesus. When you meet the new, you get the power to say good-bye to the old. You will never be able to break the grip on your life that those old ways have until you know Jesus Christ is the real way. You will never get it straight without Jesus. You must come to Him just as you are. Knowing Him will give you the power to break away from the old self and the ties that bind.

If you have something that has attached itself to you that is not of God, you won't be able to break it through your own strength. Submit yourself unto God, resist the enemy, and he will flee from you {James 4:7}. As you submit to God, you receive the power to resist the enemy.

This woman didn't even go back home. She ran into the city telling everyone to come and see the Man who had told her about her life. You do yourself a disservice until you really come to know Jesus. He satisfies. Everyone else, well, they pacify, but Jesus satisfies. He can satisfy every need and every yearning. He heals every pain and every affliction. Then He lifts every burden and every trouble in your life.

YOU HAVE BEEN BENT OVER LONG ENOUGH

You have had enough tragedy. You have been bent over long enough. God will do something good in you. God kept you living through all those years of infirmity because He has something greater for you than what you've ever experienced. God kept you because He has something better for you.

You may have been abused and misused. Perhaps all those you trusted in turned on you and broke your heart. Still, God has sustained you. You didn't make it because you were strong. You didn't make it because you were smart. You didn't make it because you were wise. You made it because God's amazing grace kept you and sustained you. God has more for you today than what you went through yesterday. So don't give up. Don't give in. Hold on. The blessing is on the way.

I dare you to realize that you can do all things through Christ who strengthens you {Philippians 4:13}. Once the infirm woman knew that, she didn't have to be bent over, she stood straight up. When Jesus told her to be loosed, she stood up and glorified God. He also told the woman at the well to get rid of the old. He wanted her to step away from that old pattern of selfishness. Then suddenly, she recognized that she didn't have what she thought she had.

GOD'S BEST GIVES US HIS REST

Just like the woman at the well, the sinful things that you have fought to maintain in your life are not worth what you thought they were. I'm referring to some to those things that have attached themselves to your life in which you find comfort. Some of those habits that you have come to enjoy, and some of those relationships you thought gave security. They just haven't been profitable. Often we settle for less because we didn't meet the best. But when you get the best, it gives you the power to let go of the rest.

LET GO NOW

The infirm woman didn't panic because of her crippling disease. She had been in torment and pain for eighteen years. But when she came into the presence of Jesus, she relaxed in Him. She expected that He would take care of her. And the result was a wonderful healing. What the woman at the well expected was regular water, but she left the well having found the Savior. She sought temporal satisfaction, but found eternal satisfaction!

That's what rest and Sabbath is. It is the ability to find eternal satisfaction in Jesus. The world can never give us peace and satisfaction. But Jesus offers both freely.

The woman who has struggled can find satisfaction. You can find hope for your soul. It is found in the Master of the universe. He will not deny you because of your past. He will not scrutinize your every action. He will take you as you are, and *give you rest*. He will provide a peace that will satisfy the very yearning of your soul.

> *"And the peace of God, which passeth all understanding, shall keep your hearts and minds through Christ Jesus."*
>
> {Philippians 4:7}

CHAPTER FOURTEEN

Winter
Woman

Perhaps you feel scarred by the past. Maybe you think you are unattractive and unworthy. Nothing could be more untrue. God painted a wonderful piece of artwork one day. That painting is you.

"And she said unto them, Call me not Naomi, call me Mara: for the Almighty hath dealt very bitterly with me. I went out full, and the Lord hath brought me home again empty: why then call ye me Naomi, seeing the Lord hath testified against me, and the Almighty hath afflicted me?"

[Ruth 1:20-21]

his morning when I rose, the land was still asleep. I watched the miracle of beginnings from the verandah of my hotel. The waves of the sea wandered listlessly in and dashed themselves on empty beaches where the sand smiled at the peacefulness of the breaking day. Like the initial sounds of an orchestra warming up for a concerto, the sea gulls cried and screeched out their opening solos. The wind watched, occasionally brushing past the palm trees spreading their leaves like the fan of a distinguished lady. Far to the east the sun crept up on stage as if it was trying to arrive without disturbing anyone. It peeked up over the ocean like the eye of a child around a corner as he stealthily plays peek-a-boo.

If I had not stayed perched on my window's edge, I would have misjudged the day. I would have thought that the morning, or perhaps the bustling sun-drenched afternoon, was the most beautiful part of the day. I would have thought the sound of laughing, hysterically happy children running into or away from the ocean would have, without contention, won the award for the best part of the day.

But just before I turned in my ballot to cast my vote in the poll, the wisdom of the evening slipped up on the stage. The early morning entertainment and the bustling sounds of the afternoon had distracted me. Now I looked over in the distance as the sun began its descent. When I did, I noticed that the crescendo of the concert is always reserved for the closing.

How had I not noticed that the sun had changed her sundress to an evening gown, full of color and grandeur? The grace of a closing day is far greater than the uncertainty of morning. So too, the next time you get a chance to notice a sun burst into its neon rainbow and curtsy before setting in the west, you will scratch out your early scribbling and recast your vote.

For the most beautiful part of the day, in fact the most beautiful part of a woman's life, is at the setting of the sun.

I write this with my mother in mind. Her hair has changed colors before my eyes. Like afterthoughts of an artist, lines have been etched upon her brow. Her arms are much weaker now, and her gait much slower; but she is somehow warmer at life's winter age than she was in her days of summer. All of life's tragedy has been wrestled to the mat, and still she stands to attest to the authenticity of her goals, dreams and ambitions.

THE WINTER OF LIFE

What is wrong with hanging around the stage to collect an encore from a grateful audience whose lives have been touched by the beauty of your song? Just because the glare of summer doesn't beat upon your face doesn't mean that there is nothing left for you to do. Whose presence will stand as a witness that God will see you through? Who will care to catch a glimpse of your children run their race or catch them when they fall beneath the weight of their day?

God never extends days beyond purpose. My daughters are in their springtime, my wife is in her middle of summer, and my mother is walking through autumn to step into the winter of her life. Together they form a chord of womanhood—three different notes creating a harmonious blend. To the reader I would suggest: Enjoy every note.

> *"While the earth remaineth, seedtime and harvest, and cold and heat, and summer and winter, and day and night shall not cease."*
> *(Genesis 8:22)*

Our culture has celebrated youth to such a degree that we have isolated the elderly. The Hollywood mentality accentuates the dynamics of youth as though each season of life didn't have its own beauty. But anyone who observes nature will tell you that all seasons have their own advantages and disadvantages. So it is important that we teach women to prepare for the winter.

I believe age can be stressful for women in a way that it isn't for men—only because we have not historically recognized women at other stages in their lives. Equally disturbing is the fact that statisticians tell us women tend to live longer, more productive lives than their male counterparts. And it is not their longevity of life that is disturbing; it is the fact that many times, because of the early death of their spouse, they have no sense of companionship.

HONOR WIDOWS WHO ARE WIDOWS INDEED

Although the Bible has very little to say in regard to the care of aged men, it does address ministry to widows. {See 1 Timothy 5:3-16.} So we need to invest some effort in encouraging older women. They have a need for more than just provision of natural substance. Many women spend their lives building their identity around their role, rather than around their own person. Then when their role changes, they feel somewhat displaced. Because being a good mother is a self-sacrificing job, when those demands have subsided, many women feel like Naomi. Her name meant "my joy." But after losing her children and her husband she said, "Change my name to *Mara*." *Mara* means "bitterness."

RESISTING THE "MARA MENTALITY"

Don't allow changing times to change who you are. It is dangerous to lose your identity in your circumstances. Circumstances can change and when they do, older women can feel empty and unfulfilled. This is what happened to Naomi. But in spite of her bout with depression, God still had much for her to contribute in life. So just because life's demands have changed doesn't mean your life is over. If yours has, you need to redefine your purpose, gather your assets and keep on living and giving. As long as you can maintain a sense of worth, you can resist the "Mara" mentality.

NO ONE HAS SEEN IT ALL

Naomi was a collection of tragedies. She had weathered many storms. Discouragement comes when people think they have seen it all and most of it was terrible! But no matter what age you are, you have never seen it all. There are no graduations from the school of life other than death. No one knows how God will end His book, but He does tend to save the best for last.

Israel didn't recognize Jesus because they were so used to seeing what they had already seen. God had sent dozens of prophets, but when He finally sent their King, they failed to recognize Him. So it is dangerous to assume that what you will see out of life will be similar to what you saw before.

God can have the strangest way of restoring purpose to one's life. For Naomi, it was through a relationship she had tried to dissuade. It is dangerous to keep sending people away. The very one you are trying to send away may have the key to restoring your purpose and fulfillment in life.

> *"And Ruth said, Intreat me not to leave thee, or to return from following after thee: for whither thou goest, I will go; and where thou lodgest, I will lodge: thy people shall be my people, and thy God my God.* {Ruth 1:16}

Ruth was Naomi's daughter-in-law. But Naomi thought their only connection was through her son, who was now dead. Many times we who have been very family-oriented do not understand friendships. When family circumstances change, we lapse into isolation because we know nothing of other relationships. There are bonds that are stronger than blood. {See Proverbs 18:24.} They are God-bonds! When God brings someone like Ruth into our life, He is the bonding agent. When Ruth said, "Your God shall be my God," God wanted Naomi to see the splendor of winter relationships. He wanted her to experience the joy of passing the baton of her wisdom and strength to someone worthy of her attention. But we should let God choose such a person for us, because too often we choose on the basis of fleshly ties, not godly ties.

I have noticed in the Scriptures that the strongest female relationships tend to be exemplified between older and younger women. I am certainly not suggesting that such will always be the case. However, let me submit a few cases for your own edification.

NAOMI AND RUTH

1. Ruth would have died in Moab, probably marrying some heathen idolater if it were not for the wisdom of Naomi, an older, more seasoned woman. Naomi knew how to provide guidance without manipulation—a strength many women at that stage of life do not have. Ruth was, of course, one of the great-grandparents in the lineage of Jesus Christ. She had greatness in her that God used Naomi to cultivate. Perhaps Naomi would have been called Mara, and perhaps she would have ended up dying in bitterness without touching any lives, if it had not been for Ruth.

ELIZABETH AND MARY

2.   Elizabeth, the wife of the priest Zacharias, is the biblical synonym for the modern pastor's wife. She was a winter woman with a summer experience. She was pregnant with a promise. And in spite of her declining years, she was fulfilling more destiny then than she ever had in her youth. Elizabeth is biblical proof that God blesses us in His own time, and on His own terms. But she was also in seclusion. Perhaps it was the attitude of the community. Many times when an older woman is still vibrant and productive it can cause jealousy and intimidation. Perhaps it was the silent stillness in her womb which some believe she experienced. Whatever the reason, she was a recluse for six months until she heard a knock at the door. If you have isolated yourself from others, regardless of the reason, I pray you will hear the knocking of the Lord. He will give you the garment of praise to clothe the spirit of heaviness {Isaiah 61:3}.

When Elizabeth lifted her still-creaking body, which seemed almost anchored down to the chair, and drug her enlarged torso to the door, she saw a young girl, a picture of herself in days gone by, standing there. Opening that door changed her life forever. As you open the door to new relationships and remove the chain from your own fears, God will overwhelm you with new splendor. Mary, the future mother of our Savior and Lord, Elizabeth's young cousin, was at the door! The splendor of this young girl's salutation, and the exposure to her experience, made the baby in Elizabeth's womb leap as Elizabeth was filled with the Holy Ghost. People probably wondered why these women who were so different, were so close. But it was a God-bond! God doesn't mean for you to go sit in a chair and die! *So in Jesus' name, get up—and answer the door!*

STRIPPING OFF THE OLD WAX

When I was in school, I worked at a local paint store, and of course had to acquaint myself with our products and procedures. As I became familiar with them, I became intrigued by a refinishing product that restored old furniture to its former luster. So I purchased the product to see if it was as effective as

I had been told. I learned right away that the most difficult part of restoring furniture was stripping off the old wax. It takes patience to overcome the effects of years of use and abuse. And if you are not committed to getting back what you once had, you could easily decide that the process is impossible. Nevertheless, I assure you, it is not impossible.

RESTORATION IS A PROCESS

David, the psalmist, declares, "He restoreth my soul..." {Psalm 23:3}. Restoration is a process. And only God knows what it takes to remove the build-up that may be existing in your life. But He specializes in restoring and renewing the human heart.

> *"And the women said unto Naomi, Blessed be the Lord, which hath not left thee this day without a kinsman, that his name may be famous in Israel. And he shall be unto thee a restorer of thy life, and a nourisher of thine old age: for thy daughter in law, which loveth thee, which is better to thee than seven sons, hath born him."*
> *{Ruth 4:14-15}*

Remember that Naomi had almost changed her name to Mara. She felt that God had dealt very bitterly with her. It is dangerous to be prejudiced against God. Prejudice means to pre-judge. Still, people, even believers, often prejudge God. Naomi did. However, God wasn't finished with her yet. Before it was over, everyone agreed that the hand of the Lord was upon her. Therefore, if you are being challenged with the silent struggles of winter, you can be encouraged that you're still on course. Trust God to see you through days that may be different from the ones you encountered earlier.

THE SILENT STRUGGLES OF WINTER

I believe the most painful experience is to have to look backward and stare into the cold face of regret. When doing so most people have thought, "I wonder how things would have been had I not made this decision...or that one...." To realize that you have been both the victim and the assailant in your own life may be difficult to accept—especially since most of those dilemmas are birthed through the womb of your own decisions. Admittedly, there are those who inadvertently crashed into circumstances that stripped them, wounded them and left them feeling like the victim on the Jericho road! No matter which case best describes your current situation, first pause to thank God that, like Naomi, in spite of any tragedies of your youth, it is a miracle that you survived the solemn chill of former days. Your presence should be a praise. Look over your shoulder and see what could have been. Has God dealt with you bitterly? I think not. Anyone can recognize Him in the sunshine, but in the storm His disciples thought He was a ghost {Matthew 14:26}.

TWO THINGS EVERY NAOMI CAN RELY UPON

There are two things every Naomi can rely upon as she gathers wood for winter days and wraps quilts around weak, willowy legs.

- First, God is a *restorer*. That is to say, as you sit by the fire sipping coffee, rehearsing your own thoughts, playing old reruns from the scenes in your life—some things He will explain, and others He will heal. Restoration doesn't mean all the lost people who left you will return. Neither Naomi's husband nor her sons were resurrected. It is just that God gives purpose back to the years that had question marks.

WAIT BY THE WINDOW

How many times have you been able to look back and say, "If I hadn't gone through that, I wouldn't have known or received this." Simply said, "He will make it up to you." He restores the effects of the years of turmoil. The people who heard Naomi running through the house with rollers in her hair complaining that God had dealt bitterly, should have waited with their noses pressed against the window pane as God masterfully brought His peace into her arms. If you wait by the window, you will hear the soft hum of an old woman nodding with her grandchild clutched in her arms. Perhaps she is too proud to tell you that she charged God foolishly, but the smile on her leathery face and the calmness of her rest says, "...He hath done all things well..." {Mark 7:37}.

"And I will restore to you the years that the locust hath eaten,
the cankerworm, and the caterpiller, and the palmerworm, my

*great army which I sent among you. And ye shall eat in plenty, and
be satisfied, and praise the name of the Lord your God, that hath
dealt wondrously with you: and my people shall never be
ashamed."*

[Joel 2:25-26]

- Second, the Lord will be known as your *nourisher*. This may be a difficult role for you who have clutched babies and men alike to the
  warm breast of your sensitivity. You, who have been the source for
  others to be strengthened, may find it difficult to know what to do
  with this role reversal. The nourisher must learn to be nourished.

STRENGTH TO THE FEEBLE AND WARMTH TO THE COLD

Many women pray more earnestly as intercessors for others than for
themselves. That is wonderful, but there ought to be a time that you desire
certain things for yourself. Our God is El Shaddai, "the breasted one" {Gene-
sis 17:1}. He gives strength to the feeble and warmth to the cold. There is
great comfort in His arms. Like children, even adults can snuggle into His
everlasting arms and hear the heartbeat of a loving God who says, "And ye
shall eat in plenty, and be satisfied, and praise the name of the Lord your
God..." {Joel 2:26}.

Expect God in all His varied forms. He is a master of disguise, a guiding
star in the night, a lily left growing in the valley, or an answered prayer sent
on the breath of an angel. Angels are the butlers of Heaven; they open doors.
He sends angels to minister to His own. Have you ever seen an angel? They
aren't always dressed in white with dramatically arched wings. Sometimes
they are so ordinary that they can be overlooked. Ruth was an angel that
Naomi almost sent away. God can use anyone as a channel of nourishment.
Regardless of the channel, He is still the source.

*"Do not forget to entertain strangers, for by so doing some peo-
ple have entertained angels without knowing it."*

[Hebrews 13:2] [NIV]

ANGELS IN YOUR PATH

When Hagar was lost in the wilderness of depression and wrestling exas-
peration, God sent an angel. When the labor-ridden mother of Samson was
mundane and barren, God sent an angel. When young Mary was wandering

listlessly through life, God sent an angel. When the grief-stricken Mary Magdalene came stumbling down to the tomb, God sent an angel. For every woman in crisis, there is an angel! For every lonely night and forgotten mother, there is an angel. For every lost young girl wandering the concrete jungle of an inner city, there is an angel.

My sister, set your coffee down, take the blanket off your legs, and stand up on your feet! Hast thou not known, hast thou not heard? For every woman facing winter, *there is an angel!*

> *"Are not all angels ministering spirits sent to serve those who will inherit salvation?"* {Hebrews 1:14} [NIV]

> *"Through faith also Sara herself received strength to conceive seed, and was delivered of a child when she was past age, because she judged him faithful who had promised."* {Hebrews 11:11}

THE MIRACLES OF WINTER

I think it would be remiss of me not to share, before moving on, the miracles of winter. In the summer, all was well with Sarah. At that time she knew little about Jehovah, her husband's God. She basically knew she was in love with a wonderful man. She was the luckiest woman in Ur. An incredibly beautiful woman already, she wore her love like a striking woman wears a flattering dress. The air smelled like honeysuckle and the wind called her name. Then one day, her husband spoke to her about moving. Where...she didn't know. And crazy as it may sound to those who have forgotten the excitement of summer, Sarah really didn't care. She ran into the tent and began to pack. Sometimes it's good to get away from relatives and friends. Starting over would be fun!

But soon the giddy exuberance of summer started to ebb as she began wrestling with the harsh realities of following a dreamer. And Abraham had not completely done what God said. God said to "...Get thee out of thy country, and from *thy kindred...*" {Genesis 12:1}. Still, Abraham took a few of their relatives with them.

"I am sure he had a good reason," Sarah thought. But what was really troubling her wasn't the strife between the relatives, or the fighting herdsmen. It was the absence of a child. By now she was sure she was barren. She felt like she had cheated Abraham out of an important part of life. Then when she was told she would have a baby, Sarah laughed. "If I am going to get a miracle," she said, "God had better hurry!"

DON'T SET YOUR OWN WATCH

I want to warn you against setting your own watch. God's time is not your time. He may not come when you want Him to, but He is always right on time. Twice it is mentioned that Sarah laughed. The first time she laughed *at* God. But in the winter time of her life, she laughed *with* God. The first time she laughed at the impossibility of God's promise. But after she had gone through life's experiences, she learned that God is faithful to perform His Word.

THE FIRST LAUGH

> *"Abraham and Sarah were already old and well advanced in years, and Sarah was past the age of childbearing. So Sarah laughed to herself as she thought, 'After I am worn out and my master is old, will I now have this pleasure?' Then the Lord said to Abraham, 'Why did Sarah laugh and say, "Will I really have a child, now that I am old?" Is anything too hard for the Lord? I will return to you at the appointed time next year and Sarah will have a son.' "*
> *{Genesis 18:11-14} [NIV]*

THE LAST LAUGH

> *"Sarah became pregnant and bore a son to Abraham in his old age, at the very time God had promised him. Abraham gave the name Isaac to the son Sarah bore him. When his son Isaac was eight days old, Abraham circumcised him, as God commanded him. Abraham was a hundred years old when his son Isaac was born to him. Sarah said, 'God has brought me laughter, and everyone who hears about this will laugh with me.' And she added, 'Who would have said to Abraham that Sarah would nurse children? Yet I have borne him a son in his old age.' "*
> *{Genesis 21:2-7} [NIV]*

Listen carefully at what I am about to say. It is relevant to you. I am not so much concerned with the eighteenth chapter of Genesis where Sarah laughs in unbelief. Nor am I focusing my attention on the twenty-first chapter where she laughs with "the joy of the Lord." I want to discuss with you the events that led to the miracles of her winter.

Often, we share our personal testimony by telling where we started and where we ultimately arrived without sharing the sequence of events that led to our deliverance. And because we leave out process, our listeners feel defeated because they named it and claimed it and still didn't attain it! We don't tell them about the awful trying of our faith that preceded our coming forth as pure gold. Today, however, we will share the whole truth and nothing but the truth! Amen.

In between these powerful moments in the life of one of God's finest examples of wives, everything in her life was tested. I believe that her love for Abraham gave her the courage to leave home, but her love for God brought forth the promised seed. Careful now, I am not saying that her love for God replaced her love for her husband; I am merely saying that it complimented the other to the highest level. After all, what good is it to appreciate what God gave us, if we do not appreciate the God who gave it to us? If age should do nothing else, it should help us put things in proper perspective. There is nothing like time to show us that we have misplaced priorities.

SARAH'S TRAGIC BLESSING IN GERAR

In summer, Sarah followed Abraham out of their country and away from their kindred. But as the seasons of life changed, she took another pilgrimage into what could have been a great tragedy. Abraham, her beloved husband, led his wife into Gerar. As I am a man and a leader myself, I dare not be too hard on him. Anyone can make a poor decision. The decision to go to Gerar I could defend, even though *Gerar* means "halting place." I have made decisions that brought me to a halting place in my life. But what is reprehensible is that Abraham, Sarah's protector and covering, when afraid for his own safety, lied about her identity {Genesis 20} . You never know who people are until you witness them under pressure. Now, I am not being sanctimonious about Abraham's flagrant disregard for truth. But it was a life-threatening lie.

MEN WILL FAIL YOU

Have you ever known someone upon whom you had cast the weight of your confidence, only to have your trust defrauded in a moment of self-gratification and indulgence? Someone who has a selfish need can jeopardize all that you have. Abraham's infamous lie jeopardized the safety of his wife. King Abimelech was a heathen king. He was used to getting whatever he wanted. And his reputation for debauchery preceded him to the degree that Abraham, the father of faith, feared for his life. So rather than risk himself, he told the king that his lovely wife was really his sister. Abraham knew that such a statement would cause Sarah to have to fulfill the torrid desires of a heathen. And Sarah now finds herself being bathed and perfumed as an offering of lust for the passions of the king.

GOD WILL SAVE YOU

Imagine the icy grip of fear that clutched this first lady of faith. Imagine her shock to realize that under real stress, a person can never be sure what another individual will do to secure his own well-being. Her Abraham had failed her. But God did not! Maybe there is someone in your life who selfishly threw you into a tempestuous situation. If so, take courage! Just because Satan set a snare for you doesn't mean you can't escape. The God we serve is able. His Word to you is "Woman, be loosed!"

Abraham's faith had always been the star of the Old Testament, but not that day. It's amazing how faith will come up in your heart at a crisis. Consider Sarah. She is facing the anxious footsteps of her rapist. She knows it will not be long until she will be abused. Like a frightened rabbit crouched in a corner, she realizes Abraham will not rescue her. I don't know what she prayed, but I know she cried out to the only One she had left!

Maybe she said, "God of Abraham, I need you to be my God too. Save me from this pending fate." Or maybe she just cried, "O God! Have mercy on me!" But whatever she said, God heard her, because God shut up all the wombs in the king's household, and He spoke up for Sarah when no one else would! He threatened the king and revealed the truth. "She is Abraham's wife!" declared the Lord. And He stopped Abimelech's footsteps of danger.

Very few men understand a woman's terror of being raped or sexually assaulted. I can only imagine the tears that ran down Sarah's face when she heard the door open. But when her would-be rapist comes in, he amazingly falls to the floor and cries out, "He touched me!" Did you know that the heart of the king is in His hand and He turneth it as He wills? {Proverbs 21:1} God delivered Sarah from the failure of her man.

THE GOD OF GERAR

When Sarah came out of Gerar, she knew something about life, about people, and most of all, about God. She didn't lose her relationship with Abraham, as we will soon see. But she did learn something that all of us must learn. She learned the faithfulness of God.

I am convinced that the things that worry us, would not, if we only knew the faithfulness of God. This proved true in Sarah's life, because right after her nightmare experience in Gerar, the Bible says in Genesis 21:1-2:

> *"And the Lord visited Sarah as he had said, and the Lord did unto Sarah as he had spoken. For Sarah conceived, and bare Abraham a son in his old age, at the set time of which God had spoken to him."*

You need to see that it wasn't Abraham who filled his woman with the supernatural promise of God. Without God Abraham could do nothing. Always remember that. Man may be the instrument, but God is the life source. It was God who visited Sarah, and did unto Sarah as He had spoken!

WINTER WOMAN

Because of Gerar, Sarah came to know God in a way that she had never known Him before. There are some things you can learn about God only in the winter. And Sarah won a spot in the hallmark hall of faith. When Hebrews 11 lists the patriarchs and their awesome faith, this winter woman's name is included. Abraham is mentioned for the kind of faith that would leave home and look for a city "whose builder and maker is God" {v. 10}. But when the writer discusses the kind of faith that it took to cause an old woman's barren womb to conceive, he talks about Sarah's faith! It was Sarah's faith that did it.

Sarah didn't take "faith" classes. She just went through her winter clutching the warm hand of a loving God who could not fail. So when you hear Sarah laughing the last time, she is laughing with God. She is holding her baby to her now wrinkled breast. And she understands the miracles that come only to winter women.

Have you ever spent the night in Gerar? If you have, I'm sure you now know the Lord in a way you never could have otherwise. Like Sarah, you know that He cares for you. And like Sarah you know He will protect and will work through you. Look over your past and remember His faithfulness. Look at your future and trust Him.

CHAPTER FIFTEEN

Breaking the Chain

The past is paid for. The wounds may leave scars, but the scars are only there to remind us that we are human. Everyone has scars.

here is awesome power in women. God has chosen women to serve as the vehicles through which entry is made into this world. And He has shared His creativity with women. Women are strong and willing to nurture others.

But in spite of this, millions of women continually suffer emotional, physical, and spiritual strain. The enemy has attempted to destroy God's vehicle of creativity.

You may be one of those who suffer. Perhaps you sit and wonder whether life will ever be normal for you. Maybe you feel like your circumstance has made you different from other women. Possibly you feel like you are alone, with no one to help you find healing.

It could be that your emotional strain comes from having been abused. Others have taken advantage of you and used you in the most horrible and depraved ways. You feel used and dirty. And you think, *how could anyone want someone who has been abused?* Nevertheless, **you are wanted. God wants you, and God's people want you.**

Mistakes made early in life impact the rest of our lives. Some become involved sexually without the commitment of marriage. Maybe you believed him when he told you that he loved you. Perhaps you really did think that yielding would show your true love. Or, maybe, you simply wanted to have a good time without thinking about the consequences. And now you feel less than normal.

But God has already determined your need. He looked down from heaven long ago and saw your pain and guilt. He evaluated your situation and decided that you needed a Redeemer. He knew that you would need Someone to reach down and lift you up. He saw that you needed to recognize how important you are. It is impossible to know all that was in the mind of God when He looked down on broken humanity, but we can know that He looked past our broken hearts, wounded histories, and our tendency to sin, and saw our need.

God met that need through Jesus Christ. Jesus took your abuse on Himself on the cross of Calvary. He paid for your shame and made a way for you to be clean again. He took your indiscretions and sins upon Himself and died in your place. He saw your desire to please others and feel good. Thus, He took all your sinful desires and crucified them on the cross.

When you accept Jesus, you become clean and holy. You are made pure. And don't think you are alone—everyone struggles with the same kinds of sins as you, whether they show it on the outside or not.

YOUR PAST IS PAID FOR

The abused little girl with all her wounds was healed by the stripes of Jesus {Isaiah 53:5}. The sins of the woman who wanted to fulfill her lusts were crucified on the cross with Him {Galatians 2:20}. The past is paid for. The wounds may leave scars, but the scars are only there to remind us that we are human. Everyone has scars.

GOD SEES YOUR POTENTIAL

God recognizes the possibility of what you can become. He has a plan, and He sees your potential. But He also knows that your potential has been bound by your history. Your suffering has made you into a different woman from the one He originally intended you to be. The circumstances of life have shaped your way of thinking. And the responses you made to those circumstances have often kept you from living up to your potential.

But God knows that there is a Sarah, a Rahab, a woman at the well, a Ruth, or even a Mary in you. He knows that hidden inside of you is a great woman who can do great exploits in His name. And He wants that woman to be set free. He wants the potential within you to be unleashed so you can become the person you were created to be.

GOD IS CALLING

There is only one way to reach that potential. He is calling you. He will spiritually stir your heart and let you know that He is moving in your life, if you will only respond to His call.

The power to unleash you is in your faith. Dare to believe that He will do what He said He would do. Shift your confidence from your own weaknesses to His power. Trust in Him rather than in yourself. Anyone who comes to

Christ will find deliverance and healing. He will soothe your wounds. He will comfort you in your desperate moments. He will raise you up.

Believe that He paid the price for your sin and guilt. Believe that He has washed you and made you clean. Believe that He will satisfy every need created by your history. Have faith that He will reward you when you call on Him and it shall be done.

You have nothing to lose, and everything to gain. Jesus will straighten the crooked places in your heart and make you completely whole. When you allow Him access to every area of your life, you will never be the same broken person again.

"Therefore, if anyone is in Christ he is a new creation; the old has gone, the new has come!"   {2 Corinthians 5:17} [NIV]

"And, behold, there was a woman which had a spirit of infirmity eighteen years, and was bowed together, and could in no wise lift up herself. And when Jesus saw her, he called her to him, and said unto her, Woman, thou art loosed from thine infirmity."

{Luke 13:11-12}

*And he laid his hands on her:
and immediately she was made
straight, and glorified God.
And the ruler of the synagogue
answered with indignation,
because that Jesus had healed
on the sabbath day, and said
unto the people, There are six
days in which men ought to
work: in them therefore come
and be healed, and not on the
sabbath day.*

{Luke 12:13-14}

The Lord then answered him, and said, Thou hypocrite, doth not each one of you on the sabbath loose his ox or his ass from the stall, and lead him away to watering? And ought not this woman, being a daughter of Abraham, whom Satan hath bound, lo, these eighteen years, be loosed from this bond on the sabbath day?

{Luke 13:15-16}

Woman, Thou Art Loosed!

DEVOTIONAL

TO

all the women from across the world who have received healing and restoration through the "Woman Thou Art Loosed" message. Your healing has made my life more meaningful. It is my prayer that this devotional assist you in keeping the chains of the past from refastening themselves in your life. When all is said and done you are a significant part of the pulse beat of God's divine purpose in the earth. Maintain your focus and whatever you do . . . keep moving!

CONTENTS

INTRODUCTION

It's Time for You to Be Loosed!

omeone once said to me, "I heard about your *Woman, Thou Art Loosed!* presentation. The Bible tells us that in Christ there is no male or female. You ought to just preach, *Thou Art Loosed.*" I said to this person, "I think I'm going to continue to say what Jesus said." And what Jesus said is, "Woman, thou art loosed."

One of the issues that we must come to grips with is that those of us who are born again do not have a problem in our spirit. If we have been truly born again, our essence—what I call our "is-ness"—has been changed. We have been given an incorruptible nature in our spirit and we are forever changed.

The problem lies in our soul—that part of us that gives rise to our minds, emotions, memories, affections, and desires. If we were only spirit, we would have no need to be loosed of anything once we were born again. But we are not just spirit. We still live in a fleshly body and we have a worldly soul that needs to be transformed. That is a process that continues after our salvation experience.

Some of those things that tie up a woman in her soul are directly related to her feminine heart. They are part of her feminine nature, not her spirit.

God wants to loose something in the souls of women today. There's something He desires to set free. I believe that today is the day God wants to loose you in your heart,
your attitude,
your emotions,
your spirit,
your finances,
your marriage,
your work,
your ministry,
your praise.

He wants you to experience a freedom in Him—a freedom from temptation,
sin,
guilt,
things that are past,
relationships that are over

in order that you might LIVE.
God has a healing for your thoughts,
  your emotions,
   your attitudes.
He desires to heal you completely.
And then once you are loosed and made whole, His desire is that you never,
     ever,
     ever,
     ever
      go back into
      bondage again.
Jesus wants to make you whole.
Are you willing to let Him do His work in you?

PART I

Loosed From Poor Self-Image

AN UNWANTED WOMAN

Leah was the elder daughter of Laban and the older sister of Rachel. She was the ugly duckling in the family, the "old maid." When Jacob went to work for Laban, he fell in love with Rachel and was willing to work seven long years to have her as his wife. Laban, however, tricked Jacob into marrying Leah first and then he required seven *more* years of labor from Jacob for Rachel. Leah was the unwanted bride, a woman scorned in favor of her beautiful, younger sister.

God, however, had a plan and purpose for Leah. He had created her for a divine role in His eternal plan and when He saw that Leah was despised by Jacob, He opened her womb and allowed her to bear children. In all, she bore six sons and one daughter—her sons became the founders of six of the twelve tribes of Israel.

From the Scriptures:

And Laban had two daughters: the name of the elder was Leah, and the name of the younger was Rachel.

Leah was tender eyed; but Rachel was beautiful and well favoured.

And Jacob loved Rachel; and said, I will serve thee seven years for Rachel thy younger daughter.

And Laban said, It is better that I give her to thee, than that I should give her to another man: abide with me.

And Jacob served seven years for Rachel; and they seemed unto him but a few days, for the love he had to her.

And Jacob said unto Laban, Give me my wife, for my days are fulfilled, that I may go in unto her.

And Laban gathered together all the men of the place, and made a feast.

And it came to pass in the evening, that he took Leah his daughter, and brought her to him; and he went in unto her.

And Laban gave unto his daughter Leah Zilpah his maid for an handmaid.

And it came to pass, that in the morning, behold, it was Leah: and he said to Laban, What is this thou hast done unto me? did not I serve with thee for Rachel? wherefore then hast thou beguiled me?

And Laban said, It must not be so done in our country, to give the younger before the first born.

Fulfil her week, and we will give thee this also for the service which thou shalt serve with me yet seven other years.

And Jacob did so, and fulfilled her week: and he gave him Rachel his daughter to wife also.

And Laban gave to Rachel his daughter Bilhah his handmaid to be her maid.

And he went in also unto Rachel, and he loved also Rachel more than Leah, and served with him yet seven other years.

And when the LORD saw that Leah was hated, he opened her womb: but Rachel was barren.

And Leah conceived, and bare a son, and she called his name Reuben. [Genesis 29:16–32]

CHAPTER ONE

You Are a Designer's Original

I will praise thee; for I am fearfully and wonderfully made: marvellous are thy works; and that my soul knoweth right well.
[Psalm 139:14]

ne of the things that makes the high-fashion designs of the New York and Paris designers so expensive is that they are one-of-a-kind creations. A woman who buys a *haute couture* design from the House of Chanel or Yves St. Laurant knows that she isn't going to see her dress on any other woman. She knows that she is going to own a garment that is superbly crafted, in many cases hand-stitched and custom-tailored to fit her like a soft leather glove fits a hand. She knows that every aspect of the design of her garment has been carefully conceived and crafted. She is willing to pay a high price for owning an original design.

And so it *should* be when we look at our own lives. God has put us together in a way that cannot be replicated and should not be replicated. He chose every aspect of our personalities, crafted every gift and talent He bestowed on us, and gave special thought to every one of our features and traits. We were handcrafted by Him in our mother's womb. He custom-made us to fit a specific role in His sovereign plan for the ages.

Leah was created and crafted and chosen for a specific purpose in God's plan, even though for much of her life she didn't know that.

She was a "designer's original."

And so are you.

God made you to be one of a kind.

Your fingerprint is different than that of anybody else—not only anybody else alive today but anybody else who has ever lived.

The same goes for your hand print,
  footprint,
    voice print,
and your entire genetic code. Nobody else has ever had the combination of physical traits that you have. Nobody else has precisely your set of genes.

And even if you did have the exact genetic makeup as another person, you would still be unique. Nobody else has been placed by God in *exactly* your family,

in your neighborhood,

  to have your friends and acquaintances,

   in your city and state,

    or to be a part of your church. Nobody else like you has been put on the earth at exactly this moment in history. Nobody else has had the exact set of experiences that you have had in your life. Nobody else has the same set of talents and personality quirks and strengths and weaknesses and abilities and disabilities and skills and training and connections that you have.

God designed you to live in a physical body that is especially adapted to this earth. He designed you with a specific number of hairs on your head and heartbeats in your heart. He knows the length of your days and the outer limits of your potential. He designed you with facets and dimensions that you may not even know!

God didn't create you to be static and unchanging. He made you with the ability to grow

      and to develop

      and to change

      and to adapt.

Only God does not change. People change. We age whether we want to or not. We perspire whether we want to or not.

As part of your ability to change and grow, God gave you the power of free will—the power to choose and to make decisions and to exert your own creativity. He gave you the ability to *change* how you think about God and about how you think about yourself. In other words, God gave you the ability to turn from sin and turn to Him. He gave you the ability to repent of the sins of your past and to walk in the paths of holiness.

Nobody else is put together exactly as you have been put together by God. Nobody has *ever* been just like you. And nobody will ever be just like you.

God doesn't repeat Himself.

Therefore . . .

Since there are no other women who could possibly be you, you may as well go ahead and be you, and think it's good to be you!

Have you developed an appreciation for your own individuality? Do you like the you that God designed you to be?

Do you wait for someone else to give you a compliment? Or, can you look at yourself in the mirror and say, "Good God of mercy, that's a fine-looking person in that mirror. If I don't have it going on this morning then I don't know how to get it going!"

Have you ever celebrated yourself? Have you ever praised God for the way He made you? If not, today is a good day to start!

Celebrate today the fact that you are the Designer's original! There's* nobody *like you.

CHAPTER TWO

There's No Comparison!

Leah was tender eyed; but Rachel was beautiful and well favoured.
[Genesis 29:17]

eah . . . but Rachel.

Leah and Rachel were compared. Not by God. Not according to who they were on the inside. Leah and Rachel were compared by people according to who they were on the outside.

God never asks us to compare ourselves with any other person. In fact, it is a slap in God's face to look at another person and say, "I wish I was more like her."

Why? Because God tenderly and uniquely designed you to be just the way He wanted you to be. He made you for Himself. He made you in a way that can never be duplicated.

When you begin to compare yourself to another person you are saying to God, "God, You made a mistake. You failed in making me. You could have done a better job in creating me." None of us has the privilege or right to criticize God in that way. He is the Creator who looks at each of His created beings and says to Himself, "It is good."

I am always amazed that women who are so concerned about making certain that they never wear the same dress that another woman is wearing to a special function or to a church service, and who will go through all kinds of hairstyle and makeup changes to make sure that they don't appear to be copying someone else's "look," fail to apply that same principle to the way they see their own bodies, personalities, abilities, and inner attractiveness. They wouldn't dream of copying the way another woman dresses, but they desire to copy the way she is and to duplicate the way she acts, the way she talks, the way she performs, and the things that she has.

The fact is, everybody is attractive in one way or another.

The tragedy related to developing our own sense of attractiveness is twofold: we compare ourselves to others, and we allow others to define for us what is attractive.

It is dangerous to give that much power to another person—so that their opinion affects your own self-esteem and their definition becomes so contagious that if they do not affirm you, you don't affirm yourself.

We each must get to the place where we hold a high opinion of ourselves solely on the basis of the fact that God made us

exactly,

precisely,

intricately,

wondrously,

and uniquely the way we are. Each of us is a one-of-a-kind creation for which there is no comparison!

God made you for His own purposes in order that you might reflect a unique aspect of His own glory.

Are you so busy scrutinizing your faults and failures that you fail to recognize your uniqueness?

Are you so busy studying and analyzing somebody else that you fail to appreciate what God has given you?

Are you so busy trying to change yourself that you have neglected to praise God for who He made you to be in the first place?

When you cease to compare yourself to others and refuse to be intimidated by what other people think and say, you are then in the position to

birth that business that God wants you to birth,

birth that ministry that God wants you to birth,

birth that effort to change your

community that God wants you to birth.

How dare you compare yourself to somebody else! God wanted you to be you. Nobody else. YOU!

Thank God today for making you exactly the way you are and for transforming you day by day into exactly the woman He wants YOU to be. You are without comparison in His eyes!

CHAPTER THREE

God Had a Good Idea

Blessed be the God and Father of our Lord Jesus Christ, who hath blessed us with all spiritual blessings in heavenly places in Christ: According as he hath chosen us in him before the foundation of the world, that we should be holy and without blame before him in love. {Ephesians 1:3–4}

How does a designer work?

I've never watched a fashion designer create a garment but I suspect the process is exactly like that of any other person who creates something that hasn't existed before.

The first step in the process is an idea. The designer no doubt "sees" with his mind's eye what his design will look like. He may then sketch out that design or start to work with fabrics to fold and drape them to bring his design to life.

You were created in the mind of God before you were put into a womb. You were God's *idea.*

Leah was God's idea before she was ever Laban's daughter, or Rachel's sister, or Jacob's wife. Her very definition and identity came from God. And so does your identity. You are God's idea, God's choice, God's creation.

And God is the One who *made* you for a specific time and place on this earth.

You aren't an accident,
    a mistake,
    an error,
    an incident,
    or a mishap.

You were fashioned and made by Elohim—the Lord God Almighty, Creator of heaven and earth. You were meticulously and distinctly made by the Master. There are many people today who grew up hearing that they weren't wanted by their parents. They were told that they were the result of a "careless moment." If you have been told that, you need to take this position: I disagree.

Your parents may have been careless, but God was very careful. You weren't born because of something your parents did or didn't do. You were born because of something that God did in your mother's womb. He is the One who caused you to be born. He is the One who allowed that one sperm cell to enter that one egg cell for life to begin. He is the One who mixed together the genes of your mother and the genes of your father to give you an identity that is distinctly different from that of either your mother or father! He is the One who breathed life into you and caused you to come into being.

Your mother and your father didn't create you. God created you. Your mother and father set up a situation in which God had the prerogative to create or not to create. They set up a circumstance in which God had the option to make you then or to wait and make you at another moment in time. But it is God who *made* you. You are *His* creation. And God doesn't make mistakes. He doesn't err. He doesn't have mishaps or incidents or accidents. God creates only what He wants to create.

You can't force the hand of God. You can't demand that God create when He doesn't want to create. He is who He is . . . and He made you to be who He wanted on the earth as His person in a particular time and place to do a particular job.

God could have put you into any body

of any age and

of any race

at any time

in any place that He chose. His idea for you, however, was that you be put precisely into *your* mother's body, and that you emerge at a designated hour and day and year in a specific location. He held back His idea of you "for such a time as this." He brought you into this world through a specific set of situations and circumstances, and then He raised you up through another set of specific situations and circumstances, for one great purpose—to complete *His* purpose and reflect *His* glory.

It doesn't matter if you were conceived during an act of date rape and born to a welfare mother who had thirteen other children by ten different men. God is the One who ordained and authorized your birth. He created you for His purposes and His glory.

He didn't allow you to be aborted or to be miscarried. He didn't allow you to be stillborn or to die of crib death. He didn't allow any number of childhood accidents or diseases to take you out. He intended from the very first moment that He had the *idea* for you that you should live and participate in His plan and accomplish His purposes.

He never took His hand off your life. It doesn't matter if you were abused as a child. God brought you through that experience alive and He is the One who kept you from losing your sanity. He is the One who brought you to an understanding of Jesus Christ as your Savior and raised you up so that you could *still* fulfill His purposes and reflect His glory in *spite* of every effort the devil made against you to destroy you, diminish you, defame you, or discourage you.

The fact is . . . if you hadn't gone through every thing that you have gone through, you wouldn't *be* the person you are today. And God knows that! He has been in the process of creating you,

> fashioning you,
> molding you,
> designing you,
> refining you,
> and perfecting you

since the moment before the foundations of the earth
when He first thought of you!
He gave you your own personality,

> your own abilities,
> your own set of spiritual gifts,
> and your own identity in Christ so

that you and you alone might

> praise the way you praise,
> give what you give,
> minister like you minister,
> and love like you love.

Oh yes! When God thought of you, He had a *good* idea.

You are God's idea. And it is impossible for God to have anything but a GOOD idea.

CHAPTER FOUR

Your Inner and Outer Beauty

Whose adorning let it not be that outward adorning of plaiting the hair, and of wearing of gold, or of putting on of apparel; but let it be the hidden man of the heart, in that which is not corruptible, even the ornament of a meek and quiet spirit, which is in the sight of God of great price. [1 Peter 3:3–4]

*W*hen a designer sends a model down the runway of a fashion show, he or she is concerned with the total look of the model. The model isn't just wearing the designer's garment. The designer, in nearly all cases, has spent a great deal of time and effort to make sure the model is wearing the right accessories—the right jewelry or shoes or hat. Most designers pay very close attention to the hairstyles and makeup of their models. They also tell them how to walk and turn and carry themselves. And they create the overall environment in which the models are to model their designs.

And so it is with our great God. He created you as a composite. He put certain talents and features together with specific personality traits, and then He added various emotional responses and spiritual gifts. He was concerned with the overall, total you. He designed you to be a vibrant,

thinking,

feeling,

fully functioning person who has a unique attractiveness. He adorned you with far more than physical appearance.

In the early days of the Pentecostal Movement, we made a serious mistake, in my opinion, in asking women to avoid all self-adornment. Women were admonished not to wear jewelry or short sleeves in their dresses or to style their hair in any way other than in a bun or covered with a prayer cap. The leaders of the movement were so concerned with the development of the inner qualities of a woman that they failed to recognize that the way a woman expresses herself in the physical and natural realm is a part of her creativity and uniqueness.

When the next generation of Pentecostals came along, they seemed to rebel against this lack of self-adornment and they went to the other extreme. Church services almost became a fashion show—each woman eyeing and appraising the hat and dress and jewelry and shoes of the woman sitting next to her in the pew. We seemed to take outer appearance and adornment as a sign that God was blessing us. We justified our clothes and furs and jewels as being a part of our witness of God's prosperity.

What we need is balance.

God made us with flesh—an outer appearance. God has blessed us with creativity and an appreciation for beauty. We can and should recognize our appearance as an area in which we express ourselves to the glory of God.

God also made us with inner qualities—gifts and talents and traits and personalities—that are also intended to be developed and displayed *to the glory of God.*

The outer doesn't replace the need for the inner. The inner doesn't negate the need for the outer. We must have balance. And, we must always recognize that the inner qualities are those which are eternal and therefore, the more important. It is the inner qualities that should give rise to the outer ones. In other words, it is who we are on the *inside* that should define for each of us what we choose to do with our *outside.*

That didn't happen in Leah's case. She was judged only by what she looked like on the outside. Nobody saw the total Leah, except God.

Some women make that same mistake today. They define themselves by what they wear and how they look. If they have a bad hair day, they are in a rotten mood all day. If they get a run in their hose, they lose their self-confidence. They allow the outer appearance to determine their inner demeanor.

God's plan for us is just the opposite—it is the inner demeanor that should dictate and define how we adorn ourselves. The woman who is self-confident in the Lord on the inside might choose to wear a $1.50 dress that she finds at the local thrift shop or a $150 dress that she buys at an upscale department store. She is self-confident either way. Her look doesn't determine her character. No . . . her character is intact in spite of her look.

Every one of us must recognize that the greater part of our attractiveness cannot be

bought,

taken off a rack or shelf,

applied like a lipstick,

or put on like a hat or shoes. The greater part of our attractiveness lies within and it wells up from the inside and finds a creative and appropriate expression on the outside.

That's what Peter meant when he wrote that "the ornament of a meek and quiet spirit" is what has a "great price" in the sight of God. (See 1 Peter 3:4.)

God sees what no one else can see. And it's that part of you that He values the most.

Look at yourself in God's mirror. He sees ALL *of who He made you to be, from the inside out.*

CHAPTER FIVE

The Wellspring of Your Attractiveness

Be strengthened with might by his Spirit in the inner man.
[Ephesians 3:16]

he greater part of your attractiveness—the part that draws or *attracts* other people to you—is on the inside, not on your flesh.

Have you ever seen a woman walking on the arm of a man and you asked yourself, "How on earth did *she get him?*" Did you think, "If *she* got somebody, surely Lord, You can do that for me!"

One day a woman flew across the nation to meet with me. She wanted to tell me her story—how her husband had left her for another woman and was tied up in an affair. The woman who came to see me was young, vibrant, beautiful—she met all the standards of what we would call a clean-living, godly woman. She sat weeping in my office and then in her frustration as she told me what had happened, she opened up her pocketbook and pulled out a photograph and said to me, "Just look at her!"

I didn't want to look . . . I didn't *need* to look in order to understand what was happening. She insisted. "Just *look* at her! He left me for *that!*"

I said, "The tragedy, ma'am, is that what you have been trained by our society to think is important, really isn't all that important. Appearance doesn't mean all that you think it does. Outer appearance isn't always the issue."

If you don't believe that, I encourage you to go to the nearest mall and sit for a while and watch the people go by. You'll see some of the strangest couples holding hands!

Our society spends billions of dollars a year to convince you to buy hundreds, even thousands of dollars a year worth of clothes and makeup in order to fix up something that doesn't really matter all that much. We spend countless hours at beauty salons and spas and malls in order to buy, acquire, or create the very things that we *think* will draw other people to us, but which actually have very little drawing power. What you create or design on the outside of yourself may turn a head or two, but it has very little power to turn a mind or a heart.

We are bombarded on a daily basis with messages that tell us that if we only

go to the right weight-loss center

and get down to the right size
and dye our hair the right shade
and go to the right spa
and use the right toothpaste
and put on the right makeup
and wear the right outfit
  at the right time
and be seen in the right places
  with the right people
  then we most certainly will be able to get for ourselves the right man
  and have the right children
  and live in the right neighborhood
  and enjoy the right kind of life!

When we do this and nothing "right" happens for us, we are puzzled. We sit back and ask, "What went wrong?"

What went wrong was this—we became merchandise for those who were selling us merchandise!

The average woman—yes, even the average Christian woman—will spend literally thousands of dollars this year on

hats
and nails
and tints
and weaves
and earrings
and dresses

and sadly, spend virtually nothing to build up and support those inner qualities and character traits that truly are what attract others to us

. . . and to Jesus Christ our Savior.

If you are only concerned with your outer appearance, you are going to be a very shallow, superficial person. People are going to find that once they have quit playing with you, the box in which you came was beautifully wrapped . . . but it was empty.

Now, I believe in women looking good. If you were to ask my wife about this, she would tell you that I spare no expense in helping her look good. I want her to look as good as she can look. Not only do I appreciate looking at her, but I like the way people look at *us* when we are out together. When she's looking good, she makes me look better than I otherwise look! Most men know this, by the way. They know they look better to other people when they are seen in public with a woman who has a great-looking outer appearance.

What most women don't know about most men, however, is that outer looks don't matter nearly as much as inner qualities once that man is home alone with his wife.

I did not marry my wife for her good looks. I married her for her *self*. Her *self* included far more than her good looks.

Shortly after my wife and I married, my wife was in an automobile accident. Her ankle was badly crushed. The doctors told us that she might never walk again. Now, I love the way my wife walks, but when the doctors told me that my wife might never walk again, I wasn't devastated. I was just glad my wife was still alive. I was glad she still had all her inner qualities that drew me to marry her in the first place.

For the better part of that next year, I carried my wife just about every place she went. She was in such pain she could hardly move. When she needed to wash her hair, I carried a basin of warm water to her as she lay on the sofa and I helped her hang her head over the side of the sofa so she could shampoo her hair.

The doctors finally said she might walk again but not without a metal brace up to her knee. I thanked the doctors for their opinion but then I looked the devil right in the eye and said, "You are a liar." I refused to accept that diagnosis from the doctors as the final verdict.

When my wife started to take her first few tentative steps, I'd encourage her, "Just take one step. Now just take one more." Over the process of months, I helped her learn how to walk again.

She is now wearing high heels ... and she has her walk back! She is dancing in the aisles and praising God.

As much as I was convinced in my spirit that my wife *would* walk again, I also faced the possibility in my mind that she might not. God calls us to have faith, not to be unrealistic or to live in a state of denial. And in facing the possibility that my wife might not walk, I made up my mind while my wife was lying in her bed that if she *never* walked again, I would push her around in a wheelchair and love her just the same as if she was walking by my side. Her ability to walk didn't have anything to do with my ability to love.

Go back to the SOURCE of what it is that makes you "attract" other people—the Source of your attractiveness is the Holy Spirit of God. He is the One who woos and wins the heart. When you are His woman, He will draw to you
the right people

for the right purposes
at just the right time!
Trust God today to be the wellspring of your attractiveness.

*The most attractive part of you is deep within you,
just waiting to be expressed.*

CHAPTER SIX

Agreeing With God's Opinion of You

And God saw every thing that he had made, and, behold, it was very good.   *[Genesis 1:31]*

God looked. He saw you. He saw everything He had created around you.

He saw the reason for your being.

He saw a specific need on this earth that you were to meet.

He saw the full set of traits and abilities that you would need to have in order to complete your purpose for living.

He knew what kind of environment you would need in order to develop your traits and abilities.

God looked, and then He created.

He created you.

You!

And God looked at you and said, "This is *good.*"

Do you have that same opinion of yourself? Do you agree with God's opinion of the way He made you?

It's important that you come to appreciate the way God created you because other people are going to treat you the way you treat yourself. They will respect you only to the degree that you respect yourself.

Have you ever purchased a gift for somebody who is really particular? It's a job. You can't just run to the local bargain basement and snatch the first thing you see. You know that the person doesn't settle for just anything so you spend the time to get something for her that you believe she'd choose for herself. If you truly care about a person, you tend to buy for that person the things that you think she would buy for herself. The higher the standards she has for herself, the higher the standards you place on the gift you choose.

If you are attracting people who don't treat you well, the first suspect in the case is *you.* What kind of message are you sending that allows them to treat you poorly?

There must be something deep inside of you that sends out a signal, "I *am* somebody because God made me to be somebody. I may not be twenty-one and wear a size seven. I may be seventy-one and wear a size twenty-seven. But I *am* somebody."

When you send out a signal like that, then that is the signal other people pick up.

There's something that you exude out of your spirit that gives you presence with others. There's a quality of inner strength that gives you an attraction. It causes other people to recognize you,

to pay attention to you,

to ask when you walk into the room, "Who is that?" They won't be asking because of the garment you are wearing, but rather, because of the strength of character that you project.

That attitude is not arrogance or pride. It is healthy self-esteem and the strength of God's Spirit inside you.

I once watched a woman approach a clerk in an office and ask in a weak, self-deprecating voice, "I don't want to bother you, but if you could please . . ." This woman was sending the message, "I know you won't like me and don't want to deal with me and don't think highly of me." She had an attitude of apology for who God made her to be.

And what happened? The clerk in that office treated her just the way she projected that she *expected* to be treated. She got walked on, sent off to sit in a corner for half an hour, and talked down to in a rude, put-down manner.

The way you appreciate yourself impacts everything you do. It affects the way that you

sit in a classroom

or apply for a job

or talk to people at a social

function

or go about the ministry

that God has called you to undertake. It even affects the way that you pray and the way that you study God's Word. If you think that you are a nobody with no future and no value, you are going to pray with less power and think that the promises of God are for everybody else but you.

God's desire is that you appreciate who He made you to be and to develop what He gave you—not that you try to exchange what He gave you for what He gave someone else.

Don't let anybody ever convince you that you should change yourself to be like someone else. I once heard about a woman who married a man and then after she got married, she decided that her husband would love her even more if she changed just about everything about her that could be changed. What happened? One day he woke up and said, "Who are you?" She had changed herself so much that he no longer recognized her as the person he had married.

From her perspective, she looked better, dressed better, and was more polished. From his perspective, she had become a stranger.

She had worried about some woman coming along and catching her husband's eye. What she hadn't accepted was that he only had eyes for her in the first place. She hadn't been able to fully receive his love and approval because she hadn't approved of herself.

You must also be wary if somebody begins to date you or marries you and then starts to demand that you change things about yourself to conform to what *they* think you ought to look like,

> talk like,
>
> act like,
>
> or dress like. That person doesn't want what God created. He wants

to do the creating. You're better off sticking with what God created you to be than to substitute that for what some person tries to create. Another person can never create you to be as good as what God has made.

Now, there are lots of people that I admire. I may admire some of their attributes or think they look wonderful or appreciate the way they do certain things. But I have never met anyone who had anything about them that I found so wonderful or so intimidating that I was willing to give up being ME in order to try to be THEM. No way!

Furthermore, you must develop deep within yourself the capacity and the tenacity to disagree with those who feel differently about you than you feel about you.

You must be able to say to another person . . .

You don't approve of me?

You don't like the way I look?

You don't like the way I talk?

You don't think I'm a quality person?

You don't think I have value?

You don't think I am worthy?

You don't think I have a purpose and reason for being that's just as important as that of the next person?

I disagree!

You don't have to get mad about it,

> argue the point,
>
> fight over the facts,

or spend the rest of your life trying to prove that you're right and they're wrong. You simply disagree. You take the position, That's *your* position. That's not *my* position. And just before you walk away, you simply and calmly say, "You have your opinion, but I also have mine. I disagree with your opinion. I like me. I value me. And I *know* God does, too."

It's time for you to look yourself and others in the eye and say with your attitude, if not your words:

Excuse me, but I have a right to be myself.

Excuse me, but I have the right to express myself.

Excuse me, but I have the right to have my opinions.

Excuse me, but I have the right to use my faith.

Excuse me, but I choose to agree with what God has said about me!

*Value yourself today the way God values you—
beyond measure!*

CHAPTER SEVEN

The Call for You

I know thee by name, and thou hast also found grace in my sight.
(Exodus 33:12)

 popular love song from a number of years ago was titled "Only You." Some of us need to go back and sing that song—to ourselves.

There's a role that God has for "only you." Nobody else will do.

In the theater world, actors and actresses often go for auditions and then the director or producer of the play or movie will have call-backs. Certain ones of those who have auditioned will be asked to come back and have a second, and sometimes a third or fourth audition before they are given the part or they are told that someone else has won the role.

A person in the entertainment world knows that he or she has arrived as a star when a director or producer calls them and offers them the part *without* an audition. They are being chosen for who they are to fill a role that the director believes is absolutely perfect for them and nobody else.

Leah had a role that only Leah could fill. Nobody else. When God asked, "Who should be the mother of Reuben and Simeon and Levi and Judah and Issachar and Zebulun and Dinah?" He came up with only one name: Leah.

God doesn't deal in auditions and call-backs for His children. He has something for you to do that *only* you can do. There's nobody else who can play the part or fill the role or meet the need or match the qualifications required. Only *you.*

If a person just wants a "woman," then you have a lot of competition. But when the call goes out for you, you have *no* competition. Only you can truly be you.

When people call and invite me to come and do seminars, I make sure that the person they really want is T. D. Jakes.

Do they just want a preacher?

Do they just want somebody to put on the program?

Do they just want somebody who has been on television or written a book?

I want to make sure they really want ME.

Because, you see, I know from the depths of my spirit that nobody can be ME as good as I can be me!

I never worry about anybody coming along and being a better T. D. than me. I am absolutely awesome at being T. D. Jakes. I have a doctorate degree in being me. There are no contenders in being me.

When you choose me, you get me. I am not a copy of anybody. I am a designer's original.

Now wouldn't I be foolish if I tried to be Pastor White? I would never be as good a Pastor White as Pastor White can be Pastor White. I would only be a cheap copy. And I have absolutely no desire to be a cheap copy when I can be a

first-class,
  truly wonderful,
    incredibly good,
      perfectly equipped,
        one-of-a-kind
          original!

A person could study me for hours and still not do what I do. They could make me the sole object of their scrutiny for days and still never be able to be a better T. D. Jakes than I am T. D. Jakes. They simply cannot do what I do in being the me that God made me to be.

If somebody doesn't love you enough to love you in spite of how you look on the outside or what you are capable of doing in the flesh, then they don't really love you. They only love your flesh.

If a man only loves your figure
        or the way you do your hair
        or the way you sing
        or the way you dance
        or the way you laugh

then he does not really love you. He only loves the IMAGE of you. He is not in love with the real you, because the real you is a composite of what is on the inside and what is on the outside, and what is on the inside is the more important part.

Suppose you lose your voice?

Suppose you lose a limb and can't dance?

Suppose you lose your figure?

You want someone to love you first and foremost for what is in your spirit and in your soul, not what is draped on your body.

You want someone to love you for the twinkle in your eye, not for your expensive eye makeup.

You want someone to love you for the dimple on your cheek and the funny way your voice rises at the end of your laugh and your tender touch that is unlike that of any other woman.

You want someone who will recognize your voice even if he is blindfolded. You want someone who will know your touch even if he is blindfolded and put into a sound chamber. You want someone who will love you for the things that make you *you*—not for the things that make you look like the model in the fashion magazine or act like the person on a TV show.

What we each must do is wait for the call that is specifically for us.

We aren't to respond to a blanket call

> or a generic call
>
> or a gender call
>
> or a wolf-whistle call,

but to a call that says, "I don't want anybody but *you* and the reason is that only *you* will do."

That is the call that is the one we should wait to hear from a person who wants to be our spouse. That's the call that is the one we should wait to hear from a person we make our friend.

That's the call that God puts on our lives. He calls us very individually— by name, not number—to do a very specific job and to fill a very specific role in His Kingdom. Nobody else will do. He has designed us to meet all the qualifications required. He hasn't created any other person that will fit the bill like we fit the bill.

You don't need to be jealous of or intimidated by anyone else because when God calls for you, there is nobody else who can answer that call. You have no contenders in His sight. You are the *star* He has in mind for the role He has written just for you.

God has only one person in mind to fill your role in His plan: YOU.

CHAPTER EIGHT

God Still Has a Plan

*When the LORD saw that Leah was hated, he opened her womb
. . . and Leah conceived.* *(Genesis 29:31–32)*

e each learn our own definition of beauty and attractiveness.
Attractiveness varies from culture to culture, from era to era,
and from person to person. What is considered attractive to you
may not be what I consider to be beautiful.

According to the definition of the times, Rachel was considered to be very beautiful—a bombshell, a fox. She was a rose petal, stardust, the tremor in the earthquake. The Bible says she was "well-favored." Jacob, it seems, looked at her and almost stopped breathing. Any time a man says that he is willing to work for seven years at doglike labor, that man is either in love or crazy.

Leah, whose name means gazelle, was older and lankier than her sister, and knobby and "tender eyed." My grandmother would have said cockeyed. She very likely had an orbital or lazy eye. She may have been cross-eyed.

Don't start putting down Leah, however. She was God's woman, especially chosen for a specific job.

Rachel's treasure was on her.

But Leah's treasure was in her.

People who never look in you are too shallow to appreciate what they will find there.

On the outside, it didn't look as if God had much of a plan for Leah.

Leah had been victimized. A girl's first definition of masculinity is formed when she looks at her father. Leah's father, Laban, didn't think much of her. He was almost like a pimp. He made a deal with a man for her and sold her for a favor. She was a "booby" prize, her father's joke on Jacob.

It's funny to read the story about how Laban tricked Jacob, giving Leah to him as a bride and Jacob not realizing it until the next morning. Laban then insisted that Jacob work an additional seven years—a total of fourteen years—for the privilege of having Rachel for his bride. The story is funny . . . until you look at it from Leah's point of view.

Can you imagine how Leah must have felt as she got ready for her wedding, knowing that she was about to be married off as a joke, a booby prize? Can you imagine how she felt, having waited all her life to be loved by a man, knowing that her groom didn't want her but wanted her younger sister instead? Leah no doubt had her hopes and dreams as a young woman, but in marrying Jacob, she knew that those hopes and dreams would never be realized.

Leah spent the entire night with Jacob, who never realized who she was until the following morning. She was intimate with a man who didn't really know who she was. He never looked her in the eye, much less into her soul. He wanted only what he wanted—he had no regard or respect for the total God-designed composite whole of Leah.

Have you ever been in an intimate relationship with someone who didn't really know who you were—someone who only wanted your body?

Have you worked on a job with someone who didn't really know who you were—and didn't make any effort to find out? Have you ever been involved in ministry with someone who didn't know who you were, not really, and who didn't care enough to take the time to find out who you were? It's a terrible situation to be in.

And then to make matters even worse, when Jacob found that he had been with Leah, he still wanted someone else.

Year after year, Leah was married to a man who was looking at someone else, who wanted someone else. Leah was still the invisible woman as far as Jacob was concerned. She may have done the chores around the tent and he may have used her for sex, but his desire was for Rachel.

No, Jacob didn't see Leah. But God did.

And God sees you.

You are not invisible to Him.

You are not unknown to Him.

You are not a mystery to Him.

He *still* has a plan and a purpose for your life. He still has something that He has put in you that He desires to bring to fruition.

God sees you and He intends for others not only to see you but receive from you the hidden treasure He put inside you.

You have treasure within that God desires to reveal.
He still has a plan for you!

CHAPTER NINE

Overcoming a Generational Curse

Weeping may endure for a night, but joy cometh in the morning.   *[Psalm 30:5]*

W e all know that certain physical characteristics are passed from generation to generation. A physician may ask you to give him not only your personal health history, but also that of your parents and grandparents. Did they have high blood pressure? Did they have kidney disease? And so forth. Certain physical ailments and diseases seem linked to our ancestors.

The same is true for some emotional characteristics. Some families are riddled with divorce. It seems everybody on the family tree got a divorce. Some families seem to be very powerful or financially successful generation after generation. Other families seem to have lived on welfare for generations. Some families can point to ten or more women in their family who have had babies out of wedlock.

From generation to generation, we see rage and abuse. Even those who were abused and know how painful abuse can be, have a tendency to abuse their own children whom they claim to love.

We might call these generational curses. We act out our father's sins.

Jacob's family was riddled with problems. His grandmother Sarah had been a schemer—advising Abraham to have a baby by Hagar, and then sending Hagar away. His grandfather Abraham had also used some tricks, especially in trying to convince important and powerful men that Sarah was really his sister and not his wife. His mother Rebekah had been a schemer—advising her favorite son Jacob to steal both the birthright and the blessing from Jacob's twin brother Esau.

Jacob's very name meant supplanter, trickster, con man. The ability to be "slick" was something his mother saw in him from his birth, probably because she knew what it meant to be slick herself. After Jacob had tricked his father Isaac into giving him what rightfully belonged to Esau, Rebekah sent him away to the home of her brother Laban—another trickster.

Laban was slick in the family tradition. He conned Jacob into working seven years for Rachel, and then gave him Leah instead. It was a trick, a con. And out of the con, he tricked Jacob into working seven more years.

Manipulators have a need to be in control, regardless of the cost. Laban wanted labor from Jacob. He wanted to control his life, even if it meant giving up his daughters in the process. The moment that Laban realized that Jacob was madly in love with Rachel, Laban knew the weakness in Jacob that he could manipulate. He controlled Jacob for fourteen years.

Leah grew up surrounded by tricksters and manipulated by them.

What is a woman to do in a situation like that?

She must choose not to give in to the generational curse.

You see, a person who manipulates others is a person who says, "I need to con my way into what I don't deserve and cannot earn." The way the curse is broken is to say, "God is capable of using who I am and what I have."

A little boy only had five loaves and two fishes. Jesus said, "Let me have them. I can make do with them."

A woman said I have only a little meal and a bit of oil. Elijah said, "Let me have them. That's just enough for God to make a miracle."

A woman said, "I only have one small cruse of oil." The prophet said, "Here's what God wants you to do with it."

God can take whatever it is that you have—even if it's only a little bit—and multiply it into a miracle. It can be more than enough for you to fulfill what it is that God wants you to do.

A woman once worked in an office. She was a terrible typist. She kept making mistakes and she was spending all of her time correcting them. She needed her job so she said, "I've got to do something about this." She said to herself, "I don't have all the typing skills in the world but I am a pretty good problem-solver and a pretty good artist." So she went home and began to experiment with some of her art supplies until she created the product we have come to call "white out." She became a millionaire—not because of what she *couldn't* do, but because she was willing to use what she *could* do.

You don't need a lot of talent. You only need a little bit.

Are you aware that there are models who are hired to do commercials and appear in advertisements who have only one good feature—it might be her hands or her legs or her feet or her eyes? She'll be hired for close-up shots of that one good feature, even though the rest of her may not be all that beautiful. She has found the little bit that God gave her. She's working it!

Many people are in financial trouble today because they have no confidence in the little bit that God has given them. They are waiting for manna to fall from heaven instead of working with what God has already given. I have news for them—that dispensation of manna-giving is over. God expects us to trust Him with what He has given us—and to use what He has given us—to get what it is that we need and want.

Every time I meet with a group of women, I sense an abundance of treasure that God wants to release. Each one of them has something that God is eager to bless and multiply. God wants each one to recognize what He has given them—even if it's only a little bit—and start working with what they have.

Quit crying over where you've been.

Quit crying over your mistakes and failures.

Quit crying over what you have lost.

Start looking toward where you are going.

Start looking toward what God has for you.

Start looking for what God is going to give you as a blessing.

Start looking for the way God is going to use what you do have.

Leah had just enough of what it was that God needed most. And so do you.

You don't need to con or scheme your way into your future. Give God what you have and let Him do the miracle of fulfillment in you and for you.

CHAPTER TEN

Releasing the Hidden Treasure Within You

*We have this treasure in earthen vessels, that the excellency of
the power may be of God.* *[2 Corinthians 4:7]*

*L*eah had gifts and abilities—hidden treasure—but Jacob could never see it.

The Bible says that when the Lord saw how Leah was hated, He opened her womb. (See Genesis 29:31.) When God saw how Leah was mistreated and despised, He opened up the hidden treasure that lay inside of Leah and brought it forth.

There's something in you that has been locked up that God wants to unlock today.

God knows what He has put in you. He knows what He desires to come out of you. And He knows how to get to what He has put in you and bring it out of you.

When you get beyond your low self-esteem and you stop comparing yourself to other people, and you begin to face and accept what God has given *you*, then you are in a position for God to bring to birth *all* that He has created you to be.

There are things in you that have been overlooked by you,

ignored by others,

perhaps even ridiculed by some,

but God calls those traits in you treasure. And He wants to bring them forth!

He has given every woman treasure—something that He intends for her to use in order to fulfill her purpose on earth. And in the process of fulfilling her purpose and God's purpose, she will bring God glory.

You had better find out what it is that God has put in you as treasure . . . because the devil is going to fight you for what God has put in you. The devil knows that treasure is there and he wants it—he wants it bad—for his purposes.

So many women today are fighting the devil and they don't even know why. They haven't discovered the treasure that lies within them. The devil knows it's there. God knows it's there. So the fight is on and the woman doesn't even know what the fight is all about. Discover your treasure. The treasure in you is not only what the devil wants, but it is the way you will defeat the devil in your life.

The devil will do anything he can to sabotage your self-esteem so you won't use your treasure or assert your gift because he doesn't want you to give birth to what God has put within you.

Being loosed means that the treasure within you has been released. It means that the treasure that has been bound within you has been given an emancipation proclamation. It means that you are free to blossom and bring forth fruit! When the treasure within you is loosed, you are at liberty to give birth.

Now giving birth may require intense effort on your part. You may have to push like a woman in labor. You may have to fill your jaws with air and push with all your might against the devil.

The apostle Paul said, "Forgetting those things which are behind, and reaching forth unto those things which are before, I press toward the mark for the prize of the high calling of God in Christ Jesus" (Philippians 3:13–14). Pressing is pushing.

You may have to push against what happened to you when you were a child, what your teachers said about you on the first day of school, or what your first boyfriend did to you. You may have to push with all your might to release what it is that God has put within you. In fact, it may not happen if you don't push!

The doctors tell a woman to push because there's something inside her that is supposed to come out. The same is true for the treasure in you. There's something God-conceived and God-created in you that is *supposed* to come out.

You may have to battle through years of suppression,

oppression,

and depression . . . but that which is within you is something God wants to bring to birth.

He put the treasure there. He'll help you bring the treasure out. But it is up to you to push.

Now what are you pushing against? You aren't pushing against other people. This isn't a battle in the natural. It is a battle of the spirit. You are going to have to push against the opposition of the devil. His opposition comes in the form of bad memories, low self-esteem, and feelings of being unworthy. The devil may have spent years pushing you aside, pulling you back, and putting you down. Now the Lord says to you, "I've seen how the world has hated you. I want to open you up. I want you to give birth to that which I put in you."

It is time for you to say to yourself and the world as a whole, "It's my time to conceive. It's time for the treasure that God put inside me to come up. It's time for me to be LOOSED to do what it is that God created me to do."

You may have to push against thoughts of suicide. You may have to push against years of bitterness and anger. You may have to push against your own feelings of being intimidated.

You may have to push against your own tendency to compare yourself to others. When you compare yourself to other people, you restrict yourself to a spiritual barrenness. You allow yourself to become more concerned about what people think of you than what the Spirit of God wants to do in you and through you.

The treasure in you is filled with possibilities and potentialities. Your treasure is a blessing that is just waiting to be birthed.

When a baby is birthed, it changes everything in the family. The same is true for you. When you give birth to the treasure that God has put in you, your entire life is going to be changed. Your marriage will be affected. Your relationship with your children will be affected. Your place in your church and your neighborhood and your workplace is going to be affected. God's blessing is an overflowing blessing.

I'm talking about birthing the gifts
   and talents
   and powers
and the ministries of the Holy Spirit inside you. I don't know the specific thing that God wants to birth in you but you know what it is. Every woman knows when she is pregnant. In fact, a woman often has an inner knowing that she is pregnant, even before she has any feeling of the baby moving inside her womb. The same is true for the spiritual ministries that God has put inside you. There's a knowing that you have.

Don't fail today to give birth to what God put in you. NOW is the time for the baby—that treasure—to be born.

***God has put in you something the whole world needs
and is waiting for. PUSH!***

CHAPTER ELEVEN

You Hold a Key to Deliverance

And the God of peace shall bruise Satan under your feet shortly. The grace of our Lord Jesus Christ be with you.

[Romans 16:20]

hy is it so massively important that a woman give birth to what it is that God has put within her?

Because the woman holds the key to deliverance. It is the seed of the woman that was designated by God to rise up and bruise the heel of Satan. After Adam and Eve had sinned, God cursed the serpent that had tempted Eve with this curse:

"I will put enmity between thee and the woman, and between thy seed and her seed; it shall bruise thy head, and thou shalt bruise his heel" (Genesis 3:15). God trusted the woman with deliverance in her womb. There's been enmity between the devil and women ever since. Satan doesn't want you to bring to birth that which God has put inside you. Why? Because what you bring to birth has the potential to bruise his head!

You have
talents
and gifts
and resources within you that have the power to cause serious damage to what Satan is attempting to do in this world.

When the children of Israel were about to be taken to Babylon in bondage, the prophet Jeremiah said, "Send for the women of mourning." He said—

O daughter of my people, gird thee with sackcloth,
and wallow thyself in ashes: make thee mourning, as
for an only son, most bitter lamentation: for the
spoiler shall suddenly come upon us. I have set thee
for a tower and a fortress among my people   (Jeremiah 6:26–27).

Jeremiah also said that the Lord of hosts had told him specifically to—
Call for the mourning women, that they may come . . .
And let them make haste, and take up a wailing for us,
that our eyes may run down with tears, and our eye-lids
gush out with waters. . . . O ye women . . . let your

ear receive the word of his mouth, and teach your
daughters wailing, and every one her neighbour
lamentation. For death is come up into our windows,
and is entered into our palaces, to cut off the children
from without, and the young men from the streets
(Jeremiah 9:17–18, 20–21).

Jeremiah said, "Find some women who are not so filled with hate and bitterness that they have become like mannequins, women who are not so downtrodden that they no longer feel. Send for some women who still have the ability to feel and cry so that they might wail against what the devil is doing."

Get a picture of what these mourning women were to do. They were to weep and wail, to mourn in sackcloth and ashes, as a sign to wake up everybody around them to face the fact that the devil was destroying them and that death was on the way. They were God's warning system to God's people. They were the alarm system, the tornado signal, the air-raid siren. They were the ones God was going to use to warn His people of the impending consequences of sin. They were the ones who created a platform from which the words of Jeremiah could ring forth with stinging conviction.

These were women who had a God-given destiny to destroy the power of Satan over God's people by waking up God's children and calling them to a mourning of repentance. These were women who were instructed to teach their daughters to weep against sin and the assault of the devil.

God has a destiny for women today. He wants His women loosed to open their mouths and cry out against the evil that the devil has put upon God's people.

You have ideas that haven't been voiced.

You have energy that hasn't been released.

You have abilities that haven't been used.

You have power that hasn't been loosed.

You have spiritual gifts that haven't been given expression.

The day has come for you to forget those things which are past and look toward the future. It's time to look at what

you *can* be

and what *you* can do

and what you *can* say

and what you *can* possess that will bring glory to God and cause the devil to be defeated and your destiny to be fulfilled.

The devil tried to take you out. Oh, time and again he's tried to take you out. But God let you go through everything you've been through so you might come to the place of crying out against that particular evil and in the process of crying out, bruise the head of the devil. God expects you to open up and give birth to the treasure in you so that you can turn the tables on the devil that the devil *thought* he had turned on you!

Were you abused as a child? God wants you to cry out against that abuse. He has put something in you that you can use to crush the abusing head of Satan BRING IT FORTH!

Were you raped by a boyfriend who said he loved you but only wanted to use you? God wants you to cry out against rape. He has put something in you that you can use to crush the raping head of Satan. BRING IT FORTH.

Were you pushed into a prison of failure as a child so that you became so afraid to take any risks that you have spent a lifetime cowered before other people until you became a doormat for society? God wants you to cry out against fear and failure and the loss of self-respect. He has put something in you that you can use to crush the lying, fear-causing head of Satan. BRING IT FORTH.

I don't know what it is that God intends for you to use in defeating the devil. It may be a new business. It may be a new ministry. It may be a job in a certain area. It may be a volunteer position that you are to fill. I don't know what it is specifically that you have within you or what opportunity He has given you, but I know that God has something in you and an opportunity for you. USE IT! The devil can't stand up against what God has given to you.

Is there an idea that you've had for years but have never acted upon?

Is there a dream you've held but have been afraid to voice?

Is there a drive that you feel welling up in you from time to time, but one that you've never put into full motion?

Is there an opportunity that you see but you've been afraid to reach out and grab hold of it?

It's time for you to BRING IT FORTH the treasure that God has given you.

So many women have spent years, even decades, locked up in a prison of worry over what people will say about them. The result is that they have failed to give birth to those things that they could have done, and would have done, and should have done. NOW IS THE TIME! Yes, *today* is your day.

***The time has come for the birthing of the treasure
God has put in you.***

PART II

Loosed From Past Failures

A FALLEN WOMAN

Eve was not only the first woman and the mother of all living. She is representative of many other firsts as well—

the first marriage,

the first family,

the first marital conflict,

the first offering,

the first murder,

the first family division,

and the first rekindling of a woman's dream.

We often think of Eve as being a "fallen woman"—she fell for the devil's temptation and with Adam, became the cause of the "fall" of all mankind. Because of Eve, every woman and man today is born in a fallen spiritual state and needs to be born again spiritually.

What we need to recognize is that God had a plan of redemption for Eve. He had an appointed seed for her to bear for His purposes.

From the Scriptures:

> *And Adam knew his wife again; and she bare a son, and called his name Seth: For God, said she, hath appointed me another seed instead of Abel, whom Cain slew.*
>
> *And to Seth, to him also there was born a son; and he called his name Enos: then began men to call upon the name of the LORD.*
> *—Genesis 4:25-26*

CHAPTER TWELVE

You Were Created for Wholeness and Life

Eve ... the mother of all living.   *[Genesis 3:20]*

ve was created in the man ... called out of the man ... and then presented to the man.

She was called woman, bone of his bone, flesh of his flesh, created to stand beside man to help meet his need, to help make up the difference. Together, Eve and Adam, woman and man, are a picture of the wholeness of God.

Have you heard the dispute that has been raised in recent years about whether God is male or female? Some people are seeking to change the Bible to have either neutral terms for God or to use the pronoun "She" as often as the pronoun "He" to refer to God.

On the one hand, I believe these people are onto something, in that we have been chauvinistic at times in describing God in only male terms, often to the degree that many women have felt excluded from relating to God. But on the other hand, we must understand that sexuality is related to our physical composition. And God is a Spirit.

When it comes to spiritual issues, there is neither male nor female, Greek nor Jew, bond nor free. We are all one in the anointing in Christ Jesus.

God is our Father. Jesus referred to Him that way. He manifests Himself to us as Father. But God also said that He is El Shaddai, which literally means "The Breasted One." He said, "As a mother nourishes her child, so I will nourish you." He said to His children, "I am full of whatever it is that you are crying for, My child." As much as God is the epitome of fatherhood in His provision and defense of His children, so He is also the epitome of motherhood in His nurture and love.

The only way we can begin to picture the sexual identity of God is to look at Adam before he was divided from Eve. The Bible tells us that at creation, God said, "Let us make man in our image, after our likeness: and let them have dominion. ... So God created man in his own image, in the image of God created he him; male and female created he them" (Genesis 1:26–27).

Eve, the woman, was hidden in the "womb" of man. When Adam got to the place where he needed someone, God did not need to reenter the creative process. He simply said, "Adam, I'm going to put you to sleep and pull out of you what I've already created in you. I've already made exactly what it is that you need."

Adam had absolutely no trouble in relating to Eve because she was him. When they came together, they were a picture of total godliness. They were one flesh, a mirror of one God.

When men and women come together today in the Spirit, they too are a total picture of all the characteristics of God. That is one of the reasons that the enemy wants to do everything he can to divide men and women; that is why he has declared war on our marriages. He knows that when we are separated, we do not give a total picture of godliness to the world.

Neither man nor woman can totally depict God's nature without the other. We men need the gentleness, tenderness, femininity, love, mercy, and compassion of women. Women need men to express the strength, provision, power, protection, and defense of God. When we come together, we are able to express the total nature of God to a hurting world. And the devil doesn't want to see that happen.

Anything the devil can do to divide us and make us suspicious and wary of each other, he'll do it. If it isn't wife abuse, it's male bashing. He delights in bitter, angry mothers who teach their daughters to hate men and to live individualistic lives. Just because mama had a conflict with her husband, doesn't mean you have to have a conflict with yours!

When men and women come together, God allows them to act out who He is—they are privileged to be partners with Him in the creative process of life. And the celebration of the union of man and woman is children . . . life. Just as God breathed His life into Adam, so we are allowed to breathe life into this world through the bearing of children.

You were created as a woman for a very special purpose—first, to experience wholeness and union, and then, to bear children. That dual purpose is not limited to the natural. It is a supernatural purpose. God created you to become the mother of something spiritual that will live forever!

Trust God today to make you whole and to use you to bear His life in the world.

CHAPTER
THIRTEEN

Shut the Door!

If she be a door, we will inclose her with boards of cedar.
(Song of Solomon 8:9)

 o sooner had God created Eve than the devil sought her out to talk to her. Why? Because he knew something about Eve, just as he knows something about women today. He knows that women are the door to life.

Women are the only legal entry into the earth realm. If it is going to be born, it is going to be born of a woman. If it is going to come from the eternal realm into the realm of time, it is going to come through the door of a woman's womb. The devil is waiting at the door.

Most women don't seem to understand that they are the passageway—the entry for life. It is an awesome responsibility, an awesome privilege.

We each were chosen by God from the foundations of eternity, but in order to get us from eternity into time, God has only one method—that we be born of a woman. God is so serious about this law of His creation that when He got ready to pour Himself into human flesh and live on this earth, He didn't violate His own method but rather, was born of a woman.

It is this fact that puts women on the devil's hit list. The enemy is opposed to life. He deals in sickness, destruction, denial, devastation, thievery, and death. The enemy knows that if he is going to be successful, he must conquer the legal entryway to life.

Woman, guard your doors and lock them. Slam your fence gates shut and chain them tight. Be very careful what you let come through you ...

what you let affect you ...

what you let influence you ...

and be careful what spirit you let

loose in your mind ...

in your emotion ...

in your family.

Shut the door!

Shut the door on that confusion.

Shut the door on that depression.

Shut the door on that temptation.

Shut the door on that evil spirit.

You are shutting the door in the devil's face.

Solomon wrote in the Song of Solomon, "We have a little sister, and she hath no breasts . . . If she be a wall, we will build upon her a palace of silver: and if she be a door, we will inclose her with boards of cedar" (Song of Solomon 8:8–9).

Solomon was describing a sister who was immature. He said if she was found to be "swinging loose," he would teach her how to "keep herself." He would close her in so she didn't give entrance to just any old thing or any old person that happened to come along. But if she proved to be a wall—if she was found to be solid in what she believed and how she behaved—then he would build on her.

This is the stance we need to take in the church. If we have a woman in our midst who is a little "loose," we need to surround her with strong women of faith, rather than gossip about her or shun her. We need to teach her how to keep herself, how not to put herself into vulnerable positions, how not to be "shopping" for a man every time she meets one.

So many women have been abused, and abused women don't know anything about how to have a healthy relationship with a man. Their concept of men has been shattered. They don't know about brotherly love. We need to teach them about the type of love that can exist between men and women that is not sexual—the types of love that can be brotherly and comforting and friendly. It is important that we heal the concept of family in the church, and it begins with our teaching one another what it means to keep oneself pure and to relate in ways that are right before God.

Guard the door of your life, your soul, your spirit. Shut the door on the devil today!

You have precious treasure inside you that needs protecting. You have the capacity to bear life. Don't let the enemy steal it from you.

Slam the door on the devil today. Give entrance only to the Holy Spirit and open yourself up only to those things that are from God.

CHAPTER
FOURTEEN

Stand in His Strength

God is able to make [us] stand.

[Romans 14:4]

The enemy confronted Eve in the garden. He wanted to be in the family. He wanted to get in the door of her life, in her relationship with her husband, and in her relationship with God. He wanted to gain authority over the earth realm and to be the god of this world, and in order to do so, he knew he had to have influence over the one who held the key to producing life.

The enemy said to Eve, "Girl, take a look at this fruit." And Eve did. She looked, she touched, she ate. She became a partaker in something that God had said not to do.

Now, I don't fully blame Eve for the consequences of what happened as a result of her disobedience. What Eve did still could have been salvaged, but when Adam joined Eve in disobedience, destruction was assured. Adam missed his opportunity to become a full picture of the "last Adam," Jesus Christ.

Adam, in his weakness of need, died with his bride.

Jesus, in His strength of love, died for His bride.

Every child that was born to Adam and Eve was born after Adam and Eve had sinned. Every child born to them was therefore fallen, shaped in iniquity. When the Bible says that we are all born in sin, the word is *sin,* not *sins.* We are born with a sin nature, the state of sin, not as the result of a sinful act or with a host of sins attributed to our account.

I am very weary of two kinds of people—those who brag about their old sinful nature, and those who act as if they never had one.

Some people seem to boast about what they did before they accepted Jesus Christ as their Savior. It's as if they are working for bragging rights—they seem to enjoy recounting all the details about how bad they were.

The fact is, it doesn't matter what you did before you were saved or how bad your life was. It doesn't matter how bad your sins were or how many of them you committed. God didn't save you because you had accumulated a long list of sinful deeds. He saved you because He loved you and He wanted to change your sin nature—the nature in you that is prone to disobey God.

We were all born with identically the same sin nature. We inherited it from our first parents, Adam and Eve.

There are other people who act as if they were born lily white. Let me assure you that if the Lord hadn't saved you when He did, you could have done anything . . .

run with anyone . . .

been anything . . .

or even died as the result of anything that any other person has ever experienced in the sin department. The fact that you didn't engage in more sinful acts before God reached down and lifted you up is a miracle of God!

If the truth was known, if God hadn't taken hold of us when He did we all would have committed horrible sinful acts, and more of them than we could recount. We may not have done all the bad things that we had the capacity or desire to do before we were saved, but if we hadn't been saved when we were, we probably would have done them!

There are probably some things frustrating you today that are things you didn't "get to do" before you got saved. I know many people who wrestle with those things daily. They still have a desire to sin, which is part of their flesh nature, even after they have been saved.

After a major earthquake, tremors can continue for hours, days, even weeks. They are called "aftershocks." The same is true in the spirit realm. After a person is saved, she can still have tremors of temptation from her former life.

Believe me when I tell you, those who don't tell you about their sins or who don't seem to have sinned very much . . . have thought about sinning! We all have thought about doing some bad things that we haven't actually done.

If we are born with the weakness of Eve and Adam, what are we to do when the devil comes along?

The Bible says, "Having done all . . . Stand therefore" (Ephesians 6:13–14). And in Romans 14:4 we read, "God is able to make [us] stand." Not in your strength but in the strength of Jesus Christ. You can't stand on your strength. By yourself, you are just another Eve. But in the strength of Jesus, you can stand and not give in.

about how we are to live our

lives . . .

every time we start feeling

pity that we didn't receive

everything we needed as a
child.

Some days we need a little more strength than on other days. But every time we need strength, we are to run to the Breasted One. He has what it is that we need. He longs to hold us and comfort us and impart to us the strength we need to move forward in our lives. Draw from Him the strength you need to stand.

My wife breast-fed our first daughter. I didn't know anything about what it meant to breast-feed a baby. They told us in the classes that we attended that this was nature's way and the best method for both a mother and baby. I said to my wife, "Let's do it." Seemed good to me!

My wife tried it. And it didn't take long before we found ourselves asking, "How can something so natural be so hard?" The baby didn't seem to know that breast-feeding was natural. She didn't seem to be able to get enough milk and she cried and screamed around the clock. Finally I got a bottle and said, "Here! We're going to try a new method!"

God's way isn't always easy. It may be the perfect way, the ideal way, the truly "natural" way according to God's creation . . . but you still may need to work at it. Just because something is right doesn't mean it's easy.

We often have to work at drawing from God what it is that we need.

The tremors of temptation, the moods and attitudes toward sin, will pass if you will only stand up to them in His name. The blood of Jesus Christ has set you free and will continue to uphold you, if you will just stand. On Christ the solid rock we STAND!

Announce to the devil that when he comes around with his temptations, you are going to stand in Christ. You are going to stand until the shaking quits . . .

until the thunder stops rolling . . .

until midnight passes into dawn . . .

until you feel peace again . . .

until the wave of loneliness

passes . . .

until your marriage is

restored . . .

until you come

out of debt . . .

until your

struggle

is over!

When we do the standing, God does the strengthening. Paul said, "I can do all things through Christ which strengtheneth me" (Philippians 4:13).

Christ doesn't just strengthen us once. He strengthens us again and again and again. He strengthens us every time we face a difficult challenge . . .

every time a memory comes up to haunt us . . .

every time we are reminded of our

imperfect past . . .

every time we face a decision

Drawing from God the strength you need to stand up to the devil may take effort. It may take your praise, your prayer, your getting into His Word with an intensity you've never had before.

But the fact is, you can stand if you want to stand.

Choose to stand up to the devil today in the strength of Christ Jesus.

CHAPTER FIFTEEN

Refuse to Be Killed

*My father seeketh to kill thee: now therefore, I pray thee, take
heed to thyself . . . and abide in a secret place, and hide thyself.*
                                                          [1 Samuel 19:2]

dam and Eve were created in the likeness of God but all of their
children were born in their likeness—in the likeness of sin.
Their children were born dysfunctional.

We are all from dysfunctional families. I get amused when I
watch talk shows on which they have flown in a person who has a terrible
story to tell. The person is veiled behind a curtain so you only see her sil-
houette as she says, "I came from a dysfunctional family." People in the
audience ask, "How did you feel? What was it like to grow up in a dysfunctional family? Were you emotionally upset?"

I want to say, "Ah, come on. Get out of here! Why are you asking all those
questions as if you don't know the answer from your own life?" Everybody I
know or ever hope to meet came from a dysfunctional family. Every family
on earth has something wrong with it that keeps it from being perfect. The
first family was dysfunctional and every family since then has been dysfunctional.

Quit feeling sorry for yourself because you came from a dysfunctional
family. So did every other person. Quit allowing the enemy to make you feel
guilty as if your problem is some kind of special case. All people were born
with problems regardless of their color, race, educational background, the
part of town they lived in, the type of parents they had, or the things they
went through.

Every person is born inwardly depraved, regardless of how that depravity
might be expressed. In the case of Cain, the firstborn son of Adam and Eve,
depravity was expressed as hatred, jealousy, and murder. The first child ever
born was a murderer. The first family on earth was marked by crime. The
first person murdered was a son.

Families today are marked by murder, including the family of God, the
church. In fact, you haven't really been killed until you've been killed by a
brother or sister in the church! I know some women who made it through
the worst possible life on the streets only to be driven half crazy by saints.

It's time we say to those in our family—both our natural family and our spiritual family—"I love you, I'm related to you, I care about you . . . but I won't let you kill me."

You had better adopt that attitude toward every person in your life, including your husband, your children, your friends, your boss, the people you work with, the members of your church. You need to say to them, "Jesus died for me. That's all the dying that needs to be done. I'm not going to let you kill me. I'm going to hide myself in Him. I won't let you kill me."

I'm not talking about the body. I'm talking about your resisting those who will attempt to kill something in your spirit and soul. I'm talking about people who will come at you to try to kill something in your emotions, your attitude, your inner life. They'll try to get you to sin with them, or to give into the temptation you feel to sin.

They'll say to you, "It's alright. It won't matter if you do this just this once. It's just a little thing, a one-time deal."

Others might say to you, "Nothing is going to get better. You might as well give up and sit down in your ashes because nothing is ever going to change and nothing is ever going to be right in your life."

No! Those who will say such things to you are agents of death itself creeping up on you and coming at you in disguise. Don't let them kill you! Stand up to them in the strength of Jesus Christ and say, "I'm not going to let you drive me crazy with your lies and your temptations. I'm not going to let you lead me into sin. I refuse to let you kill in me what God has birthed in me!"

Get your praise out. Start praising God for what He has done for you. Celebrate the life He has given you. Declare to God and to every person who talks death to you—"My life isn't over. There's still more that God has for me to do and to say and to be. I'm choosing life. I refuse to go back down that road of death."

Say no to those drugs . . .

say no to that sinful relationship . . .

say no to that evil desire . . .

say no to those thoughts of

depression and suicide . . .

say no to that thing or that person who is trying to lead you straight back to a life of dying instead of living. Don't let yourself be killed!

Stand strong in Christ today. Refuse to let the depravity of another person pull you down or destroy you.

CHAPTER SIXTEEN

Dealing With Your Cains and Abels

*Cain rose up against Abel his brother, and slew him. . . . And
Cain went out from the presence of the LORD, and dwelt in the land
of Nod, on the east of Eden.*   *[Genesis 4:8, 16]*

hen Eve gave birth to Cain, she no doubt thought she was receiving her miracle. The prophecy over her life had been this:
her seed would bruise the head of the serpent, the one who had
deceived and beguiled her. (See Genesis 3:15.)

So, when Eve saw that she had given birth to a son, she probably said,
"Here it is! This is my miracle. This is what God promised. Here is my savior, the one who is going to straighten out this mess that I created, the one
who is going to undo what I have done."

Then when she gave birth to Abel, she no doubt said, "Why, here's another miracle—another opportunity to defeat the serpent. One of these two
has got to be the Messiah! Surely one of these boys is God's answer."

But things didn't turn out the way Eve had hoped. In fact, things didn't
turn out right at all.

Have you ever raised someone who didn't turn out right? When a woman
raises a child who falls into sin and gets into trouble, she feels responsible.
She feels as if their outcome is her fault.

Eve probably had an idea early in their lives how Cain and Abel might
turn out. The rebellious, quick-tempered, proud, easily-upset Cain didn't get
that way overnight. He didn't develop his strong work ethic and his drive to
achieve success in a day. His violent streak didn't appear suddenly.

Likewise, Abel's desire to please, his humility, his obedience, his nurturing and "tending" traits weren't the product of spontaneous combustion.

I suspect that Abel was always Eve's favorite. We see mothers everywhere
who say, "Oh, Abel's making good grades. Abel's on his way to college. Abel
always does what I tell him to do. Abel does the nicest things for me. Now I'm
praying for Cain, but Abel is doing just fine." In every family, there always
seems to be a Cain and an Abel.

The day came, however, when Cain killed Abel. The first woman, who
had become the first wife, and who was the first mother, now attended
the first funeral. She had lost her baby son. She knew the pain—a pain

like no other pain—of lowering the body of her beloved child into the ground.

Not only that, but her elder son was as good as dead—marked for destruction and living on the run. Cain was alive, but he was dead as far as she was concerned. He wasn't there for her either.

There is one kind of pain that we experience when we lose something we thought we would always have. There is another kind of pain in having something that you are perpetually in the state of losing. Cain represents that second kind of pain for Eve. He is alive, but he isn't. He survived, but he didn't. There is no loneliness like that of feeling alone even if you aren't alone.

I hear so many single women say, "I want to be married." They sing the praises of marriage with a high-C pitch. They think that if they just get married their loneliness in life will be solved.

They don't seem to know that there are many married women who are still waiting to be "married." They don't know that there are tens of thousands of women who get up every morning and fight loneliness all through the day because they are linked to someone who isn't there. Now, their husbands may be snoring in the bed next to them. Their husbands may be sitting at the breakfast table. But they aren't there. They are present physically, but they are absent emotionally and spiritually. It's terrible to be with somebody and still be by yourself. It's far worse than the loneliness of not being with anybody at all.

Many relationships don't work, but they persist. The people in them exist, but they don't live. They are dying on the inside, even if they show all the signs of living on the outside.

Cain represents all those relationships in which a person is there, but you can't trust him or depend on him. Cain was not dead, but he was as good as dead. He was a member of the "living dead."

Eve couldn't stop grieving for Cain because his life wasn't over. She couldn't pronounce a final benediction on Cain because he was in a lingering limbo. At least she could have a funeral for Abel.

So many women I know today have "Cains" in their lives. They have unresolved issues, which is what Cain was to Eve. They have relationships that are like sustained notes—there is no melody, but there also is no ending, no conclusion, no resolution. They are unable to determine in their minds if something is over or still in process. They feel as if they are on hold. They don't know where they are at, or where things are going. One day things seem to be moving in one direction, and the next day things seem to be going the opposite way. Unless a woman learns to deal with the Cain in her life, she is in danger of cracking up.

We mourn for what we lose. But at the same time, we know where the thing that we lost is located. We know where the body has been laid. We know where the tombstone has been placed.

But in cases of Cain, there is no body, no funeral, no grave, no tombstone. You just don't know where he is. Now you see him, now you don't.

It's hard to praise if there's a Cain in your life because you don't know what it is that you should be praising God for. The reason you don't know is because you don't know where he's at, and until you know where he's at, you can't know where you're at. If you don't know where you're at, you're confused. And those who are confused find it difficult to get beyond their confusion to see the absolutes and the sovereignty of God.

If you are going to be able to receive your next blessing . . .

if you are going to be in a position to

experience the next move of God in your life . . .

  if you are going to come out of the valley

  of the shadow of death . . .

   you have got to let your past go.

You have got to bury Abel.

You have got to say "goodbye" to Cain. Otherwise you will never be able to say "hello" to what God has for you next.

You can't continue to pine away over somebody you were in love with fifteen years ago—somebody who has been married for ten years and is out roasting wieners in the park with his family while you are at home crying in your soup. You've got to let that person go from your heart and your mind. If you don't, you won't be able to say "hello" to the right man God brings your way.

When Jesus said to let the dead bury their dead, He was saying that we shouldn't be overly concerned with that which is over. (See Matthew 8:22.) We should let what is over be over.

You wouldn't let a dead man hold onto you. Why let a dead relationship keep you in its grasp? Why let yesterday pull you down and hold you back?

Today is the day to say "goodbye" to what you've lost—both to what you may have buried and to what has gone away from you. It is your day to stop grieving and go forward.

*Ask God to help you deal with your disappointment
and loss so you can be ready for the blessing He still
wants to give you.*

CHAPTER
SEVENTEEN

Let Go of
Your Past

When I became a man, I put away childish things.
(1 Corinthians 13:11)

Eve woke up a wife. Can you imagine? On her first day on planet earth she may have heard her husband ask, "Honey, where are my socks?"

She had no training for the job, no preparation—it was a matter of "well, that's the way it is." It's very difficult to do something that you've never seen done before. It's difficult to be something if you've never seen it modeled for you. It's very tough to be a good wife if you never saw a good wife in action. No wonder Eve went for a walk in the garden. She was probably stressed out!

Eve was created without a childhood, without having had an opportunity to be a little girl. She stepped right into being a wife, and then a mother. She was a woman before she had a chance to be a girl.

Now in Eve's case, that may have been alright. God had a plan and He did things His way. But in our world today, there are lots of women who found themselves being women before they had a chance to be girls. They didn't have an opportunity to know what it meant to be innocent, to feel free to trust, or what it meant to receive genuine love.

Sometimes life can come at us too fast. Sometimes we have our childhoods stripped away from us. The little girl in you may never have had an opportunity to be a little girl. And if that happened, you were robbed of something very precious.

I tell my daughters, "Be little girls as long as you can." I look around sometimes and I can't believe what I see—mothers who have dressed up their little girls to look like women, with their hair all done up and earrings in their ears and lipstick on their mouths . . . even at four months old!

I want my daughters to be innocent and free and trusting of others as long as possible.

Whether you had a girlhood or not, you must not use the past as your excuse. You must refuse to blame your past for your present and future.

The fact is . . .

You can never relive your past.

You can't go back and make it different.

You are not the person you were then and you are never going to be that person again.

You can't go back into your mother's womb.

You can't relive your first marriage.

Your past is your past.

It is over!

Accept that fact and dismiss your past and move on. Let it go!

Let go of anything that is holding you back,

> or slowing you down,
> and keeping you all
> bound up inside.

If you are holding onto your past, it's because there is something about your past that you think you still need.

I feel certain that if I needed my baby clothes, my mother could go up in her attic and find them. Up in that attic somewhere, she has my pacifier. I know she has my size-30 gym shorts from junior high. She has boxes and bags and bundles of things in her attic "just in case we ever need them."

My mother seems to have the mind-set that if we ever fall on hard times and are on skid row, she can go up in her attic and find something that will get us through. I tease her, "What are you going to do? Sew all my baby clothes into a quilt to keep us warm?"

When I go to visit her, she often pulls out something that she found. She'll say to me, "I've got a copy of your first check, the one you got for cutting grass when you were nine years old. Do you want to see it?" I say, "No." And she'll show it to me anyway. She has kept all kinds of stuff over the years.

I know my mother isn't the only woman who has done this. When I speak to women's groups, I often ask them, "How many of you hold onto stuff from the past?" Just about every woman in the room looks guilty.

When my wife was expecting our first child, she was given all kinds of stuff from people who stopped by the house, saying, "Here's this, here's that—just in case you need it." They'd tell her how their baby or their grandbaby had used the items, or how they themselves had worn the item as a child. I said to my wife, "They aren't blessing us. They're cleaning out their closets!" We had stacks and stacks of stuff for our baby daughter, including a whole stack of little boy clothes!

My wife has this tendency, too. After each pregnancy, she wanted to keep her maternity clothes, just in case she might need them again. After our last baby, I said, "Throw them away!"

As a man, I don't understand that tendency. As far as I am concerned, when you hold onto things like that, they keep you tied to the past.

Have you ever noticed that when you visit old people, they spend most of their time talking about the past? They'll say to you, "Do you remember the time? Do you recall how we used to . . . ?" They want to relive those times. I suspect that it's because they think those were the best times of their lives and they aren't expecting anything better ever to come along. There is something about the past that they need in order to give meaning to their present.

People who don't let go of things easily, have little faith. They cling to things because they fear they will never be able to replace them. They won't give you the last twenty-dollar bill they have in their purse or pocket because they fear they won't ever have another one.

Don't you know that God has more for you? He has something else for you. If you are trusting God for your future, then you have not yet seen your best days. There's more before you than there is behind you.

It doesn't matter how young you are, or how old you are. If you are alive today, then God has kept you here for this very hour and He has something more for you.

He has something more for you to be . . . something more for you to say . . .

something more for you to do . . .

something more for you to
experience . . .

something more for you to praise.

You are alive today because God still has a reason for you to be alive.

I want you to get it into your heart, in your mind, in your spirit . . . there's a reason for you to go forward. You may have lost the Garden of Eden, you may have buried your Abel, you may have lost your Cain . . . but God has something ahead for your future. He has something good planned for you. You aren't dead. You're alive . . . so LIVE!

***Let go of your past so your hands and heart are free
for what God has for you NOW.***

There's More Life Ahead

I had fainted, unless I had believed to see the goodness of the
LORD in the land of the living. *{Psalm 27:13}*

$\mathcal{I}$ have no doubt that Eve was the first person who knew what it meant to feel depressed. Her hopes had been dashed. She had experienced murder in her family. She had lost both of her sons—one to death, the other to a curse. She felt the failure of having produced an outlaw from her own womb. She no doubt felt regret that she had ever become pregnant in the first place.

Regret is something that many women need to face today. There can be no recovery until a woman is willing to look at herself in the mirror and say, "I messed up." People who blame other people never recover because they live in a state of denial. Any time you blame another person for your problem, you put that person in control of your life. You are saying with your blame, "I can't get out until you let me out. I can't succeed until you allow me to succeed. I can't move forward in my life until you give me the green light." That's a lie of the devil!

You must accept responsibility for your own actions. You may not have done it all, but you contributed. It may not be all your fault, but you need to accept responsibility for the part that was yours. You must be able to say to yourself, "I wasn't without fault. I was a contributing factor."

Unless you are able to accept responsibility for your actions, you will be eaten up with unresolved guilt in your life. It will rot inside you and erupt in your life in the form of jealousy and anger and hatred and bitterness. Find the Cains in your life and deal with them. Confront the issues. Challenge the lies that the devil will try to speak in your mind, when he tells you, "It's not your fault. It's all his fault. You were right, he was wrong. Things were just out of control. You didn't do anything bad. Somebody else is to blame for all this." No! Accept your share of the responsibility for what has gone wrong and ask God to forgive you.

God is too wise and too loving to put your destiny into the hands of another person. He doesn't trust the actions of another person to control your future. What you do from this point on in your life is up to you. How you feel and how you react and what you do and what you say and what you choose and how you deal with the past is solely your responsibility. It's your decision.

If you will face up to your own sin and take hold of the hand of our forgiving God, you can overcome anything. You can overcome the past influence of any person . . . the evil of any circumstance . . . and live and not die!

You don't need to live with depression,

oppression,

or suppression. God wants you to come out of your feelings of failure and rejection and regret, and start living!

A number of years ago I went through a time of great depression in my life. I'd preach and then go back to my room, sit on the floor with the lights out, and cry in the dark. Nothing was wrong, but everything was wrong.

I didn't care what I did or what others did to me. I didn't care if I got up in the morning. I didn't care what I wore or what I looked like. I didn't care what other people thought of me because I didn't have any thoughts for anything but the way I felt. And I felt so low that I didn't care if I lived or died. When people were around, I'd smile and praise the Lord. But when I was alone, I'd go back into the dark and cry.

I preached a lot about heaven because that's where I wanted to go. I read about heaven and studied the Scriptures about heaven and wrote songs about heaven because that's the only place I wanted to be. I didn't want to be here on this earth. I wanted out.

That time in my life was before my ministry began to flourish, before I wrote any books, before I started speaking across the nation. There were many things that I had already overcome at that point in my life, but there were still many things that I had to face. I was so overwhelmed by discouragement that for months, I wanted to die.

I asked the Lord, "What's wrong with me? What is happening to me?"

He said, "Son, your heart has fainted. You've been through so much that your heart—not your physical heart, but your emotional and spiritual heart—has fainted."

I said, "What shall I do?"

He said, "Wait on Me. Be of good courage. I'm going to strengthen your heart."

Let me tell you something about the way things work. Just before you birth that new seed, just before you see your miracle, just before your promise is fulfilled ... that's the time when all hell seems to break out against you.

Just before you come into your purpose, that's when others will do their best to nail you to the tree.

Just before you experience the fullness of God's power working in you, that's the time when the devil will try to break you.

Just before the baby arrives, that's when the labor pains reach their peak.

All the while, however, you have all the symptoms of a miracle growing in you.

Before I ever wrote a book, I wrote a letter to myself. I said to myself, "Don't die. Don't die. It's going to get better in a minute."

I told myself, "You can make it. You can make it. Don't give up."

I said, "You have gone through too much to die now. You may cry, but don't die. There's got to be something else for you. There's got to be a reason for you to feel the way you feel. There's got to be a blessing that is better than anything you have ever felt before."

Those are the very words I believe the Lord wants me to say to you.

Don't die.

Don't die.

Don't die.

Keep standing.

Keep standing.

Keep standing.

God is about to give you another seed to birth. He's about to open up the windows of heaven to you and pour you out a blessing that will be so great you won't even have room enough to receive it all.

I can't tell you what day I came out of my depression. When God restores you, He does so in a way that suddenly you are walking in the light and you can hardly recall how dark your life had been.

I suspect it was just that way for Eve. When she held Seth in her arms, her thoughts of Abel faded. Her burden about Cain lifted. She had another miracle, another opportunity.

When you move into the fullness of your appointment with God's destiny for you, you won't think any more about those things that are in your past. You won't have time—you won't have the inclination—to dwell on your failures, your mistakes, your former life. You will be so busy raising up your miracle and living in your blessing that all the former things in your life will be not only out of your sight and out of your mind, but out of your heart.

You will be free. You will be loosed at last to do and be what it is that God has appointed you to do and to be!

Don't quit or give up. Give birth to that promise that God has put in your life. Look for it to be born in you and to be a blessing!

Your
Appointed
Seed

God, said she, hath appointed me another seed instead of Abel.
[Genesis 4:25]

You have a predetermined appointment with God that has been set from the foundations of the earth, and that appointment isn't over until God says it's over. You may think that all of your good days are in the past, but the very fact that you are alive says that God wants you to be alive. He is not through with you yet. You have an appointment.

The angels of the Lord are going to keep you here as long as God wants you here.

No weapon formed against you is going to prosper as long as God wants you here.

Your appointment isn't over until God says it's over!

Even after all she had been through with Cain and Abel, Eve still had an appointment with God. In spite of all that she had experienced, all the heartache and hard times she had known, she had an appointed task. Eve said, "God has appointed me another seed." (See Genesis 4:25.) Her appointment involved having another baby, another son. She named him Seth.

God has another promise with your name on it today. He has appointed you another seed.

In spite of all that you've been through,
   all that you've suffered,
   all of your tears,
   all of your failures and mistakes,
   all of your misjudgment and mismanagement,
   all that you've lost,
   all that has left you . . .
   God has another "baby" for you to birth.
Don't give up.
Don't give in.
Don't give way.
God has another method to bring you the blessing He has destined for you to receive.

When you make an appointment, you set a date and a time in the present for something that is going to happen in the future. And that's exactly what God has done in setting His appointment with you.

God's destiny for you is preset. He has known all along that you would go through what you've been through to get to the place where you are right now. Even so, He still has an appointment with you. He has not cancelled out. There's still something on His calendar that has your name on it.

The devil knew that God had a plan for you. That's why he worked so hard to wipe you out. He didn't want you to live long enough to keep your full appointment, to live out all that God had in store for you. He knew there was more ahead. He knew it was good. He knew it had to do with life. That's why he tried so hard to deal you a death-blow early on.

He sent trials . . .

troubles . . .

and tribulations to destroy you—and if you refused to be destroyed on the outside, he tried even harder to destroy you on the inside.

Start looking ahead. There's something coming up on God's calendar and it's got your name on it. There's something good just over the horizon of tomorrow that's for your life,

your marriage,

your family,

your work,

your ministry.

For everything that you have lost in your life . . . God has another seed.

For everything that you loved and that died . . . God has another seed.

For everything that you lost and can no longer hold . . . God has another seed.

Every time the devil tells you that you are going down, that you are going to die, that you are going to cave in, that there's nothing else for you, tell him, "You are a liar. There's got to be something else. I have an appointment with God. He has another seed for me to birth. He has another miracle for me to hold."

God has called you with an eternal purpose. Where you are right now is not where you are going. He still has an appointed task for you to finish.

God still has an appointed seed for you to birth.

CHAPTER TWENTY

Keep Your Appointment

Then began men to call upon the name of the LORD.
[Genesis 4:26]

t seems that every time I get ready for a major appointment, something comes up to try to slow me down. People will call and just want to chit-chat. I'll be pacing the floor trying to find a way to get off the phone, but the person will just go on and on.

Problems always seem to come up. The car keys won't be anywhere in sight. The gas gauge will read empty. Traffic will be heavy. An accident will block the highway. It seems everything possible will arise to slow me down.

When God has an appointed seed for you to birth, there may be obstacles you have to hurdle. There may be delays you have to endure. There may be things you have to refuse.

When God appoints a task for you, there's no time for idle talk. There's no time for gossip. In order for you to receive what God has for you, you are going to have to hang up on some folk . . .

you are going to have to hang up on some situations . . .

you are going to have to outlast or
outmaneuver some circumstances . . .

you are going to have to say "no" to
some activities that will pull you
away from your appointment or
delay you from keeping it.

You will have no time for foolishness,
pity parties,
or side shows.

If you are going to hold onto your miracle, your dream, the fulfillment of God's plan for your life, then you are going to have to keep moving, keep moving, keep moving. Always keep moving toward what God has for you.

You may have to crawl to get there, but keep crawling.

You may have to cry a lot of tears along the way, but keep walking.

You may get knocked down, but get up and keep going.

Don't let anything keep you from keeping your appointment!

The thing that God has for you must be done. That's the way God feels about His plan for you. Write yourself a note, "I have an appointment. It must be kept."

Eve kept her appointment. She had a son named Seth and he had a son named Enos. The Bible says that it was with the birth of Enos that Eve's descendants began to "call upon the name of the Lord." That means that they began to trust God with their lives and to identify completely with Him. Seth was God's man. Enos was God's man. The people of Enos were God's people.

Eve lived to see her son and her grandson walk in holiness before the Lord. She lived to see her miracle. She lived to see her son and her grandson turn back to God and live in obedience, reversing the tide of disobedience and reversing the curse on her family.

There's a reversal ahead for you, too, if you will only keep your appointment with God.

Don't let anything keep you from your appointment with God today.

PART III

Loosed to Express Emotions

A CRYING WOMAN

Hannah was deeply distressed over her failure to bear a child. She was the wife of Elkanah, who was also married to Peninnah. Peninnah had children and in her jealousy at Elkanah's great love for Hannah, she ridiculed and provoked Hannah because she was childless. In a word, Peninnah made Hannah's life miserable.

Hannah took her grief to the door of the tabernacle, the closest she could go to the holy of holies sanctuary. There, she poured out her heart to God, with such anguish that Eli the priest thought she was drunk. When she explained that she was in anguish before the Lord, Eli blessed her and assured her that God would answer her prayer. Hannah had touched the heart of God with her tears.

Hannah became the mother of Samuel, the last judge and a great prophet of Israel who anointed the first two kings of Israel, Saul and David.

From the Scriptures:

[Elkanah] had two wives; the name of the one was Hannah, and the name of the other Peninnah: and Peninnah had children, but Hannah had no children.

And this man went up out of his city yearly to worship and to sacrifice unto the LORD of hosts in Shiloh. . . .

And when the time was that Elkanah offered, he gave to Peninnah his wife, and to all her sons and her daughters, portions:

But unto Hannah he gave a worthy portion; for he loved Hannah: but the LORD had shut up her womb.

And her adversary also provoked her sore, for to make her fret, because the LORD had shut up her womb.

And as he did so year by year, when she went up to the house of the LORD, so she provoked her; therefore she wept, and did not eat.

Then said Elkanah her husband to her, Hannah, why weepest thou? and why eatest thou not? and why is thy heart grieved? am not I better to thee than ten sons?

So Hannah rose up after they had eaten in Shiloh, and after they had drunk. Now Eli the priest sat upon a seat by a post of the temple of the LORD.

And she was in bitterness of soul, and prayed unto the LORD, and wept sore.

And she vowed a vow, and said, O LORD of hosts, if thou wilt indeed look on the affliction of thine handmaid, and remember me, and not forget thine handmaid, but wilt give unto thine handmaid a man child, then I will give him unto the LORD all the days of his life, and there shall no razor come upon his head.

And it came to pass, as she continued praying before the LORD, that Eli marked her mouth.

Now Hannah, she spake in her heart; only her lips moved, but her voice was not heard: therefore Eli thought she had been drunken.

And Eli said unto her, How long wilt thou be drunken? put away thy wine from thee.

And Hannah answered and said, No, my lord, I am a woman of a sorrowful spirit: I have drunk neither wine nor strong drink, but have poured out my soul before the LORD.

Count not thine handmaid for a daughter of Belial: for out of the abundance of my complaint and grief have I spoken hitherto.

Then Eli answered and said, Go in peace: and the God of Israel grant thee thy petition that thou hast asked of him.

—1 Samuel 1:2-17

**CHAPTER
TWENTY-ONE**

You Were Made to Express Emotions

*[She] stood at his feet behind him [Jesus] weeping, and began
to wash his feet with tears.* *[Luke 7:38]*

od made men and women very differently. He brought us forth at
different stages in His process of creation. The woman was at the
peak of God's creative crescendo. God outdid Himself when He
brought her forth.

God waited until everything was in place before He brought forth woman.
When He made Adam, Adam had everything in creation under his dominion,
but he did not have a helpmate.

Adam had existed without a relationship, although he did have authority.
Men today often find that they can exist without a relationship with a woman.
They tend not to be as relationship oriented as women. They direct their energy instead into their work, their career, in which they have power and
authority. Positions and titles are important to men, often far more so than
relationships.

When women get together, they talk about relationships. They don't even
have to know each other very well before they are willing to whip out baby
pictures of all their children and grandchildren. Those children might be
forty years old now, but they still carry their baby pictures! Women are happy
to tell all the details about their family members—how old they are, where
they go to school, what they are doing in their lives, whether they are married or not. You won't see an average man whipping out his wallet to show
another man his grandbabies.

This doesn't mean that men don't love their children and grandchildren.
They just have a different way of expressing that love. They don't spend the
majority of their time talking about relationships. Women do, however.

Because women are so relationship oriented, they have a sensitivity toward worship—about nurturing their relationship with God—that men don't
have. They have a degree of understanding about spiritual matters that most
men don't have. Women seem to understand readily what it means to enter
into praise and to long for intimate relationship with God, but men have to
be wooed into that desire.

Now what does this have to do with your emotions?

Women are more emotional than men because emotions are the language of relationship. In fact, the more relationship oriented you are, the more emotional you are likely to be.

There's nothing wrong with our being emotional. It's a part of our creation to express our emotions. Emotions are a key part of the way we relate to one another and to God. What's wrong is when we allow ourselves to be led by our emotions—when we allow our emotions to be more important or to carry more weight than our spirits.

Men are often conditioned not to express their emotions. They are taught from an early age to stifle and suppress their emotions. I've seen mothers tell their eighteen-month-old sons, "Stop crying and be a man!" When that boy grows to be a fifty-year-old man, he's likely to have trouble hugging his wife or raising his hands in praise.

When God saw that it was not good for Adam to be alone, He put Adam to sleep and said, "Adam, everything you need has already been put within you. I'm going to pull what you are thirsting for out of you." When Adam opened his eyes, he saw Eve and instantly he was attracted to her.

Adam wasn't attracted to Eve because of her beauty—her figure, face, or her form. He said, "She is me. She is bone of my bone and flesh of my flesh. She is me, only with a womb. She is me with the ability to carry life. She is the feminine expression of my masculinity. She is my release. She is the silk, the rose, the lace, the fragrance, the softness of my life." Adam found in Eve all of the emotions he had longed to express but hadn't been able to release.

Women, don't let anyone convince you that you need to stifle your emotions.

Don't let anything happen to you that makes you so cold you lose your ability to love.

Don't rehearse old memories until you become imprisoned by them to the point where you can no longer cry or shout or laugh.

You have a great capacity as a woman to express feelings and affections. God gave you that capacity so you could relate more fully to other people and to Him.

Some women today are in shock. They've lost their sensitivity, their femininity, their ability to feel. When that happens, they've adopted a male stance. They've lost part of their identity, the part that makes them uniquely woman. In fact, when a woman begins to display masculine tendencies, I consider that something has put her femininity into shock.

A person who has been in shock sometimes appears as if she has passed out. She withdraws. She loses touch with the reality around her.

She needs to be warmed and helped and comforted. She needs to be encouraged . . .

Come out of it.

Come out of it!

COME OUT OF IT!

Some women go into shock because they have been mistreated.

Some women go into shock because they have been abused.

Some women go into shock because they have been hurt or rejected.

The time is now for them to come out of it! If you are such a woman, hear me clearly: The time has come for you to come out of your shock! Allow yourself to feel again. Allow yourself to cry again. Allow yourself to cry out to God again.

A person in shock is immobilized. She has let a part of her become paralyzed. She has let her emotions die.

Don't let that happen to you.

If it's already happened, then don't stay in that condition! It's time for you to come out of the state of shock that you are in.

If you have lost your tears, ask God to restore them to you. Ask Him to bring your femininity out of shock.

CHAPTER
TWENTY-TWO

Your
Emotions and
Your Spirit

*And the very God of peace sanctify you wholly; and I pray God
your whole spirit and soul and body be preserved blameless unto
the coming of our Lord Jesus Christ.　　[1 Thessalonians 5:23]*

We must understand the difference between our spirits and our emotions. They are linked, yet they are separate. Our emotions are part of our soul realm.

In our spirits, we have God-consciousness. Jesus said, "But the hour cometh, and now is, when the true worshipers shall worship the Father in spirit and in truth: for the Father seeketh such to worship him. God is a Spirit: and they that worship him must worship him in spirit and in truth" (John 4:23–24). Paul wrote, "The Spirit itself beareth witness with our spirit, that we are the children of God" (Romans 8:16).

The spirit realm is the realm in which we relate to God intimately and fully.

In our bodies, we have world-consciousness, an awareness of our physical world. If we didn't have bodies, we wouldn't know whether it was a cold day or a hot day. Our bodies are our means of relating to everything in the natural realm.

In our souls, we have self-consciousness. We know that we exist. When God made man, man became a living soul. He became aware of himself.

Now, we each know who we are. It is our self-consciousness, our self-awareness that separates us from oak trees and rushing streams and mountain peaks. It is in our soul realm that we become aware of our emotions and our appetites and our dreams and our memories and our affections. We know we are alive because we have a soul. It is from our soul that we relate to one another as human beings.

How we each express our soulish lives is just as unique as our fingerprints. Even if we were all gathered in one room and shouted "Hallelujah" at the same time, we each would mean something different with our shout of praise. We would have different reasons for voicing our praise. We would have a different understanding of the object of our praise. Only God is capable of hearing the same word from the mouths of a thousand people and understanding fully the thousand meanings that are being expressed.

Truth seems to come to the body of Christ in waves. The Bible says that the "earth shall be full of the knowledge of the LORD, as the waters cover the sea" (Isaiah 11:9). The waters cover the seas with currents and waves.

We see one aspect of God's truth come into the church as a wave, and then another aspect of God's truth comes in as another wave. At times, it seems as if opinions in the church swing like a pendulum. We need to wait until there is a balance before we come to a conclusion about certain teachings. We need to watch the overall pattern of the waves to see how the tide is falling or rising.

The church went through a time in which there was a great emphasis on what the Greek or Hebrew words mean in the Scriptures. It was an intellectual wave that allowed for very little emotional expression of praise and worship. People could explain what the Bible meant, but they didn't know how to do what the Bible talked about when it came to miracles and to the various gifts of the Spirit. During that wave, if a person broke out into praise and worship, their behavior would be denounced as "too emotional." The church didn't know how to handle emotions. We are still learning a lot about how to express our emotions in the church.

To tell a person not to be emotional is to tell a person not to be human. It is to deny that person's God-given right and privilege to enter into adoration of the Creator. It is to deny the soul realm. Don't ever try to tell me that God doesn't care about how I feel. I know that He does.

That is one of the reasons I'm in the church. I'm tired of being around people in the world who don't care how I feel—or how anybody else feels for that matter. I want to be in a place where at least some of the people care about how I feel, and where I know I can be with God who always cares about how I feel.

Because of the uniqueness of woman's femininity and her ability to express emotions, there were times in history that God specifically called for women. For example, Jeremiah said, "Call for the mourning women, that they may come" (Jeremiah 9:17). God wanted to see tears and brokenness on the altar. He wanted to hear expressions of sorrow over the fact that His people were being carried away in bondage. He said, "Get the women and tell them to cry."

If ever we needed women to lay on the altar and wail in response to God's people being taken into bondage, it is now!

God knows the power of tears, of feelings. Jesus said about prayer, "What things soever ye desire, when ye pray, believe that ye receive them, and ye shall have them" (Mark 11:24). When you desire something, you don't just "want" it. To desire something is to want it with passion. Jesus said, "Make known to Me the things that you can't do without, the things that you want with a passion."

Man looks on the outer appearance but God looks on the heart. He is looking to see what we desire with all of our heart, not what we want as a whim or an idea in our minds.

Is there something today that you want so much that you are willing to lay on the altar and cry for it?

Is there a desire in you to see God move in your life—a desire that is burning in your innermost being with such a passion that you can't forget it, can't get away from it, can't dismiss it, and can't ignore it?

Is there something that you want to see God do with such intensity that you awaken in the middle of the night with the thought of it?

Is there something that you feel so certain that God wants to do and will do that you just know that it is going to be done, even if every indicator around you says otherwise?

That is your desire. It arises from your spirit and it's meant to be expressed by your soul. It is something God expects you to be emotional about!

What is it that you want God to do for you today?
Do you want it with all of your heart? Do you want
it with passion and intensity?

CHAPTER
TWENTY-THREE

Touching God With Your Feelings

Seeing then that we have a great high priest, that is passed into the heavens, Jesus the Son of God, let us hold fast our profession. For we have not an high priest which cannot be touched with the feeling of our infirmities; but was in all points tempted like as we are, yet without sin. Let us therefore come boldly unto the throne of grace, that we may obtain mercy, and find grace to help in time of need.   *[Hebrews 4:14–16]*

ome things are things that only God can do. Hannah knew that.

From the world's standpoint, Hannah had a good life. She had a good husband. He was a rich man. He was a good man. He was generous to her. He loved her greatly. He said to her, "Am not I better to you than ten sons?" But he hadn't given her a son.

Hannah didn't have the one thing she truly desired—a son who could worship God as a priest. And she knew that only God could give her the desire of her heart. She went to the right place with her prayer request.

There are many things that God expects us to do, but there are some things that only God can do. And God expects us to call upon Him to do those things that are His "job."

Is there a need in your life that is a job for God? Have you taken that problem to Him? Or have you taken it to everybody else and sought out every other solution but God? If so, it's time to stop playing games and get serious with God.

Stop running to this group or that group. Stop trying to use this method or that method. Go to God. There are jobs that only God can do. Going to anybody else and trying any other method is a waste of your time.

Don't even think about going to the palm reader . . .

   the dope man . . .

     the crack house . . .

       or the loan shark. Go to the altar and cry out to God! Express yourself with intensity.

God gave you feelings so you could light the altar of incense—so that you might "burn" about something to the point that when you put your believing to your feeling, it's as if you have put a match to incense. Your prayer then floats up to God like a sweet-smelling savor!

No two blends of incense smell the same. And the same is true for your prayer. The way you pray and the words you use and the intent of your heart are all about you. Don't pray the prayer of someone else. Don't say to yourself, "Well, that prayer worked for her. Perhaps it will work for me." God is looking for a prayer that comes up out of your passion, your desire, your emotions, your soul!

You may have read all the recipes for prayer that have ever been written. There are a lot of them around. Five steps for a miracle. Three steps to a blessing. Four steps for binding the devil over your house. Four steps to come into financial prosperity. Two ways to evoke the power and the love of God.

Before we had all those recipes, however, we had women who were willing to cry upon the altar of the Lord and say nothing more than, "Do this for me, Jesus! If You don't, I will die!" They didn't have a process or a formula. Just the power of their passion. And God heard their prayers and answered them.

Do you really want to see God move?

Really?

Really?

Really?

Then touch God with your passion . . . touch Him with your feelings . . . with your getting up in the middle of the night and pacing the floor . . . with your tears that flow like a flood from your eyes . . .

 with your groanings and wailings.

We have a High Priest, Jesus Christ, who is not touched by your outer holiness, your degree, your BMW, your fur coat, your diamond ring, or by how cute you are. He is a High Priest who is only touched by your boldness to come before His throne of grace and cry out with your faith for what it is that you need from Him.

He is not swayed by the fact of your need. You may be broke, busted, and disgusted, but those conditions don't sway Him. He is moved by the depth of your desire that is matched by the depth of your faith! He is touched by your feeling and your believing.

You may say, "I can't touch God. I messed up and I had a baby out of wedlock and I've been divorced three times." God isn't touched by how good you've been or by how bad you've been. He is touched by the feeling of your infirmities. He is moved by your cry that comes up out of your weakness.

If there is any ember still glowing in your heart, any flicker of faith still burning in your spirit, fan that ember, fan that flicker into a flame of desire and call out to God.

Can you still feel?

Then God can still be moved on your behalf.

You may be weak.

You may have failed.

You may have sinned.

But if you still have feeling toward God and you still have a desire in your heart to see God move on your behalf...

Then God can still be moved.

You may not have what someone else has.

You may not look like that other person looks.

You may not have that woman's talents or another woman's skills.

You may not have her education or her personality or her background.

But none of that matters.

None of that moves God.

He is moved by the feelings of your infirmities.

God is not moved by what you have.

He is moved by how you feel about what you don't have and what you need. He is moved by what you are believing for with your faith.

***Go to God today with your need and express
your need to Him with the full force of your
feelings and faith.***

What Do You Want Enough to Cry for It?

Hannah answered and said . . . I am a woman of a sorrowful
spirit: I have drunk neither wine nor strong drink, but have
poured out my soul before the LORD.   *{1 Samuel 1:15}*

annah was a woman who wanted something so much that she was willing to cry for it.

She slipped into the temple one night and folded up her face like a towel and wrenched her tear ducts like a garment and wept until the high priest Eli thought she was drunk. She said, "No, I haven't been drinking. I am a wounded woman with a sorrowful spirit!"

Are you so filled with the idea that your life might be different that you are willing to stagger to the altar and pray while others play?

Do you want something from God with so much desire that you are willing to risk the opinions of others who might say that you are too emotional in your asking God to give it to you?

Do you believe with such a passion that you are intoxicated with the hope of what God has for you?

What hope or dream do you have that consumes your thinking, your feeling, your believing? Pray about that . . . because if your prayer request doesn't move you, it probably won't move God.

Use your trouble, too, to fuel your passion.

The very fear that has been tormenting you . . . the very problem that has been traumatizing you . . . is the very thing that is going to enable you to touch God.

How can that be?

The depth of the trouble you have been experiencing is likely to be equal to the depth of the desire that drives you toward God.

The greater your problem . . .

The more intense your fear . . .

The deeper your discouragement . . .

The more you are willing to risk crying out to God. When your trouble is great enough and your desire is strong enough, you will feel that you have nothing to lose, and everything to gain by pouring out all your passion to God.

There are women who need to stop worrying so much about being Miss Wonderful that they stifle their emotions before God. There are women who need to stop weighing everything they do with the idea that they need to uphold their reputation so they can belong to the right club and get in with the right group and have the favor of the right crowd.

God wants women who will humble themselves before Him, who will come to Him, who will cry out to Him—without any thought to what other people think or say.

Make a decision that you are going to allow yourself to touch God with intensity. Don't hold anything back. Cry for what you want as if your very life depends upon it.

Rachel said to Jacob, "Give me a child, lest I die." She wanted something so much that if she couldn't have it and live, she would rather die. Go to God with that same attitude.

God is looking for women who want to see God's will done on this earth so much that they will cry for it. He is looking for women who want to see right become victorious over wrong, good win over evil, Jesus reign over the devil. He is looking for women who want to see God act on their behalf—and who want it so much they will cry aloud for it and will refuse to be silenced. He wants women who will cry and not shut up!

The power of life and death is in your tongue. Refuse to be silenced. Speak life! After you have prayed, speak God's words of life to yourself. Speak them to your problem. Speak them to your circumstance . . .

your situation . . .

your need . . .

your problem . . .

your lack of supply.

Don't allow yourself to be intimidated into remaining quiet about what it is that you want God to do for you. Cry for it!

God will bear and answer the cry of your heart.

PART IV

Loosed From a Spirit of Infirmity

AN INFIRM WOMAN

While teaching in a synagogue, Jesus encountered a woman who had been "bent over" or "doubled up" for eighteen years. She was bound by a spirit of infirmity. When Jesus saw her, He was moved with compassion toward her and called to her, "Woman, thou art loosed." He laid His hands upon her and immediately she could stand up straight. Her response was to glorify God in spite of the criticism that followed for Jesus having worked this deliverance miracle on the Sabbath.

From the Scriptures:

And he [Jesus] was teaching in one of the synagogues on the sabbath.

And, behold, there was a woman which had a spirit of infirmity eighteen years, and was bowed together, and could in no wise lift up herself.

And when Jesus saw her, he called her to him, and said unto her, Woman, thou art loosed from thine infirmity.

And he laid his hands on her: and immediately she was made straight, and glorified God.

And the ruler of the synagogue answered with indignation, because that Jesus had healed on the sabbath day, and said unto the people, There are six days in which men ought to work: in them therefore come and be healed, and not on the sabbath day.

The Lord then answered him, and said, Thou hypocrite, doth not each one of you on the sabbath loose his ox or his ass from the stall, and lead him away to watering?

And ought not this woman, being a daughter of Abraham, whom Satan hath bound, lo, these eighteen years, be loosed from this bond on the sabbath day? {Luke 13:10–16}

CHAPTER
TWENTY-FIVE

The Nature of Your Deliverance

*Help us, O God of our salvation, for the glory of thy name: and
deliver us . . . for thy name's sake.*   *[Psalm 79:9]*

he woman whom Jesus encountered on the Sabbath was a
woman who came to the synagogue with a spirit of infirmity, and
who left the synagogue that day loosed from it.

Now I want you to notice that the Bible does not say that Jesus destroyed the infirmity itself so that it could never exist again in her life or the life of another person. Rather, He simply separated this infirmity from this woman. He removed any influence of the infirmity from her life.

I know many people today who are waiting for the thing that has restricted or inhibited them to be destroyed. They don't think they can be loosed, or feel free unless the source of their infirmity dies. They must awaken to the possibility that a source of infirmity can continue to exist, and yet have no influence or impact upon them.

The Bible says that Jesus was manifested to "destroy the works of the devil." (See 1 John 3:8.) That word *destroy* in the Greek language means to dismantle, decompose, or break down. Whatever Satan has built up, Jesus breaks down. Something may exist, but be powerless to work against you. It's still there, but it doesn't work. It ceases to be effective.

Hell becomes very confused when Jesus delivers a person from a spirit of infirmity. Satan has a file that is supposed to predict precisely what is going to work on you. If it doesn't work, there's confusion.

Satan starts grilling his demons . . .

Didn't you catch her at a weak moment?

Didn't you make the temptation enticing enough?

Didn't you make the accusation strong enough?

Didn't you bind that spirit of infirmity to her with strong enough chains?

And the demons reply "yes" to all the questions and then add, "But this time it just didn't work."

It isn't that Satan doesn't try to bind a person who has been set free. But rather, that what had worked on you in the past no longer works. You have been loosed from its effectiveness.

In Mark 2:1-12 we read about a man who had palsy. Four of his friends brought him to Jesus and lowered him through the ceiling so Jesus could heal him. Jesus said to him, "Arise, and take up thy bed, and go thy way into thine house" (Mark 2:11). This man was carried to Jesus while he was lying on his bed. He left Jesus carrying his bed on his back. The two—the man and the bed—traded places!

We are never going to be entirely free of all problems. And, there are some specific problems from which we may not be entirely freed. But Jesus comes to heal us and deliver us so that the problem ceases to control us, diminish us, hold us back, or keep us down. Instead of the problem controlling us, we have control over the problem in the name of Jesus.

I believe that many people have been taught incorrectly about deliverance. As a result, they expect something that is unrealistic. They expect to walk down a prayer line and have somebody lay hands on them with such power that the devil will never be able to say another word to them for the rest of their lives. They think if they get in the right church or sit under the right ministry, they will become so mature in Christ that they will never be tempted again—they'll be completely "delivered" from any possibility of the devil ever getting their attention or speaking to them. It'll never happen. That isn't what deliverance means.

Deliverance means that the thing that used to control you is now under your control. Deliverance means that the thing that sat on the throne of your heart and ruled with power over your life has been dethroned and replaced by Jesus Christ. It still exists, but it isn't in charge.

Every now and then, Satan will attempt a coup. He'll try to regain control over the throne of your life. And at that point it is up to you to resist his effort and trust in God and exert control with your will. Satan isn't going to stop trying. Deliverance, however, puts you in position to keep him from succeeding.

For example, God isn't going to remove your temper from you. If you have struggled with angry outbursts and have desired to be delivered from your own temper, God will give you power over your tongue and control over your temper. But He isn't going to remove your temper from you. You need to have a temper or you would never feel compelled to rise up and do spiritual battle against evil. There's some evil in this world that you need to get "hot" about so you will pray against it and stand against it and battle against it in the spirit realm.

We find the word *wrath* linked to God in a number of places in the Bible. That word means "angry with fire." God gets angry with fire when He is challenged by evil or when He sees evil destroying His innocent children. It's good for you to get upset over evil when it comes at you.

What God will do in delivering you from your own temper is to impart to you the Holy Spirit's anointing in your life so you can deal with your temper and control it.

I once had a woman come to me and say, "Bishop, I have a problem with the flesh." Now there are many things that are rightfully associated with the flesh but when a person says that she has "problems with the flesh" we always tend to think of one thing, right? We think of sexual lust. She said, "Bishop, I want to be delivered from this flesh problem. I want you to pray that the Lord will just take it away!"

I said to her, "Are you sure that is what you want? Are you sure you don't ever want to feel any sexual feelings or sexual desires again?"

When I explained it like that, she had second thoughts! She didn't want to lose her sexuality; she just wanted to have control over her sexual desires and appetites. She wanted God to impart to her the power to say "no" to her own lust.

What we want is not to be a slave to our own passions, our own emotions, our own desires, our own appetites, but to enjoy them and let them serve to glorify God. That is the true nature of deliverance in the vast majority of cases.

From what do you desire to be delivered today?
Over what do you need to manifest the power of
the Holy Spirit in your life?

CHAPTER
TWENTY-SIX

An Inner
Work

He halted upon his thigh . . . because he touched the hollow of
Jacob's thigh. {Genesis 32:31,32}

acob wrestled with an angel of the Lord one night and came out of that experience with two things: the blessing of God and a limp in his walk. He limped all the rest of his life.

The limp didn't mean Jacob hadn't been blessed by God. It meant only that he had a limp.

Your struggle with sin doesn't mean that you aren't saved in your spirit or healed in your soul. It means only that you still have a limp.

And the fact is, you may never lose your limp entirely. Most of us won't.

We may learn to walk, and even to skip and run with our limp. We may learn to get around so well that nothing about our limp slows us down.

We may be able to get a built-up shoe that disguises our limp and enables us to function as near to normal as possible.

We may forget that our limp is there—it may come to mean absolutely nothing to us.

When that happens, and we feel no pain and no self-consciousness about our limp, then we are healed, even though the limp may remain.

My children recently saw a man who had lost the use of his legs. They said, "Why don't you come to have our daddy pray for you."

The man said, "Oh, I'm alright now. I am healed."

They didn't understand what he meant so he explained, "You see, when this first happened, I was in pain all of the time. I know I'm healed because it doesn't hurt any more."

Don't let the limp fool you. You can be healed and still have a limp. The limp is only a sign that you have been through something, not that you are still struggling with something or in pain over something.

If you can think about something and it doesn't hurt any more, you have been healed.

If you can talk about a painful experience in your past and it doesn't cause you to feel anger or hatred, you have been healed.

If you can see that person who wronged or hurt you and you don't feel bitterness, you have been healed.

You may still have scars on your body. You may still be divorced. You may still have a need. You may still have the "limp," but on the inside you have been healed.

Don't confuse the outer symptoms with the inner work. The symptoms are not what define you. What God has done in your innermost being is what defines you.

Don't let lingering symptoms fool you. Your deliverance is sure when the pain has been taken away from your heart.

CHAPTER
TWENTY-SEVEN

Loosed From Whom?

Lead us not into temptation, but deliver us from evil.
[Matthew 6:13]

 ong after I was saved, I still thought I needed to be delivered from the devil. The popular phrase at the time was, "The devil made me do it." Well, I didn't want the devil to make me do anything so I prayed hard to be delivered from the devil.

After a while I realized that the devil wasn't the problem. I stopped wasting my time and breath praying about the devil. I changed my prayer, "Lord, save me from me. Please don't let me kill my crazy self. Please don't let me do myself in—physically, emotionally, mentally, or any other way. Deliver me from my own evil tendencies."

Sometimes people don't blame the devil, but rather, they blame other people or a specific person or group of people. The greater fact is this: It isn't what people say about you or to you that's going to matter in the long run. It's what you say about yourself to yourself.

A spirit of infirmity is not a bondage that another person places on your life. It's not a bondage of chains and shackles and prison bars on the outside of you. It's a bondage on the inside. And you can't walk away from a bondage that is on the inside of you. It will keep you locked up . . . until you quit agreeing with the person who has mistreated you.

My wife and I counseled a woman that literally couldn't leave the house even though her wife-beating husband was gone. She'd get as far as the door and have an attack in which she could hardly breathe. His presence and his blows weren't the main reason she was in bondage. She was in bondage primarily because of the way she felt about herself. She had allowed his blows to beat down her self-esteem until there was virtually no self and no esteem left.

Jesus asked His disciples, "Who do men say that I am?" They gave Him all the latest gossip: Some say You are John, some say Elijah, some say Jeremiah, some say one of the other prophets. Jesus said, "I'm not concerned about what some say. Who do you say that I am?" (See Matthew 16:13–15.)

"Some say" won't hurt anybody.

"You say" will. It can make all the difference in your life.

So many people I know have made it their life's work to change somebody's opinion about them. They are determined to prove that they are worthy or valuable in that other person's eyes. Their goal in life is to show somebody that they are good, that they are a Christian, that they are important.

Never allow another person's good opinion of you to be your goal. The fact is, they might never like you. They may never approve of you, consider you to be important, or call you good. They may never change their opinion of you.

If you agree with the person who rejects you or abuses you, then you put yourself into bondage. If you say, "Yes, they were right to hit me—I'm worthy to be hit. Yes, they were right to leave me—I'm worthy to be left. Yes, they were right to hurt me—I'm worthy to be hurt" . . . then you are tying yourself up with their opinion rather than tying yourself into God's opinion of you. When their bad opinion of you becomes your bad opinion of you, there's a prison built inside your soul with only one prisoner in it—you.

Are you prepared to deal with the fact that the person you've spent your entire life trying to impress may never be impressed? Are you prepared to face the reality that from God's perspective, it doesn't matter one way or the other if he or she is impressed or not impressed?

I encourage you to come to the conclusion I reached a long time ago: People are crazy.

That's not a great theological truth but it's good practical common sense. You will never be able to figure out why some people do what they do. You'll never be able to predict all the foibles and quirks and eccentricities of human nature. You'll find yourself shaking your head all the way through life saying, "Why did she do that? Why did he allow that?" The only explanation is that people are crazy.

That's why God called you to worship Himself, not people. You won't get anywhere by worshiping a person, which is what you are doing if you are seeking that person's approval as the most defining opinion about your life.

You see, the wonderful thing about God is that He doesn't meet with the board or a committee before He decides to bless you. He doesn't have to get anybody else's approval before He pours out His love to you. He doesn't consult anybody about you!

Don't get me wrong—I like people. I just know what to expect and what not to expect from them. If you're not careful, the craziness of other people will drive you crazy. If you are going to deal effectively with people in this world, you have got to be able to work right alongside them but not allow yourself to be controlled or governed by their opinion of you.

The deliverance you likely need most is not a deliverance from the devil or a deliverance from another person. The deliverance you probably need most is a deliverance from something in your own heart and mind.

Ask the Lord today to open the prison doors of your own soul and set you free.

CHAPTER
TWENTY-EIGHT

Your
Tailor-Made
Infirmity

Woman, thou art loosed from thine infirmity.   *[Luke 13:12]*

very woman has her own tailor-made infirmity. The enemy has been studying you all your life, checking you out, figuring out which temptation will work best on you. He's not going to bring you ice cream if you like chocolate. He knows your weaknesses and what is most likely to tempt you to sin.

In case you haven't experienced this truth yet, let me tell you that church people are very prejudiced when it comes to sin. They tend to classify sin into two categories: acceptable and unacceptable. The particular sin you have will fall into the acceptable category if a person can relate to your sin—in other words, if he or she has that sin in their life, too. It will fall into the unacceptable category if it's not their particular weakness or experience.

They will forgive you quickly if it's something they can relate to, but if it's something they can't relate to, they will condemn you to hell without a judge, jury, or trial.

I once had an experience with another minister who I considered to be very arrogant and proud. Now, my father was from Mississippi and my mother was from Alabama so I have always considered myself to be a corn-bread, collard-green, down-home kind of guy. I consider myself an ordinary person. I don't need a lot of pomp and circumstance in my life. There's no report to be written on me. I'm just a guy who God uses and when it comes right down to it, I'm just a lump of clay in motion. I like to be "normal." I don't want to be put up on any pedestal.

This other man likes walking into a room and having everybody fall prostrate while they are singing "All Hail to Jesus." I'm exaggerating, of course—but not by much. He speaks in a deep resonating voice aimed at impressing anybody who hears him. People with super-inflated egos like that are a problem to me. You might even say my irritation with them is my infirmity. I want to get a little blow dart and aim it at them and pop their balloon and watch them fly into a fizzle all over the room.

Now this man didn't like me any more than I liked him. We were too civil to confront each other about our mutual dislike, but if I saw him coming, I'd veer left, and if he saw me coming, he'd veer right. We did our best to ignore each other. If we were forced to come face to face, we'd say, "Hi, brother! How are you? Praise the Lord!" and we'd go on our respective ways as quickly as possible.

One day the Lord spoke to me and said, "Do you know that problem you have with the minister you dislike so much?"

"Yes, Lord."

"It's your fault."

I nearly came unglued. "What? My fault? Do you know how arrogant and proud he is?"

I spent a considerable time telling the Lord how right I was and how wrong he was and how justified I was to hold my opinion. When I was done the Lord said, "Aren't you something? If that brother had a weakness in an area where you have a weakness, you'd have all the patience in the world with him. But the moment I send somebody into your life who has a weakness in an area where you are strong, you have the nerve to be judgmental."

I almost died. I could hardly breathe. I said, "Lord, I don't mind You doing surgery, but this time you punched a knife into my chest without an anesthetic."

God was right, of course. He always is.

We all tend to gravitate toward people who have our own infirmities. And there's a danger in that. If we hang around people who have our set of infirmities, we become codependent on them. We feed the sin in them and they feed the sin in us. We allow their weakness to continue and they allow our weakness to continue. Instead of healing one another, we make one another worse. It is God's mercy and God's plan to bring people into our lives who are strong in areas where we are weak, and people who are weak in areas where we are strong. That way we can help one another and bring balance to the body of Christ.

One of your greatest tests in life will be to live in a covenant relationship of God's love with a person who has a weakness that you don't have and to which you can't relate.

When Satan sends his demons out to oppress you, they already have a portfolio on you. They know just the right buttons to push in you. They know your particular infirmities.

Those demons know if your father never liked you . . . and if your mother approved of your older sister but not you . . .

and if your boyfriend rejected you and started going with your best friend . . .

and if a teacher held you up for ridicule. They have an entire profile worked up on you so that they won't have to waste time experimenting on which temptations are going to work best. They know where you are vulnerable.

Jesus said to the woman with a spirit of infirmity, "Woman, thou art loosed from thine infirmity." Jesus knew her exact infirmity. He knew the very thing that had her bound up and bent over.

He knows about your infirmity, too. His word to you today is, "I'm going to loose you."

Get ready for Him to do it.

Have you identified your infirmity? Are you ready for God to deliver you from it?

CHAPTER
TWENTY-NINE

Lose What You've Been Loosed From!

Go, and sin no more.   *[John 8:11]*

hen this woman was loosed from her infirmity, she was made straight immediately.

Don't make the error of thinking that your deliverance must take a long time. Change can happen in an instant. You can arrive immediately at an understanding of the truth. It's as if a light comes on.

In fact, I think the best form of change is sudden change. Years ago I smoked and I tried to quit smoking by cutting down to fifteen cigarettes a day and then ten and so forth. That was slow torture. One day I just threw the pack away and said, "I'm done with it." That was the end of cigarette smoking for me. The change was made!

Change means you were and now you aren't. Period.

You can be in an ungodly affair and leave that affair whether your partner in it agrees or disagrees, whether he's around or not. When you stop needing what it is that you were needing, the affair is over. When you are loosed from the need that drove you to that affair, you don't need to meet with that person or try to figure things out with that person. When you unhook from them inside yourself, you're free. You can just walk away and say, "I'm done with that. I'm not vulnerable in that way anymore."

There doesn't need to be any long, drawn-out discussion or any major confrontation or any redefining. As far as I'm concerned, you're better off without any of that. Just say, "I'm out of here" and be gone.

Now I'm not talking about husbands and wives. I'm talking about your association with ungodly people who have hurt you, rejected you, abused you, or used you. Once you are delivered, don't hang around. Get moving and get out. Get as far away as you can, as fast as you can.

People who have abused or used you aren't going to take kindly to your wanting to redefine your relationship with them. They've been on a power trip regarding you and they aren't interested in losing power or control. They aren't going to like the fact that you no longer are going to allow them to manipulate you.

Just leave.

Recognize, too, that any time God looses you from something, He has in mind something else to which He wants you to be attached. Things that are completely loosed—things that are totally on their own without any connection—die. They wither and shrivel up. Nothing can exist totally on its own and remain vital and alive.

If you pull a plant up out of the ground, it might look good for a day or two, but then it's going to wither and die. If you isolate a person and put her in an isolation chamber for very long, she'll curl up in a ball and be totally useless. We all need to be connected. It's a matter, however, of being connected to the right things. Connection isn't the issue. Connected to what is the issue.

If God looses you from an infirmity and you aren't reconnected to something good and positive in your life, you are likely to seek out any old reconnection. You might even go back to the thing to which you were originally connected just because it's familiar.

How many times do we see that happen? People are freed from a relationship that has been negative and they end up going right back to it because it's familiar—even though they don't want to return to that relationship, even though they know the person isn't right for them, even though they know God doesn't want that relationship in their life.

Often people will even reconnect with things they hate just for the sake of being reconnected. They don't like it, they don't want it, but they are used to it.

I've seen women go from one abusive relationship to another. They don't like being abused. But the pain of abuse has become familiar to them and they'd rather have the pain of abuse than remain disconnected.

Refuse to reconnect with your infirmity.

When you are loosed, stay loosed.

Don't allow yourself to go back into bondage.

Once you are free, stay free!

CHAPTER THIRTY

Give God Your Praise

She was made straight, and glorified God. [Luke 13:13]

hen this woman with a spirit of infirmity was loosed and made straight, she immediately glorified God. Nobody else. Only God.

I refuse to glorify anybody but God. I know that all of my needs are met by Him. I know that my identity comes from Him. I know that all my help and all my forgiveness have come from Him.

Therefore, don't try to put a guilt trip on me for not acknowledging all that you think you may have done for me. It won't work. I'm not going to give you any other credit than the fact that God may have used you to bless me. He's my Helper. He's my Deliverer.

Father, I stretch my hands to Thee.

I know You will remember Me.

When others forget and leave me all alone,

I know that Jesus, Jesus, Jesus will hear my
  groan.

When you give all the glory and all the thanks and all the praise to God for delivering you, people may not understand what you are doing or just why you are so excited. The main reason is that they don't truly know how you feel. They don't know what it's like to have had your particular infirmity, much less what it was like to have had your particular infirmity year after year after year. This woman had suffered with her infirmity for eighteen years. She had been crippled and bent over for so long she didn't know what it was like to look up. Once she was made straight, she couldn't help but give God the glory!

That will be true for you when you are loosed from your infirmity. Other people may not understand. They don't know how you felt then, so they can't understand how you feel now that you're delivered. That's alright.

The way you praise God is the way you praise God. You may want to yell . . .

or cry . . .

or sing . . .

or shout . . .

or dance!

You may want to praise Him with musical instruments. You may want to fall on your face or run like the wind. Praise Him the way you want to praise Him. Don't worry about what other people think of your praise. Get out your praise and give God the glory!

Let me assure you that when drug addicts and homosexuals and adulterers are delivered, they get happy. They can shout praise louder than any other people I know. They know from what they've been delivered! They know it is God who delivered them! They aren't the least bit bashful about giving God their praise.

Your praise is likely to be related directly to your former pain. The greater the pain, the greater your praise. If you have never been bound, you have no idea how good it feels to be free.

Don't criticize another person for being too emotional in praise. You haven't walked in their shoes. So you can't understand why they are now dancing in their shoes.

If you are in a church that won't let you praise God openly, get into a church that will let you praise Him. God is worthy of our praise. He commands us to praise Him. He dwells in the praises of His people. He delights in your praise.

Praise God loud and long today for all that He has done for you!

CHAPTER
THIRTY-ONE

Don't Break
Your Rhythm

I will bless the LORD at all times: his praise shall continually be in my mouth. {Psalm 34:1}

 on't break your rhythm of praise for anybody. No matter what you hear said about you . . .

No matter how people may look at you . . .

No matter what happens . . .

Keep your praise going!

This woman's deliverance caused the ruler of the synagogue to feel indignation. He spoke out against her miracle.

People may not like your deliverance either.

But . . .

It doesn't matter if some people don't speak to you any more . . .

or if some people don't come to visit you anymore . . .

or if some people don't seem to understand you . . .

or if some people don't call you.

You have been loosed by God and therefore, you have a right granted to you by God to stand straight and praise!

Are you aware that you have a God-given privilege to praise God as much as you want? And furthermore, you can be as emotional as you want to be in your praise? Find a place where you can praise God the way you want to praise Him!

People fall all over themselves with excitement about having won a prize on a TV game show, a prize they are going to have to pay taxes on and which they probably can't even use . . . and the world thinks that's okay.

People jump up and down and hug total strangers because their team won the big game in the last few seconds on the game clock—a game that will only be important to them until next week, a game for which they won't even be able to recall the score a month from now . . . and the world says such behavior is normal.

But let people get excited about the way God has delivered them, and let them praise Him with a little emotion—knowing that their lives have been changed for all eternity and that the deepest infirmity of their life no longer has control over them . . . and the world will call them lunatics.

Don't worry about what the world says. For that matter, don't worry about what someone in the church says. You have the privilege and right to praise the God of your deliverance—so praise the Lord!

This woman did the wise thing. She kept her rhythm and let Jesus deal with those who were upset at her deliverance. While she was glorifying God, Jesus dealt with her enemies.

While you are praising God today, the Lord is fighting the battle for you in the heavenlies. He is dealing with the enemy of your soul. He is pulverizing the demonic powers that sought to oppress you and bind you and keep you from God's blessings.

Your praise isn't just an expression of your joy. You actually are doing battle in the spirit realm. While you are praising God, swoop, the angels of God are coming into your hospital room. Swoop, the angels of God are surrounding your child. Swoop, the angels of God are stopping your enemy in his tracks. Swoop, the angels of God are scattering your enemy!

Have you ever praised God—singing and rejoicing—as you drove your car and suddenly, you felt as if you weren't alone? The fact is, you weren't. Swoop, God's angels were there right by your side. You may not see them, but they are there! The Bible says that "the angel of the LORD encampeth round about them that fear him, and delivereth them" (Psalm 34:7).

It's difficult to imagine that someone would get upset that this woman had been healed. It seems that as long as this woman was bent over and needed their help, the people in that synagogue didn't have a problem with her. But as soon as she stood straight and started glorifying God, she became a problem.

And yet, is that any different from what many women experience today?

There are those who like to surround themselves with weak, sick, needy people. But if a woman stands up straight and praises God, they don't quite know what to do with her.

If people are upset with your deliverance and your praise, consider their "upset-ness" to be their problem. Don't try to explain yourself or justify your praise. Don't try to show them how the healed, healthy you is better than the sick you. Just stay standing and keep praising.

There's an undercurrent of criticism that always coexists with praise.

There will always be somebody in every praise service who is sitting in the corner criticizing the praise. That critical person may be in your own home—criticizing you as you sing praises to God in the shower. That person may be in your social group—criticizing you for giving thanks and praise to God in the flow of normal conversation. That person may be someone at your place of employment—criticizing you for giving praise to God during a coffee break.

Don't pay any attention to them. This woman apparently didn't. She didn't say, "Oh, since you object to what has happened to me, I'll just take on this spirit of infirmity again. I'll just stoop over again in my crippled position for another eighteen years."

Don't give in to the criticism that other people may have about your deliverance. Don't listen to their protests, their murmuring, their gossip, or their attempt to rationalize away your deliverance. Don't let them hurt your feelings or inhibit you.

Sometimes you just have to praise God in the midst of background noise!

Stay standing tall. Keep praising. Continue to glorify God regardless of what others may say.

CHAPTER
THIRTY-TWO

Secure Your Deliverance

Stand fast in the faith . . . be strong.   *[1 Corinthians 16:13]*

esus responded to the man who criticized His deliverance of the woman who had a spirit of infirmity. He said, "Thou hypocrite, doth not each one of you on the sabbath loose his ox or his ass from the stall, and lead him away to watering? And ought not this woman, being a daughter of Abraham, whom Satan hath bound, lo, these eighteen years, be loosed from this bond on the sabbath day?" (Luke 13:15–16)

Oxen were considered very profitable to farmers in those days. They were work animals. The ass was not considered to be as valuable. The ass was often stubborn and contentious, and was useful for very little. Jesus said, "You will loose not only your valuable animal, but your nearly worthless animal on the Sabbath, and yet complain that a human being has been delivered?"

People seem to get very excited when talented folk are delivered. They don't get as excited when ordinary people are set free from their infirmities.

I've got good news for you today—God doesn't make that differentiation. He desires to see needs met for both the highly talented and lesser talented. Your deliverance does not depend upon the scope of your future usefulness or your future ministry. God delivers you because He loves you.

God has delivered countless people who have never written a book about their experience, or who never have gone on to lead the choir or sing a solo or chair a committee or teach a Sunday school class. God's deliverance is not contingent upon what you will do after you are delivered.

This woman of infirmity is never mentioned again. Nevertheless, Jesus delivered her.

I want you to notice also that Jesus reminded them that they kept their ox and ass in stalls. They were not kept close to where the water was flowing freely. If they had been kept close to the flow of water, there would have been no need to loose them on the Sabbath.

Stalls are built by men. They are designed to keep animals closed off and separated. There are stalls today that are man-made. They are used to divide and separate people. They are made to keep people from moving into areas where they can get what they need. People try to keep other people "in their place" so they can control them—so they can lead them to what it is that they want them to have, and to nothing else.

When you are delivered by God, you may need to say "no" to those who have kept you in a stall of their own making.

You may have to say, "I'm free and I'm not going back into that cage."

You may have to say, "I've decided to live close to the living water of the Holy Spirit and I'm not going to be put into a position where I have to rely on you or anybody else to lead me to what it is that you think I need or don't need."

There's a freedom that comes with deliverance that you must secure for yourself. You must refuse to be put back into a stall that keeps you from the things you need, and especially those things that you need on the Sabbath! You must stay close to the water. Stay close to where you can be refreshed.

When God delivers you, He wants you to be delivered from the entire environment in which you were kept cooped up and chained.

If God delivers you from an addiction, He desires to deliver you from the entire environment that contributed to your addiction in the first place. You're going to have to disassociate yourself from the person who dealt drugs to you and used drugs with you and encouraged you to think you needed drugs in the first place. You're going to have to move out of that circle, that environment, maybe even that neighborhood. Get out of the stall! Go where you can be refreshed in the Lord and stay there.

Once you are loosed by Jesus, refuse to return to the place where you were in bondage.

PART V

Loosed and Made Whole

A WOMAN WITH A PROBLEM

A woman who had hemorrhaged for twelve years made her way to Jesus one day. This woman had one of those problems that just wouldn't go away. She had sought help from many physicians, but none of them had been able to help her. As a result, not only was her health worse, but she had spent all of her money.

She faced not only the challenge of forcing her way through the crowd, but the stigma of being considered "unclean"—an outcast, an impure woman. She refused to let either challenge keep her from Jesus. When she touched the hem of His garment, she was healed just as she had believed she would be.

Jesus said to her that her faith had made her whole—not only healed in her body, but fully restored in every area of her life.

From the Scriptures:

And a certain woman, which had an issue of blood twelve years,

And had suffered many things of many physicians, and had spent all that she had, and was nothing bettered, but rather grew worse,

When she had heard of Jesus, came in the press behind, and touched his garment.

For she said, If I may touch but his clothes, I shall be whole.

And straightway the fountain of her blood was dried up; and she felt in her body that she was healed of that plague.

And Jesus, immediately knowing in himself that virtue had gone out of him, turned him about in the press, and said, Who touched my clothes?

And his disciples said unto him, Thou seest the multitude thronging thee, and sayest thou, Who touched me?

And he looked round about to see her that had done this thing.

But the woman fearing and trembling, knowing what was

done in her, came and fell down before him, and told him all the truth.

And he said unto her, Daughter, thy faith hath made thee whole; go in peace, and be whole of thy plague.

[Mark 5:25-34]

CHAPTER
THIRTY-THREE

The Drain on Your Life

*And a certain woman, which had an issue of blood twelve
years.*   *{Mark 5:25}*

don't know her name. I don't know who her father was or who
her husband was. I don't know where she lived or how she lived.
I don't know if she was rich or poor.

She could have been any woman. She may have been every
woman. The Bible refers to her only as a woman with an "issue of blood."
The Lord may have referred to her in such a generic manner so that any
woman could relate to her and put their name in her place.

To have an issue of blood is normal for a woman. This woman's problem
was that her issue of blood had lasted too long. She is a woman who had a
problem that lingered. It didn't go away. It stayed around, and then stayed on
and stayed on.

Have you ever had a problem that lasted too long?

Have you ever had a problem about which you said, "I'll surely be over
this by such and such a date. I'll have come out of this by then and have gone
on with my life"?

Have you ever said, "By this time in my life, I surely will be married . . .
I will have had children . . .

 I will have made my mark in life . . .

 I will have entered fully into my ministry . . .

 I will have accomplished what God created me to do"?

Problems that stay around too long are problems that drain away your life.
That's what happened to this woman. She had had an issue of blood for
twelve years. Her life had drained away from her.

When a problem stays around too long it isn't only the problem that grates
on you, but the longevity of the problem. The problem may be the same old
problem, but if it stays on and on and on, then that problem is compounded.
Any time you try to confront the problem, it will whip out its résumé and remind you that you have tried that solution before, you have been to that
source of help before, and it didn't work.

Your problem will begin to speak to you, "I'm here to stay forever. Nothing you can do will get rid of me. You might as well get used to me because

I'm not budging. Everything you have tried has failed. Nothing is going to work. I am your problem for the rest of your life."

Your problem will remind you of a pattern of failure in your life. It will remind you of how you grew up and give you all the details of every failed relationship you have ever been in. That's because your problem has been engineered by the devil. The enemy always loves to brag about how long he has been around.

Your issue may not be of blood—in fact, it probably won't be an issue of blood. Whatever it is, however, it is like this woman's problem if it is draining the life out of you, if it's diminishing your vitality, your sparkle, your energy, your enthusiasm for living. If it isn't money, it's the children. If it isn't the children, it's the spouse. If it isn't the spouse, it's the lack of a spouse. If it isn't that, it's something else.

Your issue may be a secret in the family . . . a secret on the job . . .
a secret in the church . . .
  a secret from your past . . .
    a secret that involves somebody you are
    hoping will stay a secret.

Your issue today may be a need—it may be a need to touch Jesus for salvation. It may be a need to touch Him for healing in your body. It may be a need to touch Him for a restoration or reconciliation in your marriage. It may be a need to touch Him for a blessing in your family. It may be a need to touch Him for a job. It may be a need to touch Him for a miracle in your ministry.

I don't know what your issue is, but I know this: every woman has one. There's always something. Look deep enough, look long enough, listen hard enough, watch closely enough, be sensitive enough . . . and you'll discover it. You may be in denial about your own problem. Look deep into your own heart, listen to your own talk . . . you'll find it.

It is your life-draining issue that Jesus wants to heal.

Identify today what it is that is consuming and draining your life. Then take your "issue" to God.

CHAPTER THIRTY-FOUR

Own Up to Your Problem, and Take It to Jesus!

When she had heard of Jesus, [she] came in the press behind . . .
[Mark 5:27]

he woman with an issue of blood had experienced twelve years of hurting, pain, suffering.

While other people around her were laughing, she was in pain.

While other people around her were having a good time, she was in pain.

While other people around her were making plans, she was thinking, I'm not sure I can go on like this.

In any group of women you happen to be in, look around. There are women who are there in pain. They may not identify themselves. You may not be able to tell from the outside that they are suffering. But they are hurting nonetheless.

One of the main reasons women don't share their problems is this: They are told they shouldn't have problems, especially after they are saved.

Church people will say or imply, "If you were really saved, you wouldn't have this problem."

In the eleventh chapter of Hebrews, we find a list of people who are often called the heroes of the faith. On that list you'll see Noah and Abraham and Sarah and Isaac and Jacob and Joseph and Moses and Rahab and Gideon and Samson and David and Samuel and all the prophets. The amazing thing to me is that every one of these giants of faith had a problem! Problems are a part of life.

The Bible says that some of these heroes of the faith were tortured and mocked and scourged and imprisoned and stoned and sawn asunder. Now I've been cut a few times, but I have never been sawn asunder.

It says they were afflicted and tormented, and that some of them wandered in deserts and lived in caves. I've lived in some poor places, but I've never lived in a cave.

God's people have problems. We need to face up to that. It's not a matter of lack of faith or of not being saved. It's a matter of life in a fallen world. Problems come with the turf of a world that has been turned upside down by sin.

This woman's problem was a private problem. It was not a public problem. It was a problem that could be covered up.

Oh, we are so good at hiding our problems. Not long ago I was in a meeting where the women looked so fine, you wouldn't have thought any of them had a worry in the world. In fact, if I could have exchanged the offering at that meeting for the amount of money those women had spent on their hairdos, I gladly would have made the exchange. They were wearing silk dresses and diamond jewelry and sequined jackets. They were looking good.

But I wasn't fooled. I knew that every imaginable secret was present in that room. That room was filled with private problems.

Various dignitaries and notable people were introduced from the platform that night. But I knew the names of many of the guests sitting out in the audience.

Sister Rape was present.

Sister Child Abuse came along.

Sister on Crack Cocaine was there.

Sister Battered Wife was there, too.

Sister Lesbian showed up.

Sister Oppressed attended.

Sister Depressed was sitting right by her side.

All the girls were present that night!

They are present in any large gathering of women anywhere in our nation at any time.

The fact that you have a problem is not what matters most. What matters is this: What you choose to do about your problem.

This woman made the right choice about where to take her problem.

Now, she didn't make the right choice immediately. She made it ultimately, but she didn't make it immediately.

Part of this woman's problem was that she had suffered for twelve years not only with the issue of blood but at the hand of physicians. The Bible says that she had "suffered many things of many physicians, and had spent all that she had, and was nothing bettered, but rather grew worse" (Mark 5:26).

It's one thing to have a problem and another thing to have a problem with all the people who are trying to tell you how to fix your problem. By the time she got finished with those who gave her advice, but no real help, she was worse off than she was before—because at that point she didn't have any money left!

Be careful who it is that you let treat you. That person who is so eager to treat you may just be after your money. They may just want to be able to tell others that you are their patient.

Be careful who it is that you trust to help you. That person may not be worthy of your trust.

Be careful who it is that becomes your confidant. That person may gossip about you to everybody she meets.

Beware of the counsel of the ungodly. They'll give you plenty of advice, but they can't give you any lasting help.

The ungodly counselor is not a good counselor—not about things that truly matter, not about things that affect your spirit, not about things that are eternal. David said, "Blessed is the person who walks not according to the counsel of the ungodly, nor aligns herself with sinners, nor sits in the seat of those who are scornful of the things of God." (See Psalm 1:1.)

This woman had put her trust, her faith, her hope in people who could not help her. They may have been able to describe her problem. But they had no ability to prescribe her solution.

If you are going to seek out someone to help you, seek out someone who knows the Answer. Find someone who will say to you, "Jesus is on the way. Jesus is coming. Jesus is the Healer. Jesus is the Problem-Solver. Jesus is the One who can dry up the problem that is draining you dry. Reach out and touch Him by your faith!"

Let the problem in your life hear you say, "Jesus is going to deal with you." Let the problem-causer, the enemy himself, hear you say, "Jesus is coming. And I'm not hanging around here with you any longer. I'm going to get to Him no matter what it takes."

Take your problem today to the Source of your solution. Take your problem to Jesus! Jesus has the overflow that can put a stop to your problem flow.

CHAPTER THIRTY-FIVE

Yes, A Woman Like You!

Him that cometh to me I will in no wise cast out.   [John 6:37]

 hen this unclean, bleeding woman heard that Jesus was coming, she had to come to grips with this question, "Can a woman like me touch a God like Him?"

You see . . .

The Law said that she was unclean.

The Law said that she wasn't supposed to touch anybody, much less a man, much less a rabbi.

She was considered to be lethal to a priest.

But this woman didn't pay any attention to what other people had to say about her. She refused to feel dirty about herself.

If you feel dirty about yourself, your ability to touch God is diminished—not because of anything that God has said, and not because God will reject you or deny you access to Himself. No! Your ability to touch God will be diminished because you won't reach out for Him.

The woman who feels dirty and unclean doesn't feel worthy to receive the miracle she needs. Oh, she needs the miracle alright, and she knows she needs it. But she doesn't feel worthy to receive the miracle so she doesn't pray like she needs to pray . . .

she won't praise like she needs to praise . . .

she won't worship like she needs to worship . . .

she won't reach out to seize the moment like she needs to seize the moment. A woman who feels dirty, unclean, unworthy is a woman who is going to sit on the sidelines with her problem.

When a woman has suffered from rejection, it affects the way she feels about God. She isn't sure that God will like her, that God will receive her, that God will help her.

You must reach the place where you know with certainty in your own life that God's love is for you. You must reach a place of understanding in which you say, "Yes! A woman with a past . . .

can touch a God in the present

who is able to change the future."

It's time to take a look at yourself and declare to the person you see in your own mirror, "It can be done."

In spite of your personal history . . .

  in spite of the problem . . .

    in spite of the circumstances . . .

      in spite of what others say . . .

God can be touched by YOU. And He wants to be touched by you.

In spite of your heartache . . .

In spite of your pain . . .

In spite of your depression . . .

You can get to Jesus with the feelings of your infirmities. You can touch Him.

Never let your past reputation or the nature of your problem keep you from going to God and asking for a miracle!

CHAPTER THIRTY-SIX

Seize the Miracle Moment

She said, If I may touch but his clothes, I shall be whole.
[Mark 5:28]

I like this woman with the issue of blood. She knew how to seize the moment.

We each need to learn how to seize the moment in the spirit realm. There are moments when the anointing is so strong in a meeting, you can almost cut it with a knife. It is at those times that you need to seize the moment. If you miss the moment, you may miss out on the miracle you need. There are too many things I need God to do for me to sit back in my seat when the anointing of God starts to fall. I want to jump right in. I can't afford for any of my miracles to pass me by.

This woman knew she was at the end of the line. She was out of health . . .

out of money . . .

out of physicians . . .

out of people who

could minister to her.

But, she wasn't out of faith.

She had run out of everything in her life but the one thing she needed. She had her belief that if she could only touch the hem of Jesus' garment, she'd be made whole.

This woman did not have any other human being helping her. Nobody was counseling her. Nobody was lobbying for her. Nobody was running interference for her. Nobody was ministering to her. She had nobody . . . she only had one person who could preach to her: herself.

Is that where you are today?

This sick, bleeding, wounded woman—weak in her body but not in her spirit—began to preach to herself. She said, "If I may but touch."

There are times when you have to encourage yourself. You can't sit and wait for somebody to rescue you. You have to get up and do what you can to rescue yourself!

She announced to the devil, "You may have caused something to be wrong with my body, but there's nothing wrong with my head. There's nothing wrong with my spirit. I know what to do. I know what to believe."

When the Bible says that she "said," the tense of that word means that she said and she said and she said. She kept on talking to herself. She told herself over and over and over again, "If I may touch but his clothes, I shall be whole."

She kept saying, "I can't die yet. I've got to touch Him. I can't give up yet. I've got to touch Him. I can't lay down and surrender yet. I've got to touch Him. And if I can't touch Him—if only I can touch His clothes—I shall be whole!"

I know people today are only alive because they are living on "If I may but touch" faith.

Touching Jesus today is all that matters.

There's nothing you can do about yesterday.

There's nothing you can do about all those lost years.

There's nothing you can do about all that wasted money.

There's nothing you can do about what people say.

There's something you can do, however, about touching Jesus.

This woman said, "I know that if I can get to Jesus, I shall be whole."

She may have had a little doubt about whether she had enough strength to get through the crowd. She may have had a question about whether she could get close enough to touch Him. She may have had some self-doubts.

But she had no doubt about Jesus. She knew that if she could get to Him, He would heal her. She believed with every ounce of her being that if she could only make contact, she would be whole.

She knew that she didn't need any other physician . . .

any other counselor . . .

any other helper . . .

any other person to minister to her . . .

if she could just get to Jesus.

Let there be no doubt in your heart today. Jesus IS the One. He IS the Healer. He IS the Savior. He IS the Deliverer.

*Seize the opportunity that God is giving you
to touch Him!*

CHAPTER
THIRTY-SEVEN

Press On!

[She] came in the press behind, and touched his garment.
                                                    —Mark 5:27

he woman with the issue of blood faced two major challenges. One was the challenge of confronting her own self-doubt, Can a woman like me touch a God like Him? The answer to that question is always "yes."

The second challenge she faced was getting through the crowd.

Once you make up your mind to get to Jesus, the devil will do everything he can to put obstacles in your way.

There's always the flesh realm that you have to break through to get to God in the spirit realm.

You have to say to those who doubt what you are doing, "Excuse me, but I'm on my way to Jesus no matter what you say."

You have to say to those who want you to stop and stroke their egos, "Excuse me, but I don't have time for your games. I'm on my way to Jesus."

You have to say to those who offer you their expert but ungodly opinions, "Excuse me, but I know where I'm going and if you'll just step out of my path, I'll be on my way."

Don't let anything stand in your way. Step right over everything of the flesh that the devil puts in your way and keep pushing forward to Jesus.

When justice says you can't get to Him, God's mercy lets you by.

When the Law tries to stop you, God's grace opens up a door.

When the world says, "Don't go," the Spirit of God says, "Come on!"

Our part is to press.

God's part is to make a way, to open up a path.

The enemy may be telling you that it is impossible for you to get up, get out, or get on with your life. I'm here to tell you that the devil is a liar!

This woman pressed through the crowd. She pressed through the naysayers and the doom-sayers.

She pressed through the doctor's report
    and the pile of bills
    and the laws that were
    intended to shut her out.

She made her way through the crowd of
    doubters
    and discouragers
    and the bad-news reporters.
She pressed right on through the drug dealers
    on her doorstep,
    the pimps on her corner,
    and the gang circling her car.
She pressed through!

When this woman with an issue of blood touched Jesus, she touched His life. His life poured into every area of her body in which life had been draining away to nothing. His life filled up her lack of life.

And His life will fill up your lack of life when you touch Him today.

***Press on to God today. Don't let any thing or any
person stop you!***

PART VI

Loosed to Live in the Now

GOD'S BABY GIRL

God spoke through the prophet Ezekiel to tell His people how He regarded them—as if they were a baby girl who had been cast away upon her birth. God found her—unwanted, uncared for—in an open field, exposed to ridicule, destined to die. He called to her to live. He cared for her, washed her, salted her, and wrapped her up in swaddling clothes.

God said, however, that His baby girl hadn't been destined to remain a baby. She was intended to grow up and mature and become a mother. Just as He had nurtured her, she was to nurture others. Just as He had ministered to her, she was to minister to others. His image of her was not of her past, but of her present. He expected her to be a "woman in the now."

From the Scriptures:

And say, Thus saith the Lord God unto Jerusalem; Thy birth and thy nativity is of the land of Canaan; thy father was an Amorite, and thy mother an Hittite.

And as for thy nativity, in the day thou wast born thy navel was not cut, neither wast thou washed in water to supple thee; thou wast not salted at all, nor swaddled at all.

None eye pitied thee, to do any of these unto thee, to have compassion upon thee; but thou wast cast out in the open field, to the loathing of thy person, in the day that thou wast born.

And when I passed by thee, and saw thee polluted in thine own blood, I said unto thee when thou wast in thy blood, Live; yea, I said unto thee when thou wast in thy blood, Live.

I have caused thee to multiply as the bud of the field, and thou hast increased and waxen great, and thou art come to excellent ornaments: thy breasts are fashioned, and thine hair is grown, whereas thou wast naked and bare.

Now when I passed by thee, and looked upon thee, behold, thy time was the time of love; and I spread my skirt over thee, and covered thy nakedness: yea, I sware unto thee, and entered into a covenant with thee, saith the Lord GOD, and thou becamest mine.

—*Ezekiel 16:3–8*

CHAPTER THIRTY-EIGHT

We All Are Born "Unclean"

*Except a man be born of water and of the Spirit, he cannot
enter into the kingdom of God.* —*John 3:5*

n Ezekiel 16, the Lord likens His people to an abandoned baby
girl. He says, "When I first saw you, you were a mess. You had
been birthed, but you hadn't been cared for. You had been
through the birth canal, but you hadn't been cleaned up." God
says, "I was shocked at your neglect—the things you should have received
but which you hadn't received. You were born, but you had not been
washed."

Being a man, I didn't know very much about the birthing process before
my wife became pregnant. Going into that delivery room for the first time
was a trip!

I'm a veteran now. I just put on that mask and walk in there and say, "Step
aside. I'm ready to deliver that baby." I don't deliver the baby, of course, but
I feel ready to do it!

Before my first experience in the delivery room, the only newborn babies
I had seen were ones I had seen on television. Those babies on television
come out weighing about twenty pounds and they have full heads of hair.
They are holding suckers and looking all around and talking to the nurses—
all the time with big smiles on their faces. The babies on television all are
born looking like the Gerber baby-food babies.

That was what I was expecting.

I was so shocked!

When my wife pushed out that baby I nearly screamed. I was rebuking the
devil and calling for the blood to be removed and the gook to disappear. That
baby didn't look at all like what I expected.

When they washed the baby, however, she started looking pretty good. I
said, "Yeah, this might be alright after all."

The appearance of the baby wasn't the baby's fault. The fact is . . . she
looked just like what she had been through!

The church has been trying to birth Gerber babies for centuries. But newborn babes in Christ don't look like that. They look like what they've just
been through. They have just pushed their way through all kinds of mess to

get to God and when they arrive in the church, they still have some of that mess clinging to them. We must not be shocked at this. Rather, we must be prepared to clean them up and care for them.

The church, by its very definition, attracts hurting people, just as a hospital attracts sick people. I recently told the congregation of my church, "Everybody in here is sick. If you're not sick, get out. Because the criteria for getting in here is that you know you are sick. Those who do not think they are sick do not feel any need for the Great Physician."

I want to be surrounded by people who know they need God. I don't have any desire at all to be around people who think that God is a theological, fanciful, abstract concept and who think it is nice to dress up and go someplace on Sunday. I want to be surrounded by those who are lame, deaf, blind, incapacitated, restricted, handicapped people who feel a need for God every hour of every day.

Jesus was attracted to hurting people. He didn't hang around the religious people who thought they were clean. He said, "You may be clean on the outside, but inside you are filthy." (See Matthew 23:25.)

At least hurting people know they are hurting. They know they are a mess when they are birthed.

Unfortunately for women, it seems the church has a special desire to see that its female babies look like Gerber babies. A double standard has developed. A man can come into the church with a long string of sins trailing behind him and the prevailing attitude is, "Well, boys will be boys. Naughty, naughty. He finally quit sowing his wild oats. Praise God." But if a woman has had two or three babies by different men and then she comes into the church and word of her past gets out, people treat her as if she has leprosy.

Pastors often make elaborate altar calls to bring in afflicted people, but once those afflicted people are saved and become a part of the church, we seem embarrassed to have them in our midst.

A shroud of secrecy is put around those who have had pasts that we are ashamed to recognize. If a woman has been scarred, raped, abused, molested, or been involved in unnatural affection, she dare not admit it.

Do you remember the woman who was taken in adultery and was brought to Jesus for Him to judge? The Bible says that the woman was caught "in the very act" of committing adultery. (See John 8:3-4.) Now if she was caught in the act, there had to have been a man there! But nobody brought him half-naked and wrapped in a blanket to a public place in the presence of the Lord. Nobody seemed ready to stone him to death although they all were eager to put her to death. The man apparently was allowed to take a shower, shave, dress himself, and crawl out the back window.

Do you know how horrifying it is to have other people judge your sins? Have you experienced that in your life? I know you have. We all have. People tend to be merciful toward their own sins, but when it comes to your sins, your reputation, your guilt . . . they can be ruthless.

We have placed a veil over the feminine heart in our churches. We insist that women smile and look good and say, "I'm living a victorious life in Christ." We allow them no opportunity to say, "I'm hurting. I'm wounded. I'm struggling."

When a painful issue arises in a woman's life, or in the life of her child, or in the life of her sister . . . she doesn't tell anybody. She is forced to keep a secret because no platform has been created that allows women to be real with one another without fear of being "stoned" to death. The secrets that lie untold in women's hearts are killing the church.

Can you imagine a woman coming into your church and saying during a testimony service, "I was abused as a child. I was the victim of incest and then when I got a little older I was raped. I've had four children now by three different husbands. I've had about twenty-nine boyfriends in my life and I'm presently divorced and trying hard to raise my kids. I know the Lord has saved me and here I am. I'm struggling, but I know I'm saved."

No, we expect a woman to say, "Praise God, He's with me all the time and He makes every minute of my life glorious and I thank Him for the opportunity to serve as chairman of this committee."

It's time to get real.

It's time that people heard your real testimony.

What drove you to the altar?

What nightmare experience drove you to fall upon His mercy and cry out to God?

Nobody cries out "Save me!" unless they are drowning.

It's time that we start looking at each other with an eye toward seeing what they've been through. It's time we see their brokenness and their heartache. It's time we see their tenacity, their ability, their faith. It's time to look inside ourselves and inside one another and to admit, "We all are born 'unclean.' "

Take a look at someone today and see her as God sees her. See all that has made her who she is, and then look even deeper to see all that God has created her to be!

CHAPTER
THIRTY-NINE

Cut the Cord

As for thy nativity, in the day thou wast born thy navel was not cut. —*Ezekiel 16:4*

 od said that when He first saw His baby girl she hadn't even had the umbilical cord cut away from her body. And that's the state for many newborn Christians. They are still tied to something in their past. They are still linked to things that they need to break away from. They are still being fed emotionally by relationships that need to be severed.

The cord to the past is cut only when a woman realizes that what she needs, she can get from a better source. We need to hold out to women the love and forgiveness and healing power of God. We need to encourage her to come to El Shaddai—the Breasted One—to receive the nurture that she needs. We need to show her how to draw from God a flow of life that will replace and nullify her need for her former life.

So often I want to tell women, "Go out and buy yourself a pair of scissors and write on it, 'Cut the cord!' " There are things you need to cut away from your life. There are relationships that you need to sever. There are habits that you need to amputate from your daily life.

Don't allow a guilt trip from the past to strangle you or cling to you or trip you up. Cut the cord!

God wants to free you from cords of manipulation . . .

cords of blackmail . . .

cords of emotional slavery . . .

cords of bondage to someone who

seeks to control your life.

Cut the cord that ties you to the old mud holes of your past.

If a little lamb and a pig fall into the same fly-infested, dirty, oozing mud hole, the pig will wallow in the mud, but the lamb will cry to get out. It's the same mud but a different nature.

If you are a child of God and you fall in the mud, you'll start to cry, "I don't like this. I want out of this. I'm not really like this. I hate this! Help me!"

The fact that you fall into the mud or someone throws you into the mud is not the issue. What you do when you are in the mud is what matters.

Say goodbye to Joe's Bar and Ruby's Lounge.
Say goodbye to the pimp and the pusher.
Say goodbye to the drinking girls and gambling friends.
Put that addiction . . .
  that abortion . . .
    that sickness . . .
      that divorce . . .
        that failure . . .
          that loss . . .
            behind you!

Pronounce your own benediction on your former life. Pronounce your own last rites on your failures. Conduct your own funeral for the "old person" you were before you were saved.

Declare that the old you—the you who existed before God found you and cleaned you up and grew you up to be His woman—is dead. She doesn't exist anymore.

Declare that the old sinful patterns of your life, the old sin-producing relationships in your life are dead and gone. They don't exist for you anymore. Declare any dominating evil spirit evicted from your life. The only spirit He wants at work in your life is the Holy Spirit!

Declare that you are a new creature in Christ Jesus. The old you has died and has been buried. The new you is being resurrected!

As you cut the cord get ready for a
new enthusiasm . . .
  a new outpouring of faith . . .
    a new freshness of anointing!
  God will release you to live in freedom.

***Being born again means you are out of the womb
of sin. Cut the ties that will seek to draw you
back into darkness.***

CHAPTER FORTY

Washed, Salted, and Swaddled

Neither wast thou washed in water to supple thee; thou wast not salted at all, nor swaddled at all. —Ezekiel 16:4

he Lord was shocked that His little baby girl had not been washed. It's not the baby's responsibility to wash itself. It's not the newly saved person's responsibility to wash herself. It's our responsibility.

How should we care for a new babe in Christ?

First, we must do some washing. The Bible says we are washed by the water of His Word. (See Ephesians 5:26.) When we give the Word of God to a new babe in Christ, we wash that person. So many women have been helped by the simple application of the words of Jesus, "Woman, thou art loosed." That word of God is powerful to them; it washes something off them, out of them, and away from them.

The Word of God, spoken in mercy and by the power of the Holy Spirit, regenerates us. (See Titus 3:5.)

Second, we must do some salting. In Bible times, salt was rubbed into the skin of a newborn baby. When someone tells us today, "You have the skin of a baby," we start grinning and take it as a great compliment. Let me remind you of something you know—the skin of a newborn baby can be anything but beautiful. It can be red and chapped and bruised and peeling. Salt was applied to both heal and toughen the skin. Salting allowed the baby to be handled without bruising.

So many people need to be salted today! They are so sensitive that they can't be handled, they can't be touched, they can't be corrected or admonished. No matter what you say to them, they swell up and get defensive. They have not been salted.

When a person has been salted, she can take a licking and keep on ticking. Nobody has to call her name for her to feel good about herself. Nobody has to acknowledge her for her to know she's worthy. Nobody has to compliment her for her to feel loved.

Jesus said that those who followed Him were the salt of the earth. (See Matthew 5:13.) We get salty by our association with salt. The newborn Christian gets salty by being around salt. It is our job to accept that new believer into our midst—to make a place for her, to surround her, to include her, to allow her into our circle of friends. The way she is going to get salty is by hanging around salt!

The more a woman knows that she is accepted and loved by other women who will be honest with her and with whom she can be honest, the less she needs to be handled with kid gloves. When she feels that it's alright to be herself, she will be less defensive about hiding who she has been or who she really is on the inside.

Third, we are to do some swaddling. We each are born naked into this world but the moment we are born, we need to be covered and protected against the elements.

Some women have been exposed to too much. They've seen too much, heard too much, and experienced too much. They were too young to learn some of the things they learned. They were exposed to the hard facts of life before they could handle that exposure.

When we swaddle a newborn Christian, we are to wrap that woman up in our arms of supernatural love and say to her, "You don't need to go back to that old life that was so painful. You can start over. You can be healed of those old painful memories and start experiencing something different. You can start having good times in your life to replace those bad times. You can start having good relationships in your life to replace those bad relationships."

To swaddle a person is to give her a continual dose of God's love . . . and to give her hope for her life.

To swaddle a person is to cover her in prayer and to intercede on her behalf.

But what if you are the baby who hasn't been cared for properly?

If you are the person today who needs to be washed and there's nobody who is washing you . . .

If you are a woman who needs to be salted and there's nobody salting you . . .

If you need to be swaddled and there's no swaddling being done for you . . .

Then you need to wash, salt, and swaddle yourself!

Wash yourself by reading God's Word. Get into a church where you can hear His Word preached with Holy Ghost power. Get around people who are studying His Word and who are speaking His Word and who are living His Word.

Salt yourself by getting right into the middle of a group of godly women.

Find a group of women who are living up to what Paul described as being a good setting for sound doctrine: "The aged women likewise, that they be in behavior as becometh holiness, not false accusers, not given to much wine, teachers of good things; that they may teach the young women to be sober, to love their husbands, to love their children, to be discreet, chaste, keepers at home, good, obedient to their own husbands, that the word of God be not blasphemed" (Titus 2:3–5).

Swaddle yourself by refusing to turn on that television set that fills your mind with filth and unrealistic expectations and lusts. Swaddle yourself instead with praise music and teaching tapes and videos of conferences in which God's Word is taught and God's delivering power is manifest.

When the devil tells you that you can't be cleaned up . . .

when he tells you that you can't be salted . . .

when he tells you that you can't be swaddled . . .

look the enemy in the eye and say, "Devil, you are a liar!"

When you desire to be cleaned up, God will help you get cleaned up!

As you wash yourself, He will wash you with His forgiveness.

As you salt yourself, God will salt you with His power and presence.

As you swaddle yourself in garments of praise, God will swaddle you in His love.

Ask God today to provide for you the exact nurture and care that you need.

Have Compassion on Yourself

None eye pitied thee... to have compassion upon thee; but
thou wast cast out in the open field, to the loathing of thy person.
—*Ezekiel 16:5*

od said that He was surprised at the attitude of people toward His baby girl. He said, "No one took pity on you. No one helped you."

When a woman is abused as a child, she grows up not only with the pain of that abuse, but with the anger that nobody helped her, nobody intervened on her behalf, nobody stepped in and rescued her. People may have murmured, but nobody helped.

God said, "You were cast out into the open field, and everybody loathed you." (See Ezekiel 16:5.) That's the way a woman feels if she was abused as a child. She feels as if she was a throw-away baby.

It's not only abused women who feel this way. Divorced women, rejected women, and abandoned women feel this way. In fact, virtually every woman goes through this experience at some time. She feels as if she has been tossed out into an open field. She feels that nobody values or appreciates her. She feels vulnerable and despised at the same time.

There's a difference between being cast away privately and being cast away into an open public field. If someone rejects you privately, you will hurt, but you won't feel nearly as much pain as if that person rejects you or denounces you publicly. It's much more difficult to overcome the shame that attaches itself to you when you are publicly cast away.

When people reject you, it's very difficult for you to feel good about yourself. You start thinking, "Well, if they don't think I'm worth anything, I must not be worth anything. If they are willing to throw me aside, I must be of no value."

Never allow another person's actions to control how you see yourself. That's too much power to give to another human being.

If people don't have the ability to discern the inner riches of your treasure, that's their problem. But if you sit at home and wallow in self-pity because they have no discernment, that becomes your problem.

Recognize that those who reject you have no ability to see inside you. They have no ability to hear the meaning behind your words. They have no ability to feel the quality of your touch. They have bought a lie—either willfully or unconsciously—that the devil has told them about you.

Refuse to adopt their opinion of you. Because if you adopt their opinion of you, you are adopting the very opinion the devil wants you to have. He wants you to buy into the lie he has told them. Don't do it!

The fact is, if you buy that lying opinion and come to the conclusion that you don't like yourself, you can't like anybody else. If you don't treat yourself well, you won't treat others well. If you don't care for yourself, you won't care for others. We treat other people out of the well of our own self-esteem. And if your well is dry, you don't have any esteem that you can give to another person. You can't value someone else because you have no value for yourself.

The Bible says that we are to love our neighbors as we love ourselves—which means we are to love other people to the degree that we love ourselves. (See Matthew 22:39.) If we don't love ourselves, we don't have any love to give to our neighbors.

In my work as a pastor, I have counseled a number of wife-beaters. I discovered again and again that the abusing man didn't hurt his wife because he hated her. The reality was, he hated himself! He was angry at himself. He loathed himself.

The Bible says that a man is to love and nurture and care for his wife just as he loves, nurtures, and cares for his own body. (See Ephesians 5:28.) But what if he does not like his own body, his own self? How can he nurture anything inside his mate if he doesn't nurture anything inside himself? It can't be done.

People who have been treated with hate become full of hate and can only give hate.

People who have been criticized become filled with a critical spirit and can only give criticism.

People who have been abused become full of anger and can only give abuse.

Refuse to accept the loathing of other people. Don't allow their opinion to creep into your inner person.

Refuse to loathe yourself.

Face the reality that if no one has had compassion on you, you can still have compassion on yourself.

Even if no one in the entire world has compassion on you . . . God does. He will help you if you will only turn to Him for help.

CHAPTER
FORTY-TWO

Live!

I said unto thee when thou wast in thy blood, Live.

—*Ezekiel 16:6*

God said that when He found you, you were such a mess that you were in a state of emergency. In emergency situations, rules often change.

In normal situations, all vehicles stop at red lights. In a state of emergency, ambulances and police cars and fire trucks roar right through them. If you are driving to get away from a tornado that is closing in on you, a stop sign isn't going to mean anything at all to you!

Many of the things that God desires to do for you, He will bypass in times of emergency. He said to His baby girl, "When I found you, you were dying in your own polluted blood." (See Ezekiel 16:6.)

When He found His baby girl He found her covered with blood, bruised and raw, naked, and strangling on the cord of her birth. She was lying out in an open field, cast away by everybody, dying!

When God found you, you were in a deplorable state, too. I don't know the circumstances of your life or what it is that drove you to the altar to accept Jesus as your Savior, but I know it was something deplorable. I know you were dying. You had been polluted by life, strangled by sin, bruised and raw because of the treatment of other people. Your past made you naked and exposed. You were cast away in loathing.

There was no time for God to tell you all that He wanted to say to you. He had only one word to speak to all of your abuse . . .

all of your trauma . . .

all of your trials . . .

all of your tears . . .

all of your pain . . .

all of your addictions.

God had only one word to speak to you in answer to your depression, your thoughts of suicide, your feelings of unworthiness.

There was no time for Him to teach you Hebrew or Greek or to define for you redemption, substitution, election, predestination, justification, or sanctification. In your state of emergency there was only one word God could speak to you that would matter.

He said to you, "LIVE!"

And that's the foremost word we each need to speak to those who are suffering or who are in pain today. It's the word we each need to hear when we feel the raw bruising pain of rejection and isolation and abuse. The word is "LIVE!"

To the woman who has just been told that she is going to be divorced, God says, "LIVE!"

To the woman who has just been beaten to a pulp by her husband, God says, "LIVE!"

To the woman who has just buried her infant child or her beloved husband of forty years, God says, "LIVE!"

To the woman who has just been raped, God says, "LIVE!"

To the woman who has just been fired from her job, God says, "LIVE!"

To the woman who is overwhelmed right now by her past, her outer problems, or her inner pain, God says, "LIVE!"

To the part of you that seems to be dying in sorrow or grief right now, God says, "Live!"

CHAPTER
FORTY-THREE

Move From the Past to Now

Beloved, now are we the sons of God.   *—1 John 3:2*

 od said to the orphaned girl that He had rescued, helped, and raised, "Now when I see you, I see what you have become." (See Ezekiel 16:8.) God knew all along that His baby girl was going to become a woman. He expected it to happen. He helped it to happen. And it did. He says, "Now when I see you, I don't see you as you were. I see you only as you are."

Focus on that word *now.*

People often talk about a woman being "in the know." I like to talk about a woman being "in the now."

There comes a time when you have to draw a line between then and now.

There comes a time when you must say, "That was then. Now is now. I used to do that. Now I do this. I used to be that. Now I am this."

Part of your maturity—part of your growing up to be God's woman—is to draw a line between the unwashed, unsalted, unswaddled, cord-bound baby that you were, and the mature, ornamented, breasted woman in Christ that you are."

There will come a time when you must declare that the crisis in your life is over.

You didn't die.

You didn't lose your mind.

You didn't fall off the end of the earth.

You didn't crumble into a heap.

You are alive. You are strong. You made it. You are a survivor of whatever it was that the devil tried to do to you to keep you from God's salvation and take you out of God's plan.

There will come a time when you must get rid of the rotting, decaying, dead bodies that you have been carrying around. Some women have been carrying around old relationships and old experiences so long that they've become accustomed to the stench of them. God declares that thing to be dead in your life. It's time for you to bury it so you can get on with the resurrection He has planned for you.

Make a decision today to bury anything that has pulled you down, held you back, kept you in despair, limited you, deceived you, or made you vulnerable. Throw it into the coffin. Lower it into the ground. Declare it over in your life.

Everything you can't change and can't fix . . .
Every childhood trauma . . .
Every secret disgrace . . .
Every memory of abuse . . .
Every instance of rejection . . .
Every addiction . . .
Every fear . . .
Every failure . . .

Must be buried in Christ Jesus! Commit those things to the Lord once and for all. Give them to Him. Seal them up in a grave forever. And rise up.

You have been cleaned up . . .
 freed . . .
  salted . . .
   clothed . . .
    loved . . .
     and raised to
     maturity in Christ.

It's time for you to experience His resurrection power and live in the now.

Draw a line between who you were and what you are—and step over into the NOW!

CHAPTER
FORTY-FOUR

The Process
of Wholeness

. . . Unto the measure of the stature of the fulness of Christ.
—Ephesians 4:13

irth and growth are two different processes, both naturally and spiritually. There's a difference between being saved and being healed until you are whole. Salvation happens instantly. Healing can be a lifelong process.

When God saves you, He quickens the eternal part of you. He calls it to come to life and it springs to life in a moment of time. Your spirit is immediately changed by the Holy Ghost and you can never be any more saved than you are in that moment.

If you compare a person who just died with a person who died twenty years ago, there's no difference in their state of "deadness." They are equally dead. The same principle holds for your salvation. You are either saved or you aren't. It's a state of being, not a state of becoming. If you were made alive in Christ, then you are alive in Christ.

When you were saved, God gave you everlasting life and illumined your innermost being with an eternal light. Your salvation was a supernatural impartation of God in your most secret place—your spirit.

Even though your spirit has been saved, you can still have some areas in your mind, your emotions, your appetites, and your desires that need to be healed.

In every one of us, there is something that needs to be healed. And until it is healed, you will continue to fall back into the same cesspool of sinful behavior again and again and again.

There are those who will tell you, "If you were really saved, you wouldn't act like that. You wouldn't want to do that. You wouldn't sin like that." Lapses into error have nothing to do with the salvation of your spirit. They have to do with the healing of your soul and the fact that you are not yet whole.

There are also those who say, "Well, if she knew it was wrong, she wouldn't do it, but she doesn't know any better." No . . . you can know what is right to do and still struggle with doing it.

A preacher friend of mine once said, "It's not enough to preach against sin, because sin is not the real issue. Sin is not the problem. Sin is merely how a person seeks to medicate their problem."

In other words, whatever sin seems to plague you the most, that sin has become your method for medicating your inner pain. And the reason a person keeps sinning after they are saved is because they are still hurting.

We preachers tend to offer seminars and conferences and classes and counseling sessions that tell people to stop sinning and to start living right. The people who attend those meetings try . . . and then fail. So we teach again, and they try again . . . and fail again. So we teach some more, and they try some more . . . and fail some more. Why? Because we never get down to the real problems. We never get down to the real void. We never get down into the mouth of the lion.

Sin is how we medicate the need we have for validation. It's how we numb our pain.

We go to the marketplace seeking to buy intimacy and we end up coming home with only sexuality. You can have sexuality without having intimacy. And when that happens, there's guilt, there's shame, there's disappointment. The need for intimacy remains—in fact, it grows. And all the while, the secret need for intimacy never finds expression and is never cured.

We go to the marketplace seeking to buy peace and we come home with a fifth of alcohol. You can have numbed senses without having peace. And when that happens, there's guilt and shame and frustration and disappointment in the aftermath of your getting sober. The need for peace remains—yes, it grows. And all the while, your secret need for peace lurks in your soul and is never really addressed.

It doesn't make any difference how much money you make, or where you live, or how big your house is, or how cute you are.

You can be suicidal as you drive your Mercedes down the street.

You can be depressed as you sit in your big house.

You can be depressed whether you are married or single.

Your answer does not lie in people or in things. It lies in the presence of God.

Wholeness comes when you turn to Him in your weakness, your pain, your suffering, and you allow Him to do for you what no one else can do.

Only God can regenerate the human spirit. And only God can raise a person to spiritual maturity and wholeness.

Trust God today to FINISH the good work He has started in you.

Raised to Maturity for the Purpose of Ministry

Freely ye have received, freely give.   —*Matthew 10:8*

od said to His grown-up girl, "I caused you to multiply as the bud of the field and to increase and to become great. I have given you ornaments so that you are attractive to other people. I have caused you to grow to maturity." (See Ezekiel 16:7.)

The Bible paints a very graphic picture of the little girl who has now grown up because of God's care. She has breasts. She has passed through puberty into adulthood. She now has the capacity to bear children and nurse them.

That's what God desires for every woman who comes to Him as a newborn baby Christian. He wants to raise her up so that she can birth spiritual children and then nurture those spiritual babies so that they grow up in Christ. He wants to prepare her to give to others of her love, not her anger, pain, or bitterness. He wants to mature her so that she can say to others, "The God who rescued me and delivered me and gave me life and raised me up is the same God who can and will do all that for you."

God wants to raise up women who will declare:

"The same God who brought me through can bring you through."

"The same God who helped me can help you."

"The same God who saved me can save you."

"The same God who is healing me can heal you."

God wants His women to have milk so they can nurse and nurture spiritual sons and daughters.

I believe that if you ask Him, God will show you why you had to go through what you went through so you would be who you are right now.

I believe that if you desire for Him to tell you, God will reveal to you all that He still has to give to you and all that He wants for you to do in ministry to others.

Now that He has brought you through the crisis and raised you up to maturity, you are ready to enter into the fullness of His destiny for you.

All the while that He was cleaning you up and cutting away from your life what needed to be cut away, He was preparing for you the blessings that He now wants you to receive.

He brought you to the bloody cross and through the cold tomb of death, and now He is ready for you to enter into the glory of resurrection time.

Your eyes have not yet seen and your ears have not yet heard and neither has it entered into your heart all the things that God has prepared for you! NOW is the time to see, to hear, and to believe. NOW is the time for blessing.

Believe God today for His NOW blessing in your life. Ask Him to reveal to you how you might help and bless others. NOW is your time to enter into His service—no longer as His orphaned baby girl, but as His woman. He has loosed you so that you might loose others in His name.

Devotional Notes

Devotional Notes